M000280379

Stand & Deliver

ADAM ANT is one of the most successful British pop stars to hit the charts in the last thirty years. Between 1980 and 1995 he had thirteen top-twenty hits in the UK, including three No.1s and seven Top 10s.

Unusually, Adam was also a major star in America, where he not only scored a string of hit singles and albums, but was once voted sexiest man in America by the viewers of MTV. He lived in Hollywood for several years and has acted in sixteen movies. He has dated some of the most beautiful women in the world, played live on five continents and is still one of the most instantly recognizable faces in Britain.

ADAM ANT

Stand & Deliver

THE AUTOBIOGRAPHY

PAN BOOKS

First published 2006 by Sidgwick & Jackson

First published in paperback 2007 by Pan Books
an imprint of Pan Macmillan, a division of Macmillan Publishers Limited
Pan Macmillan, 20 New Wharf Road, London N1 9RR
Basingstoke and Oxford
Associated companies throughout the world
www.panmacmillan.com

ISBN 978-0-330-44012-7

Copyright © Stuart Goddard 2006, 2007

The right of Stuart Goddard to be identified as the
author of this work has been asserted by him in accordance
with the Copyright, Designs and Patents Act 1988.

All rights reserved. No part of this publication may be
reproduced, stored in or introduced into a retrieval system, or
transmitted, in any form, or by any means (electronic, mechanical,
photocopying, recording or otherwise) without the prior written
permission of the publisher. Any person who does any unauthorized
act in relation to this publication may be liable to criminal
prosecution and civil claims for damages.

9 8

A cip catalogue record for this book is available from
the British Library.

Typeset by SetSystems Ltd, Saffron Walden, Essex
Printed in the UK by CPI Mackays, Chatham ME5 8TD

This book is sold subject to the condition that it shall not,
by way of trade or otherwise, be lent, re-sold, hired out,
or otherwise circulated without the publishers prior consent
in any form of binding or cover other than that in which
it is published and without a similar condition including this
condition being imposed on the subsequent purchaser.

Visit www.panmacmillan.com to read more about all our books
and to buy them. You will also find features, author interviews and
news of any author events, and you can sign up for e-newsletters
so that youre always first to hear about our new releases.

For my mother,

BETTY KATHLEEN

Acknowledgements

To Clare F, whose love, faith and support saw me through to the last page.

With love to Lily Caitlin, my daughter, for inspiration.

Thanks to my agent Mal Peachey, my business manager Richard Cohen and my Great-Aunt Mary, whose memory and stories gave me plenty to write about.

I'd like to thank Ingrid Connell at Macmillan for believing in the book and giving great feedback.

I'd also like to thank all the Antfans who continue to send me good wishes and hope that you enjoy reading this. It's not over yet . . .

ADAM ANT
May 2006

Contents

Prologue

ADAM ANT was born in 1976, in the grey, cold, echoing emergency ward of Friern Barnet Hospital, North London. He was smacked into consciousness by a hard-faced and overworked charge nurse, who calmly said, 'Wake up, you little bastard.'

I groaned.

Satisfied that I was awake she left me alone. Somewhere out of sight down a winding, peeling corridor a woman was screaming. There was no one else in the emergency room. As I sat up, groggy and feeling lost, I saw the name Stuart Goddard written in chalk on a board next to a door marked ECG.

But I had killed Stuart Goddard. A handful of my mother-in-law's pills taken from the yellow cabinet in her bathroom had done the job.

A few hours earlier as Stuart, I had sat, white and trembling, in the little room that I shared with my wife Carol on the ground floor of her parents' house in Muswell Hill. Adam was preparing for his big entrance. Not that anyone noticed anything unusual. Carol was cutting some cloth on the swirl-patterned orange carpet. Somewhere in the two-bedroomed, mid-terraced house there was an argument going on between my brother-in-law and his dad, just like always.

The tension in that house was so thick that it was suffocating me. It was all too familiar, all too much like it had been when I was a kid. I'd been living with my jaw clenched, my stomach in a knot for I don't know how many weeks. I had no appetite, I felt disorientated and seemed to be falling even when I was lying down. College wasn't open for long enough for me to feel I could really escape from the house, and when I did get out, I couldn't concentrate on anything, couldn't create. If I went to a gig it always ended in time to get the last bus home – and there was nowhere else to go except home. Pubs closed at eleven, which was when the television closed down, too. The house was bigger than anything I had ever lived in before, but at times it seemed to be smaller than the two rooms that Stuart had grown up in. This was one of those times.

I looked at the pills for a while, not really thinking anything. Then I snatched the bottle, took a handful, I don't know how many, and swilled them down with tap water. After a while – it was hard to tell how long – in our room at the back of the house, sitting on the bed watching Carol, time seemed to stop; her movements were all in slow motion. I heard myself speak as if it were someone else.

'Carol, I've taken a load of your mum's pills.'

She looked scared.

'I can't do this any more, it's just not possible. I can't be Stuart Goddard, I can't be married, I can't play bass in bands, I can't finish college. I have to get away from all the shit that my life is and has been.'

I might have said all of that, but it might just as easily have stayed trapped in my head because at some point I blacked out.

The next thing I know, I'm Adam and they want to put a few thousand volts through my head in Friern Barnet hospital. Fuck that, I thought, I'm off.

The funny thing is, no one at the hospital tried to stop me. No doctors told me that I should see someone about what I'd just done. At the reception desk I just said 'I'm leaving'. The place was in the process of being closed down for good, and no one seemed to care if the patients felt well enough to leave. I climbed into my father-in-law's car and settled back in the seat next to my wife of only a few months.

'Why did you do it, Stuart?' Carol asked me.

'Call me Adam,' I replied.

'Why Adam?'

'Because . . .'

1

FAMILY OF NOISE

'HAS SHE HAD IT YET?'

'Yes, Mr Goddard. At six-twenty this morning. Congrat—'

Before the nurse could finish, my father Les had dropped the receiver, raised a clenched fist to the heavens and raced to the nearest pub to celebrate with his mates. Only after much toasting and backslapping did it dawn on him that he hadn't asked if 'it' was male or female. The news that he had a son prompted an even more joyous return to the bar, where Les continued drinking with renewed vigour. Why shouldn't he? After all, it was what Les did. Everyone knew that. Les Goddard could drink for England and didn't have to be asked to volunteer, either.

His first and only son had been born at Middlesex Hospital, Mortimer Street, London W1. It was 3 November 1954. Scorpio rising, whatever that means. My mother remembers it as being a 'difficult' birth, her memory not made any sweeter by the fact that after several hours of agony she passed out, exhausted, before her firstborn appeared. My father was the first to see me; he eventually left the public bar and stumbled into the maternity ward in order to hold me in his arms. It was just one other thing that Mum never forgave him for.

They named me Stuart Leslie – Stuart after my Scottish uncle Mac, who was a sergeant in the legendary Black Watch Regiment, and Leslie after my father. Had I arrived two days later, on Guy Fawkes Night, Mum swears she would have called me Guy.

Guy Goddard.

So I'll always be grateful for my date of birth.

My parents met in 1947. Mum, or Betty Kathleen Smith, was just fifteen years old at the time, a sultry, dark-haired, brown-eyed beauty working as an embroiderer for Norman Hartnell, Queen Elizabeth's dressmaker. Dad, Leslie Alfred Goddard, was twenty and an ex-RAF corporal just back from National Service in Iraq, Iran and Palestine. Now earning a living as a driver for the *News Chronicle*, he was apparently something of a snappy dresser, a picture of sartorial correctness. 'Always cravats,' my mum recalls. 'He was lovely, so handsome in his double-breasted suits with the big shoulders. Very smart.'

That first day they met, my mum was taken with this sharp-dressed man and he with her. He was waiting by his car in Nottingham Place, W1, when Mum, on her lunch break, walked past him and he let out a low whistle. She stopped, called him cheeky and they got talking.

Photographs of Les from the time show a cocky-looking young man, often with a beer in his hand, and always with Brylcreem in his hair. Les seemed to believe that without a head full of the white greasy stuff you were somehow undressed. (A belief that he held to his last day.) His job was to get *Chronicle* reporters to the scene of the big story first. Very Raymond Chandler he liked to think it was, screeching around corners in big black Buicks carrying reporters with names like Ronnie Fortune, hungry for a story and a sensational photograph. During his time in the job Les covered the infamous Christie and Hanratty cases, the death of King George VI, and the tragic Ruth Ellis murder case. He once told me that he met Ruth Ellis, the last woman to be executed in England for shooting her unfaithful lover outside a pub in Hampstead, a few years before her death. 'Such a nice woman, a bloody shame if you ask me,' he'd say, shaking his head and having another pull on his pint.

When my parents met, Les was a keen motorcyclist. Some of their Friday evening courting took them to the Crystal Palace speedway races. Unable to afford his own car at the time, like many ex-servicemen he made a very sound investment by acquiring a classic AJS motorbike instead. What Les didn't know about cars, bikes or their engines was not worth knowing, so they always got my mum and dad there and back, despite his rather unorthodox riding style which meant that Les always had to drop Mum home a few streets away from where she lived. He had to do that, to prevent my grandfather killing the both of them – a threat he had sworn to carry out if he ever caught her riding on the back of 'that bastard dangerous thing'. It was hardly a surprising threat, made as it was after he had seen Les riding his bike up and down the street standing, Eros-like, on the seat.

Four blissfully happy years after their first date, Les and Betty went and spoiled it all by getting married at Marylebone parish church on St Patrick's Day 1951. After a brief and predictably romantic stay at a room above a shop in St John's Wood High Street, they moved to the infamous De Walden Buildings just around the corner, in Allitsen Road, NW8. Why my mum fell for this I have no idea, but I guess it was love and this was only just the 1950s. There was still rationing in England, and after several consecutive winters of murderous smog and with scores of servicemen still stationed overseas, number 4 De Walden may well have seemed like a little slice of heaven on earth to 21-year-old Betty.

In fact it was a two-roomed chambers in a big, brown-bricked Victorian slum. When they moved in there was no electricity or gas, no toilet or running water. Mum intended to use her thirteen pounds maternity money putting the electricity on, she told me. But Les was arrested and jailed for drunken driving just after I'd been born, so he needed the money to bail himself out. Only much later did she discover that there had been no fine, and he'd spent the money on more booze.

In the mid-1960s a cold-water sink unit was put in the flat, but until then the only water supply came from an ancient brown stone sink with a rusty, mildew-coated tap on the landing outside. This was shared with eight other families, all as hard up as us. However, by far the biggest worry for all the families on our floor was the community 'crapper', aptly named and situated at the darkest and coldest end of the landing. It was a black hole that warned you off from several feet away with a stench guaranteed to give you instant constipation. Until I was almost twelve, we would have to use buckets of water to flush it out every morning. Number 4 was, to say the least, cosy, consisting of a kitchen/living room area, and a bedroom.

That was it, there was no more.

The kitchen had a single window, framed by red-striped 1950s curtains with a floral motif. Mum had made matching seat covers, tablecloths and casing for the folding Z-bed that I later slept on. Nearby stood a huge kitchen cabinet, which contained everything that we owned and needed. I pulled this cabinet down on top of me when I was eighteen months old or so, trying to reach a bottle of garlic salt I'd taken a liking to which lived inside. I lay there surrounded by the smashed remains of my mum's favourite Wedgwood dinner service, milk, red varnish and blood from the gash on the back of my head. All over the lino, it was. My mum took it quite well, I guess, by which I mean I'm still here to tell the tale.

The kitchen table was the focal point of the room, because there we not only ate and drank, we leaned. We leaned on the table to watch the almighty television that stood right next to it in the corner by the bedroom door in a place all its own. It became very important to me, that television. At times it would seem as if it was the light of my life.

A door separated the two rooms of our flat. On it was a brass doorknocker in the shape of a bust of Charles Dickens, in profile. Behind Charles was the bedroom, a very simple affair, as the double bed took up two-thirds of the available space. A chest of drawers and a glass-topped dressing table were squeezed in there too somehow. The lack of furniture was supplemented by the quality of Mum's hand-crafted surrounds: her pleated bed-spreads and cushion covers. The flat was always immaculate, reflecting my mum's house-proud nature.

By the time I arrived, Dad was a private chauffeur for a wealthy family named Wallace. With the job came two uni-forms, complete with a peaked cap. One was a dark blue pinstripe, the other grey. Each morning Les would don a clean white shirt and then lift up the mattress and remove the trousers he'd placed there the night before. It was a primitive but effective method of getting a good crease.

The thick lingering smoke of my father's roll-ups was always present throughout the flat. Old Holborn tobacco wrapped in green Rizla papers, lit with an old chrome Zippo lighter and smoked down to a soggy butt, too wet for his attempt at a mouse-coloured moustache to burst into flames. Not that I was always averse to Les's cigarettes, apparently. My mum tells me that she would often find a blissfully happy baby Stuart staring at the blank screen of our huge television set, clearly entranced and sucking and gumming his way through an ashtray full of cigarette butts. I had some strange habits, and I was a far from gorgeous child. 'You weren't a very pretty baby,' my mum later told me. 'People would come over to have a peek at you and say, "Oh . . . what a lovely pram".'

The lovely pram, which must have been hell to carry up and down the four flights of stairs to our flat, was a source of amusement for me when I was small. One day I managed to unclip the undercarriage of it as we were crossing the main road by Lord's Cricket Ground. 'The wheels fell off and rolled away. You just laughed as the cars hooted. It cost me fifteen quid, that pram did.'

My mum tells horrible tales of a horrible child with horrible ways. Those early months at De Walden still bring painful memories flooding back for her. 'Oh Jesus, you were never one for much sleep. Wanted attention all the time. Had to be played with, and only a half-pint of full (and she stressed the full) National Dried [milk powder] would shut you up.'

In the flat I would strip off and throw my baby clothes out of the window, so they moved my cot away from the window. But that didn't stop me. En route to the clinic, beautifully fresh, immaculate knitted outfits would also hit the dirt. I'd arrive a complete disgrace, while all the other babies and their mothers looked down their noses at us. Locking my mother out of the flat was another of my great feats. The most serious occasion involved leaving her stranded on the landing as, inside, a cauldron of boiling water attempted to bleach my soiled nappies back to a respectable whiteness.

'I'm a good boy,' I gurgled.

'Yes, you are, my darling,' my mother lied, shoving dozens of chocolate Smarties under the door at me in order to keep me away from the boiling pan. She needn't have worried, though. My appetite far outweighed my enquiring mind. I bawled my eyes out when an exhausted policeman, having climbed up the drainpipe and broken the window to get in, tried to pull me away from the foot of the door.

I had little practical musical experience as a baby. Rattles, drums or any other slightly percussive toys were entirely out of the question at my house. No sooner had some kind heart been thanked for the lovely present and assured that I'd have hours of fun playing adorable little tunes on it than my new musical toy would be wrenched from my stumpy hands and thrown in the nearest dustbin.

My childish pranks could have contributed to the fact that my mum went out to work when I was barely out of nappies, but it's a less likely reason than one of pure need. My dad's job may have paid very well, but since he could never pass a pub on the way home without popping in for an hour or five, by the time he got home with a pay packet there was significantly less in it than when he had left work. So Mum took a job in a small restaurant called the Black Tulip, situated in the High Street, St John's Wood. The place did a good business serving a variety of dishes centred mainly on bacon, eggs and chips, although not necessarily in that order. There was always just enough grease to please everybody. She wore a black dress with the white frilly collar and cuffs like the other waitresses Joan Pockett and Kathleen Hanzewiniak, both of whom would become lifelong friends of hers.

These two delightful women became my surrogate aunties and were somehow closer than the real ones. Auntie Joan was a 'Forces favourite'-style of lady with an hourglass figure, and she sported not only the biggest, reddest head of intricately rolled hair I'd ever seen, but wore make-up thicker than a kabuki actor. Her face was literally painted on. This both delighted and fascinated me. (I'm convinced that this is one of the reasons why I was attracted to make-up in later life.) Auntie Kathleen on the other hand was a Bette Davis type, who for her sins was divorced but still plagued by her crazy Polish husband, Michael. He was an architect, very tall, skinny, and with a big crooked nose and a big black moustache. His clothes hung off him as he sat in Kathleen's parlour chain-smoking and demanding endless cups of tea. Once considered (mainly by himself, I suspect) quite a ladies' man, he ruled the roost. He claimed he could never return to his homeland because of his mysterious activities in the Polish Underground during the war. I'd wonder if this 'underground' business referred to a career as a partisan or as a platform porter.

While Mum, Joan and Kathleen waitressed I was looked after by Nanny Smith, at 17 O'Neil House, just around the corner in Cochrane Street. Even by my tiny standards Nan was small, with a face similar to Geraldine Chaplin, Charlie's actress daughter. Then in her late sixties, Nan looked much older, with a thin, kindly face and a body so delicate you wondered how she had borne seven children (four boys – Tommy, Tony, Wally, Bert – and two girls – my mother and Peggy, who had died at two years old. There was also a stillbirth, 'but we don't count that,' said Mum).

Born Lily Ada Jopson, in Tiptree, Essex, Nan had spent her life as a nurse. She began nursing during World War I, when she met my grandfather. Later on she worked at the Children's Hospital in Paddington Green. She had been one of the first supporters of the Marie Stopes movement demanding birth control for women. (It's a pity she was never able to practise what she preached.) Almost stone deaf and constantly peering over wire-rimmed granny spectacles, she would fuss over me in her own silent way.

Lily Ada had married by far the most important man in my life as I grew up, my maternal grandfather. Born a Romany gypsy, Walter Albany Smith came into this world in a caravan in Oxford in 1898, and his life reads like a romantic lead in a D. H. Lawrence novel. It's impossible to trace his family tree before this time as, in true gypsy tradition, the less contact with officialdom or society in general that his people had, they considered, the better. It is believed they were of Rumanian heritage. Judging by the thickset Slavic head and jawline that the whole family inherited, I think this is quite possible. The young Walter, or Wally as he became known, lived through a childhood of abject poverty. He wore no shoes on his feet until he ran off to join the army in 1914, aged just sixteen. Thankfully his mother reported him to the military authorities, and he was saved from almost certain death when he was returned home by MPs before he could get to the front.

Food was so scarce for his family that often they would be reduced to eating an obnoxious soup made from dandelions stewed in water. Despite the old Queen being long dead, the discipline employed by his father was thoroughly Victorian and he fully believed that sparing the rod meant spoiling the child. So Wally would be beaten with his father's huge leather belt, the buckle of which would tear into his back, scarring him for life, at the merest hint of dissent from the boy or the silliest, mistaken, 'bad' behaviour.

Great-Grandma Smith was a much kinder soul altogether. My mother remembers her as a strikingly dark woman with a thick head of gypsy hair and large earrings dangling from her ears. She wore a ring on every finger and a black shawl embroidered with large flowers in vivid colours which was fringed around the bottom. In later life Great-Grandma Smith lost her sight, but before she did she was able to read fortunes from the tea leaves. She warned my mum not to marry Les, as it would be 'stupid, and you'll never be happy', she told her. She then told my mum that she would bear one child, and one day meet an older man and be happy. All of which came to pass.

Given his father's brutal nature, it's little wonder that Wally was desperate to join the military and go off to fight someone his own size. His second attempt to join up, this time in the Royal Navy in 1916, was successful, and at last he owned his own pair of boots. While serving on HMS *Colossus*, Granddad spotted a torpedo, let out the warning, and saved the ship, for which he was decorated. He then fought at the Battle of Jutland before transferring to the new and very fragile submarine fleet. He did extremely well there, eventually earning the rank of leading torpedoman as the result of a peculiar incident. One day, apparently, the submarine's engines gave out and the craft sank quietly to the bottom of the ocean. After a few hours without power and with the air running out, along with any hope of survival, the crew, in a true display of wartime heroics and British Bulldog mentality, broke out the rum ration and decided to meet their maker as painlessly as possible. They were all soon blind drunk. But Granddad and another torpedoman kept working at the engines and were eventually successful in getting them going. So the crew woke up in an afterlife all too familiar to them.

Because of his tough background it's perhaps unsurprising

that Wally became a champion in the Navy boxing team. It's also unsurprising that back on civvy street after the war, Granddad was considered by those who came to know him as rather a tough cookie. My mother describes him as being a 'bit of a villain, with a hot temper'. She tells a story of how 'once Tony, Tom and me were at the Odeon [cinema] Edgware Road, and met him at the Westminster Pub. All of a sudden Dad was in a fight with a couple of blokes in an alley. He came out a few minutes later. They didn't.'

Wally swept Lily Ada, the nurse, off her feet, married her and went out to try and bring home the bacon. Right after World War I this was no easy task. Three long years of unemployment followed until he landed a job as a driver for Broads, a building company. At first Wally drove a horse and cart. Then came the early lorries that he learned to drive by trial and error. For three consecutive days he crashed into three unsuspecting milk carts. 'Then I got the hang of it,' Granddad would comment laconically. He spent a whole lifetime working for Broads and earned enough to support his wife and kids. They weren't well off, but there was always food on the table, and a love that bonded them together.

Wally became my first true hero when I discovered that he was the reason that my father Les wore dentures where his four front teeth should have been. Granddad Smith had dragged Les out of a pub and knocked the teeth (and him) out with a single punch after he'd found out that he'd hit my mum. Wally was a person to be looked up to, respected. And feared – if you were bad, that is.

My father's father, Granddad Tom Goddard, was an unlikely combination of musician, immaculate taxi driver, drinker and heavy gambler. He was a fine musician and led his own band; legend had it that he could play any instrument he tried. However unlikely this may seem, Granddad Goddard was an excellent pianist and probably could have squeezed a tune out of every instrument in his own band's line-up. At their top-floor flat at 151 Bravington Road, Paddington, my grandparents would play host to many a World War II knees-up. Granddad's upright piano stood against the front parlour wall, just up the stairs from the landing of their large flat. On Sunday afternoons as a child I'd sit up there mercilessly banging away at the keys. The noise was made worse by my use of the foot pedals, which would echo and extend the disastrous chords I'd concoct as I 'played'. Every now and then I'd try to remember how to play 'Chopsticks', an impressive tune requiring the use of only two fingers that my dad repeatedly tried to teach me. A certain record entitled 'Sparky's Magic Piano' had convinced me that it was only a matter of time before my chimp-like compositions would suddenly transform into a classical masterpiece. Funnily enough, that never happened.

Granddad Tom was memorable for his nose more than anything else. A huge, outstanding one it was, which at my young age seemed to me to be quite out of the ordinary. I can remember when it first came at me in my pram, through blinding white sunlight in the courtyard at De Walden. It was potato-shaped, with red veins mapping out curvy roads around the bulbous fleshy mainland to the hidden caverns of his nostrils. Secondary roads of green skipped around these high-ways. Every part of it seemed to throb, and I wondered if he was in pain of any kind. But no, for here was a prime example of the true cockney boozer's conk, made so famous by the legendary wartime actor Stanley Holloway (along with the great W. C. Fields, of course). Years of knocking back alcohol of every description had left its mark, the particles of distilled sugar travelling to the furthest extremities of his nose. A gout of the face, it was to be worn with pride, almost.

Otherwise, Granddad was a bit of a dandy, especially when driving his cab. He always wore a pinstriped suit, freshly pressed, with a starched white shirt, regimental tie in a Windsor knot, a fresh carnation, highly polished brogues, bowler hat and gloves. When my mum first met him, she thought he resembled former British prime minister Sir Anthony Eden. There, unfortunately, any similarities ended. He was a difficult man for my gran to live with. A heavy drinker, he ruled the home with a fist of iron. Over the years he developed stomach ulcers, which by the time I arrived had restricted his drinking to an unlikely mixture of Guinness and milk. But he'd drink as much of that as he could.

Tom loved a gamble, and card games were a regular feature at Bravington Road. This must have been torture for my gran, who often saw her housekeeping money change hands the wrong way in her own parlour. Whatever happened, though, outside appearances had to be kept up, and Tom would just continue, feathers unruffled, never mind that he didn't have a pot to piss in. Without doubt, the most tragic consequence of this was the time he gambled away the beautiful house they owned in Golders Green. There ended the family's prospects of lower-middle-class status, comfort, security or fortune. Instead the taxi was loaded up and off they travelled to bombed-out, filthy old Paddington. Not that Tom seemed to be too bothered, and he always seemed to have money, laying out rounds of drinks for his mates.

My gran told me in the 1990s that he had been a Freemason, in a Scottish lodge. 'Because it was cheaper to join and easier to get in,' she recalled. It fitted with Granddad's image of himself – that of a successful tradesman, looking to do his secret buddies a favour whenever he could. The truth about the organisation, however, is less impressive, according to my gran. She apparently had an argument with someone at the annual Masons' ladies' night, and was never invited back. Not that she considered it any great loss. When Granddad died she was assured by the Brotherhood that she'd never have to worry about money with the Freemasons behind her. 'They sent me a fiver,' she remembered years later, adding, 'I was going to put it on the wall and frame it.'

Granddad Tom had a pathological dislike of my father, his

son. Through no fault of his own, Les suffered for the death of his elder brother Charlie. Granddad had worshipped Charlie, his firstborn. By all accounts the boy was something of a prodigy, well behaved, intelligent and loving. Perfect. When he died of pneumonia at the age of five, Les didn't stand a chance. To my heartbroken granddad, Les was nothing more than a poor substitute, and a constant reminder of his great loss. My father, a remarkably pretty child with curly blond hair, was referred to as a 'girl' by his father, and as soon as he could string a sentence together (and Tom could scrape the money) Les was sent off to private school. All Les's efforts at school were dismissed by Tom as never being up to scratch, while any display of love from my grandmother towards her son was punishable by Tom. I gathered all this information from my Great-Aunt Mary, who would look after Les in London at the time. She firmly believes that his father's behaviour led to Les's drinking problem as well as other problems he suffered from in later life.

My father's mother, my grandmother Caroline Anne Goddard, was usually referred to by her nickname, Bill. (I think that after six daughters my great-grandfather just decided it was time he had a son, and my gran, being a bit of a tomboy, was the closest he could get.) One of eleven children of the Hutchens family, her childhood was truly happy and not particularly hard. The family moved from Romney to the delightful village of Cookham in Berkshire just before World War I. She recalls running from her classroom to see a Zeppelin float over the town of Dean.

As old ladies, Grandmother Billy and her sister, my Great-Aunt Mary, would describe their life in service to me, and I was riveted from the start. Their family had long been 'in service', that is, working as domestics to the upper-middle-classes of Victorian and Edwardian England. Like her sisters and family before her, Billy left school at the age of fourteen and went directly into service as an under-parlourmaid for a wealthy family nearby. Up at five, her duties were scrubbing floors, polishing everything that could be made to shine, helping to prepare the food, and generally doing the shit jobs no one else wanted. Only Sunday afternoons were free, and even then, if she wanted to go out on a date, she had to have permission from 'the missus'.

One term of employment ended rather dramatically for her when she fell prey to the amorous designs of the master of the house. This was not an uncommon occurrence at the time, and many an innocent working-class girl was seduced, used, then thrown out in disgrace when the bump began to show. My gran was chased but not caught, rescued by her younger sister Mary, who was working in the room next door. Both were dismissed the following morning, disgraced but still pure.

I used to bear this sort of thing in mind when watching the endless sagas of our British aristocracy on TV or in the cinema. *Upstairs, Downstairs, Maurice, Room with a View, Brideshead Revisited* or, worst of all, *Howard's End* never quite impressed me as they glorified a corrupt society, stereotyping and patronising working people. I couldn't care less about the turn-of-the-century rich and their problems trying to occupy their time or deal with their sexuality. I always found myself more interested in the faithful servants, and the extras with no lines who portrayed people like my grandmother, treated with all the respect of a well-behaved dog, tugging at a greasy forelock or curtseying.

Eventually Billy progressed through the ranks to the position of cook, for a Prussian archduke, no less. Then she met and married Tom and carried on doing the same thing, but without a wage.

As far back as I can remember, the food prepared by my gran was (and remained) of the most exquisite quality. Her Sunday roasts are memorable to this day. Perfect sides of roast lamb, beef and pork have passed my grateful lips, dressed with lashings of vegetables. Leeks, swede, parsnips, carrots, peas, as well as perfectly roasted potatoes and the ultimate Yorkshire

pudding were all part of her repertoire. I was very lucky to have
a forward-looking gran, who preferred the new to the old and
who possessed a wonderful sense of humour. With the help of
a gin she could also be encouraged to sing a song or two. There
were no charming little folk songs in her set list, but, being a
boisterous ball of energy, she'd belt out her own compositions
and arrangements of old vaudeville tunes. Among them was
'The Fiddle Is My Sweetheart', which went like this:

> The fiddle is my sweetheart
> I play and play all day
> But when the strings are broken
> THROW THE BLEEDING THING AWAY.

Gran would let out a wonderful naughty laugh. Or rather, a
cackle. She was like a high-pitched 'Singing Policeman', laughing at her own jokes.

Billy was tough and smart and she had to endure an incredibly hard life, which she did with humour. Her life, like that of
my mother, was blighted by her husband's drinking to excess
and the effect that had on the family.

•

Because both my parents worked and there wasn't always
someone around to leave me with, I would spend hours, possibly
all day, alone and creating an imaginary world. I'd imagine
the bed was a huge steamship, for instance, and stand on the
imaginary bow, my father's chauffeur cap on back to front. I
was a sailor and the floor surrounding me a turbulent sea,
filled with the most dangerous of sharks and exotic fish. I memorised every inch of that flat. Every corner offered a particular challenge for me to get to. A white, one-eyed teddy bear
named Chessy would accompany me on Amazonian adventures
through the infamous Bedstead Pass to the Plains of the Kitchen
Table or Sideboard Mountain. Over the years I became quite
partial to being away from the other kids at school or in the

yard, for I knew nothing could match the excitement of my imaginary games.

My nights were spent sleeping first in my parents' bed, and then on a folding Z-bed in the kitchen, to which I'd be carried after Dad got home. Dad never got home before the pubs closed. That was the golden rule. Together with the rule that he ruled. I'll never forget the sound of his footsteps crossing the yard below. That low, boozy cough as he approached the stairs. These sounds would wake me up like a terrible alarm clock. Then I'd have to pretend that I was asleep, because I knew what followed would be awful, and I wanted no part of it.

His key twisted in the lock and in would come that night's Mr Hyde. The mighty arguments soon followed the first icy moments of silent hatred that stood between them. Mum was in a no-win situation. If she didn't start up the proceedings with a, 'So what time do you call this?' he'd pick on her with, 'What are you looking at?'

Then he'd attack her with a stream of vile, abusive language, making hurtful, unjustified accusations about anything he considered her guilty of. Slow, ugly words spat out of his purple, puffy, twisted face. It wasn't an experimental concoction that transformed this Doctor Les Jekyll, the kindest of men, into the nightly Beast, but a dozen or so pints of Whitbread light ale. Angel to Arsewipe. Every night. Like some sick magic.

The magic was at its sickest when I'd hear my mum's screams suddenly turn into a low moan. Then I knew he'd hit her. In the stomach or in the face were the usual places. It was only this that stopped my pretending to be asleep, and I'd run to her where she'd fallen, crumpled in the corner, holding her stomach, fighting for breath. I'd press my face to hers, still wet with tears and streaked by comical streams of running make-up.

All the nightly nonsense eventually affected me. I started to sleepwalk and hallucinate. It began at an early age, although exactly when is hard to say. I may have been two, three, four or six when these moments of pure hallucination started occurring. The sleepwalking, so I am told, usually took the form of me desperately trying to open the front door and get away. To be fair, it's quite common in growing children, but the hint to my father couldn't have been stronger.

The hallucinations were terrifying. To this day I can recall what used to happen. Sitting wide awake in the early hours of the morning, I'd be in the middle of a giant aquarium. Perfect, three-dimensional, technicolor fish would swim all around the room. Sharks, stingrays and Portuguese men-of-war would slide past within inches of my pyjamas. I would shake my parents awake to ask them what was going on, pointing at the different creatures as they passed. This usually scared them enough for Les to promise that he would mend his ways. Which indeed he would, for about two days. Then he was back on form, soaking his bread in it, as my gran used to say.

As the child of an alcoholic I find it easy to be a teetotaller. After twenty years I began to feel a certain amount of empathy with my father and the millions like him. Empathy, yes; sympathy, no. As a man, at any social gathering I attend there will inevitably be people who try to get me to have 'just a sip of wine or champagne and not be such an antisocial bastard'. I have always refused, and continue to do so because I am perhaps lucky to have first-hand experience of this disease and to see that there's no romance in it. I'm not brave enough to believe that I might not have inherited this gene after all, given that my father and his father both suffered from alcoholism. I'm a coward when it comes to drink.

•

Our flat was one of four situated on the first floor at De Walden. The stairs leading up to it were lined with old brown tiles that had only sparse patches of the original enamel remaining. The hard, grey, stone steps were cold in both summer and winter. Always dark, there was a single bulb throwing out just enough light to determine the numbers on the doors in each corridor. With its lack of sunlight, the hallway was always damp, the air moist and smelling of cheap, strong disinfectant. However, a true spirit, reminiscent of the Blitz a little more than a decade earlier, existed between the families who lived along it. This sense of belonging lifted us out of our surroundings, offering some relief from what could otherwise be described as a Dickensian scenario.

The neighbours were an interesting bunch of characters. Next door at number 3 lived the Hill family. Brenda was a mother of two daughters, Susan and Sandra. She was a big, powerful woman. Her ebony beehive hairdo and plump, voluptuous figure gave her a most imposing authority. Under skin-tight pencil skirts, her great fleshy white thighs would rub together as they fought for space and air, and beneath the skirts her white ankles were always overflowing from stiletto shoes. Brenda took shit from no man, woman, child, animal, vegetable or mineral. But especially man, and in particular her husband, who lived, shall we say, under the thumb.

Her youngest daughter Sandra seemed to adopt her mother's approach to boys from an early age. 'Boys' in this case being me. Putting up with her superior behaviour was never easy, and one sunny day my patience gave in. I struck her on the back of the head with the polka-dot handle of my Lone Ranger cap gun. When Sandra returned from the hospital, bravely bearing eight neat stitches, she forgave me instantly and we became closer than I'd ever dreamt we could be. I had, incidentally, cried my eyes out at the sight of what I'd done to poor Sandra. So upset was I that neither Brenda nor my mum could stop the tears. Promises that they wouldn't punish me, that it wasn't my fault or even that she deserved it made no difference whatsoever. Only the sight of my bandaged victim and her ultimate forgiveness put me out of my misery.

At number 2, the flat opposite ours, lived the Dumbletons. Mary was a tiny, attractive platinum blonde, with big eyes enhanced by loads of make-up and plump lips. Her husband Terry was an authentic Teddy boy, always combing his thick, oily, rolled-elephant-trunk DA into a kiss-curl just below eye level. They also had two daughters, Kimmy, the eldest, and Tracey-Lee the baby. The girls were the spitting image of their mother, and playing with Kimmy always felt special.

Around the corner at the end of the landing lived Anna, a mysterious Dutch woman who kept to herself. A kind enough person if you took the trouble to get to know her, I fear she was the subject of much gossip due to having a live-in lover and a son no one ever saw. (My mother was, however, godmother to the poor boy, so poor Anna was not without her allies on the landing.) Of course, at this time, merely having a European accent gave rise to ample suspicion amongst the cheeky, chirpy, cockney fraternity – 'salt of the earth', my arse.

The 'black sheep' family of De Walden was, without question, the Stewart clan. Originally from Scotland, they lived at either end of the building. On the top floor of our block lived Susie, the eldest Stewart sister, with her husband, two daughters and a baby son. A slight, fair-haired woman, Susie was a firm but fair type who possessed enormous strength of character. This was just as well, for it was poor Susie who had to bear the brunt of responsibility and embarrassment resulting from the scandalous activities of the rest of the family, situated a hundred yards away in the end block. They were nicknamed 'the gruesome threesome', and not without some justification, for here were three truly intimidating people.

To begin with there was Jim, the alcoholic father, a tiny, inconspicuous man, never without a cigarette pinned between thin lips. Unassuming and polite when sober, he would transform into a wild, abusive, violent little shit after a visit to the pub. One night he burst into our flat by mistake after leaving the pub. He was so drunk that he'd staggered right instead of left at the main gate. An enormous crash heralded his entrance, when, unable to open the door with his keys, he simply kicked it in. After a quarter of an hour of vicious swearing, belching and farting, Susie was able to convince Jim of his error and drag him to his home. 'Fuck aaaallaya anyway,' were his parting words as he tripped down the stairs, hit his head on the wall and threw up all down himself.

And so to his two other unfortunate offspring, Rita and Dave. I liked Rita enormously, as did all the other kids. She always gave us a good tip to buy ourselves sweets whenever we ran errands for her. We could never understand why our mothers warned us against her. Perhaps it was because of the loud plastic raincoats she favoured, or the regularity with which she changed her hair colour. I thought she was very beautiful. (Not as beautiful as Kimmy Dumbleton maybe, but an eyeful all the same.)

One afternoon a number of policemen turned up asking for Rita. Then we didn't see her for a while. Our mothers seemed to be unsurprised by all this, and they kept whispering the word 'prostitute' under their breath. It appears that Rita was a working girl whose profession, although one of the oldest in the world, coupled with the abortion she'd supposedly had, out-raged the hypocritical morals of the De Walden majority.

This left only Ian, who was the closest twentieth-century London has come to producing an authentic Dickensian street urchin. Had Fagin existed he would certainly have keenly wanted to enrol someone like Ian instead of the twerpish Oliver Twist. And if he had, then the Artful Dodger would have had the shit beaten out of him, and Fagin's gang would have gained a new and far more formidable leader. Dave was without doubt a blueprint for the professional criminal. Dirt poor, filthy and motherless, he roamed the streets as he liked. His clothes were threadbare, and even in the middle of winter, in the snow and slush, he'd run around wearing just a T-shirt, a pair of shorts and worn-out shoes. Many of the mothers took pity on the boy, feeding him a hot meal whenever they could. The trouble was that Dave was a very talented thief, and if you weren't careful the meal could turn out to be rather expensive. Watches, cutlery, clothes or anything saleable would disappear like magic after he'd visited.

At the front of the buildings, in a basement flat, lived a kindly old woman known to me as Scotch Annie. A big, fat old dear she was too, and would occasionally babysit me. I always loved my stays with her, as they invariably meant a slice of cake or a cup of cocoa, or some chocolate, as long as I 'didna tell ma mother'. She talked lovingly of her dead husband, Noel Tinnison. Born on a Christmas day, and appropriately named, Noel had the distinction of having served as a navigating officer on the disastrous maiden voyage of the *Titanic*. He had survived but never fully recovered from the injuries or the awful memories. He gave my mother a Bible he had carried with him on the trip, which she still has and cherishes. Scotch Annie also introduced me to the fortifying wonders of porridge, which I still consider a delicacy (when it's made right) and a close favourite behind rice pudding, the culinary delight of my life.

The only other family of note in the buildings were the Palmers, who lived on the top floor of the block opposite. Harry, the father, was a sour-faced, bald-headed, bolshy type. Barbara, his wife, was a thickset European. You could imagine her at home serving huge kegs of beer to a rowdy band of Bavarians in a bierkeller. Fitting the stereotype of a 'Fraulein', her thick Slavic accent didn't exactly endear her to the rest of the community. Despite her continual assurances that she was Polish or Westphalian, she was considered to be an undercover Nazi. She didn't help matters much by dressing her son François in lederhosen and parting his hair to the side. But in my eyes, all of Harry and Barbara's faults were forgiven by the fact that this unlikely pair had managed to produce the lovely Sonya. Sonya, with her plaited hair and braces on her teeth was the first time love of my life.

After television, of course.

Television, the big brown box tucked away in the corner of our room. Just below it, almost as holy, almost as important, sat the red Dansette record player with white plastic piping. My other saviour, music, often filled the air at De Walden, providing comfort, adventure, excitement and escape (at least when Les wasn't around). Here was my first education, leaving images and sounds so strong in my subconscious that they still flash into my mind today, crystal clear. I shut my eyes and think back to those times and feel a warm glow inside, especially when I remember Ricki, another babysitter. A blonde beatnik, she played down her considerable looks and figure wearing slacks, huge 'sloppy Joe' pullovers and wild, ornate glasses which swept out at each side of her face like the wings of a Cadillac. I grew very fond of Ricki. She brought her teenage energy with her, along with a sense of joy and laughter, when she came to see me. But above all, she brought her record collection, and with it my introduction to the wonderful world of rock 'n' roll. And just in time. For up until then I'd been exposed only to the more sober tastes of my parents. Not that I minded Perry Como's sugary invitation to catch a falling star or pass some magic moments with him. They still rate as two of my all-time favourites. There was also the high-kicking mensch himself, Frankie Vaughan (looking like Sylvester Stallone's older brother), asking sex-starved housewives everywhere to give him the moonlight. Frankie also recorded an extremely nifty Elvis-type rocker entitled 'Honey Bunny Baby', which would surprise a few people listening to it today.

Mum adored the cheeky cherub Dickie Valentine, the wholly underrated and tragic Michael Holliday, Big Frank (Sinatra), Nat King Cole, and Frank Ifield, the yodel master, who blamed his girlfriend for the state of his voice. She taught me to yodel, he claimed. (I'm convinced that it is as a result of listening to his 'I Remember You' record that in my early recordings with Adam and the Ants, yodelling accounted for a large part of my vocal repertoire.) But by far the most played song at our house was by the late great Matt Munro – 'Softly As I Leave You'.

Les considered all this stuff to be 'crap', of course, insisting that trad jazz was the world's only legitimate form of popular music. In reality his interest went as far as his collection did – that is, one copy of the single 'Midnight In Moscow' by Acker Bilk and his Paramount Jazz Band. This disc was sacred. Mum and I knew better than to even dare to look at, let alone touch it. 'Knackers to Acker', Mum would often quip, from a safe distance.

On Sundays, as the roast whatever cooked away in the oven, we would listen to the radio, usually 'Three-Way Family Favourites', when the poor, lonely, brave members of Her Majesty's forces could listen to requests sent from their more idiotic relatives back home in Crawley, Bristol, Burnley, or even up there in bonnie Scotland. For some reason, every tune played was middle-of-the-road, light orchestral or a showtune. However, worse than this had to be Les's other favourite radio programme, 'The Billy Cotton Band Show'. A throwback to wartime vaudeville, the show began with Billy's memorable cry of 'Way-kee wake-aye!!!', delivered as if he'd just coughed up a wad. Billy would then treat us to his own very special brand of third-rate comedy sketches. Now, I'm sure that Billy could have got away with his dull jokes during the Blitz, when a fucking great bomb could fall on your head at any second, but we were now living in the age of the comic genius. The Goons (including Peter Sellers and Spike Milligan), Tony Hancock and Norman Wisdom were all performing and making people laugh about an apparently different Britain from the one in which Billy Cotton seemed to live. Yet still Billy would make ancient jokes and Les would laugh along. Maybe it made my dad recall a time when he wore a uniform that commanded more respect than the one he wore as a chauffeur.

Ricki saved me from all this. Suddenly a new wave of music filled the air when she was around, and it was the real thing: Elvis, Gene Vincent, Eddie Cochran, Sam Cooke. All down and dirty and American, from the land where everything was bigger and better. Like any other English new-breed teenager, Ricki also subscribed to the rock 'n' roll gospel as sung by home-bred idols. British rockers were a bunch of lightweights compared with the real American article, though. Only the chirpy cockney Tommy Steele stood out to my infant, but no less discerning, ears. Blasting away at 'Rock With The Caveman' or 'Elevator Rock', Tommy managed to at least match some of the Yankee efforts. He did so despite the musical backing of the Val Parnell type of big bands, which, like the rest of the British music establishment at the time, thought the rock 'n' roll revolution a passing comedy fad and performed accordingly. But the boy from Bermondsey had captured my imagination, and a few years later, when I saw Tommy Steele leaning on a Wurlitzer 1800 jukebox in the coffee bar scene from *The Duke Wore Jeans* at the Saturday morning pictures, Odeon Swiss Cottage, my interest in becoming a singer began.

Lonnie Donegan was also a regular performer at De Walden. With his unique vocal range, and in the best spirit of Woody Guthrie, 'The Battle Of New Orleans', and 'Rock Island Line' were belted out, even louder later with the humorous 'Does Your Chewing Gum Lose Its Flavour (On The Bedpost Overnight?)' and 'My Old Man's A Dustman'.

Ricki was obviously inspired by the skiffle craze (in 1958 garage bands sprang up all over the land, equipped with three chords, cheap guitars, tea-chest and broom bass and kazoo) and bought me a plastic Woolworths guitar. Ricki would stand me on our table, in front of the polished side of the TV. Here, looking at myself aged six in the mirrored wood, I was encouraged to mime and sing along with the music. The bright light thrown from a table lamp above created a truly stagelike setting, as I strummed away at the imaginary strings (Mum had removed them right after I'd unwrapped the guitar).

Ricki eventually married a technician who worked at the St John's Wood television studios and was gone from my life, but the influence she had on me was not. I was too young to realise it, but the rock 'n' roll education I received buried itself deep inside me; it was forever under my skin. There it waited, maturing, always capable of lifting me out of boredom or a bad situation: I would simply hum the opening bars of the songs I knew by heart.

After Ricki left, I returned myself to the power of the great god Television. I was a member of the first true television generation. Rationed though my viewing was, the telly was the ultimate in early 1960s pleasure and entertainment. I never argued with it. Whatever it had to offer suited me just fine, particularly the Sunday film, with its Gainsborough Studio releases, or Ealing comedies. These black and white films were usually something to do with the recent war, and always starred John Mills, Jack Hawkins, Anna Neagle, and Sam Kydd in a bit part. In a league all their own stood the marvellous Alastair Sim at his creepy best and Alec Guinness in many guises. Thrown in with these were Hollywood's finest, Errol Flynn, John Wayne, Clark Gable, and James Stewart, and, all too often, the second-division stuff too, with Stewart Granger and Victor Mature. To me, they were all sheer pleasure.

I witnessed the first TV shows catering solely for children, all of which came courtesy of the BBC. The *Watch with Mother* series, which showed twice a week, was a marvel for kids like me. Compulsive viewing, addictive, and speaking my sort of language. The big paper flower that opened at the start of each show, and the charming piano tune that went with it, guaranteed perfect silence and a hundred per cent attention from children who only seconds before would be shouting, screaming or smashing things up. For the next twenty minutes I was in another world entirely. As the primitive wooden puppets, strings clearly visible, hopped around the screen, a woman sounding remarkably like Queen Elizabeth II would tell us a story. Unfortunately, television was inevitably replaced in my daytime schedule by the legal necessity of attending school.

•

My first school was Robinsfield Infants, situated around the corner from De Walden in Townshend Road. One of the prefab-style 'modern' structures, the school was large, new and boasted two enormous grey concrete playgrounds. Mum took me to school on the first day with surprising ease. There were no tears, no screaming or clinging like the bulk of the other kids. For me this was the beginning of a new adventure. Never before had I seen so many other children in one place. The deal I made with Mum was that I would have my own desk, and be on my own at school, so I went quietly. At first. Little did I know that here was a place that would introduce a number of 'firsts' in my young life.

My time at Robinsfield was happy enough – from my point of view, that is – but less enjoyable for my teachers, I fear. 'You were a little sod,' Mum recalls, and not without some justification. On two consecutive days I smashed one of the headmistress's office windows with a brick – these were plate-glass windows, about twelve foot by six foot. The first time I did it I was undoubtedly showing off in front of another boy. It was a demand for the kind of attention that I was used to getting on the landing at De Walden. That time I was given the benefit of doubt as to whether I meant it. However, when I threw a brick through the window the second time – mainly to hear that fantastic sound of breaking glass, but also because I'd liked being the centre of attention the previous day – Mrs Phillips, the headmistress, summoned Mum to the school. She demanded a drastic improvement in my behaviour, and threatened expulsion. She also informed Mum that I was 'by far the most horrible child' it had ever been her misfortune to meet, let alone teach. I remember little about the incidents, other than that superb smashing sound as the glass broke, the playground population parting like the Red Sea, and dozens of fingers pointing me out as the offender to the teacher who arrived a short while later.

Robinsfield was the first place I became aware of girls as interesting playmates. (More interesting than just people to fight with verbally or hit over the back of the head with the polka-dot handle of your Roy Rogers cap gun, that is.) The pure and innocent desire to see what it was that little girls had that I didn't have, and vica versa, took a strong hold of me. This desire was manifested in a game, played in secret, and known universally as Doctors and Nurses.

My first game took place under a table in the front classroom at Robinsfield, at the invitation of a beautiful blonde girl named Harriet. I was as impressed with her looks and knowledge of the game as I was with myself for being able to pronounce her name all in one go. There, under the formica top, we pulled at each other's elastic. 'I'll show you mine if you show me yours.' Wee Doctor Stuart examined the secret treasures of that little peach down there as Nurse Harriet peeked at nature's only acorn with balls attached. We were both very serious, almost religious in our explorations of each other's private parts. We had no idea why, but the fact that it was an area obscured by clothes suggested some naughtiness. Afterwards, Harriet and I would hold hands as if some special silent bond now existed between us.

It wasn't my first sexual experience; that had happened at a very early age. I make no ridiculous claim that I had any idea of what was stirring in my young loins, or why, but what set me going was my first look at a fine pair of women's legs. It was at a time in my life that is too early to pinpoint, but I can't have been older than five or six. A close friend of my mother, a French au pair named Vivien, was at our flat one day. I recall standing opposite her as she sipped her tea. Suddenly she sat upright and slid forward on the armchair, possibly to get closer to Mum's conversation. As she did so, her tight skirt rose up above her tanned, shapely, athletic-looking legs.

Then it happened.

My short trousers showed no sign of an erection or anything remotely smutty, but a warm, gleeful, satisfying glow started to spread all over my body. Inexplicable though it was, I had to go and tell my weather-beaten teddy bear and confidant, Chessy, all about it. I told him I was going to take him with me to meet French Vivien, and he should 'prepare himself for something special'.

The first woman I had a major crush on, though, was Mrs Joanna Saloman, my form mistress at Robinsfield School. Maybe it's coincidence, but she was not only a tall redhead of outstanding beauty, she also had the most wonderful figure, with long, shapely legs. The time I spent gaping at her became almost a religious experience for me. Of course this went unnoticed by her, as she was concerned only with helping me to learn something, and save me from the life of delinquency I was clearly headed for. But importantly, she returned my 'love' by the encouragement she showed me, especially for painting pictures.

One day she noticed my enthusiasm during the painting of a picture I called Mother Goose, which featured a large duck-shaped creature, in profile, surrounded by a bright blue sky, white fluffy clouds, and feathers of many colours, all individually painted with nifty wavelike strokes of my brush. Mrs Saloman congratulated me, and called the rest of the class over to have a look. I was naturally pleased with myself, but more elated by the belief that I'd painted my way into her heart. I imagined that regardless of my size and age, we'd simply fly off somewhere together. She would cuddle and kiss me, and let me kiss her back. I memorised every inch of her face – the pale orange and browns of her eye make-up, her high, delicate cheekbones, her small, full mouth. She was somehow Victorian-looking, like a Dante Gabriel Rossetti model, with skin so pale, enhanced by a light powder. Framing all this was her waterfall of tumbling red and auburn ringletted hair.

Mrs Saloman's son Nick was a good two or three years older than me, but we would later become good friends. He introduced me to long hair, Jimi Hendrix and electric guitars, which he played wildly, and not without skill.

My crush on Mrs Saloman was necessarily impossible, but simple and perfect in its sincerity and innocence. I had a huge desire to impress her, without quite knowing why or what to do about it, but was nevertheless blissfully happy. I tried not to think of the inevitable day when it would all end and I'd have to go to big school. Barrow Hill.

2

KICK!

WITH A NAME MORE FITTING for a Saxon burial mound than an inner London junior school, Barrow Hill sat less than a hundred yards away from De Walden Buildings. A large, red-bricked Victorian castle-style affair with an almost gothic atmosphere, it was big, proud and unfriendly. It had an enormous playground, with a cricket net at the far end where my character was to be shaped, and where I first experienced a sense of worth, achievement and the desire to accept responsibility.

That I did was mostly due to the influence of Mr Perkins, the sports master. Initially, through fear alone, he became the first authority figure in my life that I admired enough to want to impress. Mr Perkins single-handedly taught me the game of cricket, moulding my primitive schoolyard efforts into a controlled style effective enough to eventually earn me the captaincy of the school eleven.

Mr Perkins was a large, overpowering man who wore a lot of tweedy colours, with leather patches on the elbows of his jacket, a checked waistcoat and suede shoes. He always appeared to be slightly ruffled, as if he'd just snapped to attention after a few minutes of illicit kip in the staff room. He could best be described as a demented Eric Morecambe type, bald, with glasses that always seemed to be a bit too small, so that they would ride up one side of his wide head and perch lopsided across the bridge of his nose. His teeth were nicotine pillars, badly gapped. He was always short of breath, a result of the cigarettes and asthma he suffered from. His big wheeze would inevitably be followed by an even bigger cough.

If you happened to be stupid enough to upset him, God help you. That round, jocular head would turn bright burgundy and the boom of his voice could paralyse every nerve in your body.

No one ever answered Mr Perkins back.

He was no tyrant, though. His anger was always justified, and I for one benefited a great deal from trying to listen, learn and act upon his advice or orders to the best of my ability. Under his tutelage I became goalkeeper for the school football team. However unlikely this may seem now, with my short, stocky schoolboy physique, I kept a lot of goals out. That was before my eyes went on the blink, which I'm convinced was caused by my receiving a high-speed cricket ball to the bridge of my nose during a Barrow Hill XI school game on Parliament Hill Fields. I was carried off semi-conscious and dumped unceremoniously beneath a big tree near the boundary line. The crispness of vision didn't seem the same as I rejoined the game a while later, to a mild round of applause. It has never been the same since.

At Barrow Hill I had my first experience of boxing. Every Friday afternoon in the main hall there would be bouts between boys, run by the headmaster, Mr Porter, who was a tall, grey-haired man in his sixties. Apparently calm, he could explode, if roused, into a most formidable creature. He had a tongue as fast and venomous as a rattlesnake, with a backhand swipe to match. These outbursts were rare, but once seen, they were never forgotten, so the boxing classes were run to his command.

It is my firm belief that Mr Porter had a bit of a sadistic streak in him, as throughout these contests, clumsy and violent though they undoubtedly were, his face was a picture of peace and joy. It was as if he was in the middle of some private and hugely enjoyable dream. First we would form a square ring, using chairs. The two gladiators once selected had no choice but to adopt the best sneer possible and aim it at their opponent. It was hard to make any type of excuse to Porter, but even harder to back down in front of your mates. The Friday that brought my turn, I took off my pullover, tie and shirt, leaving just the vest. My tie was then tied around my waist. Still scowling, which seemed a better option than throwing up or crapping myself (which would have been a more honest gesture), my arms were spreadeagled to the side, and huge, aged brown leather boxing gloves were strapped to my tiny fists. There must have been some kind of an arrangement between the London County Council and the army surplus stores, as these gloves were so old and cracked that after a fight the surface of the leather fell away in a dry powder. Perhaps they'd been used for recreation purposes at the Somme or Verdun. A chair was removed, I was pushed into the ring, and the chair was replaced.

Everyone then knelt on the surrounding chairs and looked at Mr Porter, who stood smiling as he held a bell out to one side. There was a deathly silence. Then, just before striking the bell with a drumstick, he announced in a gentle, friendly voice, 'Round One'.

Ping.

Out we both charged, swinging helicopter-style punches at each other or anything else in the ring. A long three minutes of overhead punches, slaps, hooks, forearms or vicious elbowing followed. It was non-stop aggression. The more I got hit, the angrier I got and I attacked twice as hard, completely forgetting to defend myself as I did so.

These battles went three rounds, by the end of which both combatants stood utterly exhausted, dazed, with big red blotches all over their faces and arms. The tears that had welled up during the first round and had fallen despite everything had dispersed, mixing with the dirt from the gloves or the floor, which I invariably hit several times during the bout, grazing and skinning my elbows and knees. The size and antiquity of the gloves usually guaranteed a thumb in the eye or, worse, numb ears – you'd be half deaf save for a ringing in your head for days afterwards.

In all the years of Friday boxing, Mr Porter never took the trouble to teach us any sort of technique, stance, or how to defend ourselves. Maybe he thought it might spoil the spontaneous brawling spectacle that we provided for him.

•

When I was seven, my parents separated. Les had given my mother her last beating. She went to the courts with the advice and backing of a friend and got Les kicked out of the flat. The police were never called as far as I can remember, and there wasn't a day when big men came and took him away or anything. He just didn't come home any more. Because there'd be times when he didn't come home for a few days anyway when he was on a bender, I didn't specifically know that he wasn't coming home. Mum must have told me, but I didn't believe it at first. Then, as my hallucinations stopped, I really began to believe that Les had left De Walden. It was just Mum and me in the two rooms.

However, I was soon forced to see Les at least one day a week, which was one day a week more than I could previously have been sure of.

Mum was left with all the responsibility and work needed to bring me up, but welcomed the peaceful life she now had in return. Dad felt that his four pounds per week maintenance was the be all and end all of his responsibility as a husband and father. She had always been in charge of disciplining me, even when Les lived with us. Punishment was administered never unfairly but always swiftly, effectively, and with great accuracy across the back of the head, legs or on the bum. Clean, crisp, stinging swipes they were. As each hit home, Mum would tell me why she was punishing me.

'I (slap) told (slap) you (slap) not (slap) to (slap) do (slap) that! (Slap, slap). Didn't (slap) I? (Slap).'

Thank heavens she had the determination to keep me in line. Fucked-up as I had been until Les left, with my hallucinations and nocturnal wanderings, Betty made a pledge that I would receive a proper education in life, which was something that the Blitz had robbed her and her brothers of. She was a woman true to her word. There followed years of toil for her as a result of this commitment to me. Scrubbing people's floors, cleaning up after them, doing their washing, ironing, shopping or any other task they would throw her way, all to buy the food to nourish me, the clothes and books I needed for school. It was the only way out she could give me. Through education, she firmly believed I could rise out of the squalor. (Right up until the first hit record I had with Adam and the Ants in 1980, Mum was offering me a hundred quid if I returned to Art School to get the B.A. degree that I'd lost by bailing out of the course to form the group three years earlier. Bless her.)

Of course we were on welfare, as Dad's paltry maintenance meant little in real terms. My mother was in great pain, too, and although she tried to hide it, I knew something was wrong with her. She suffered from gynaecological problems, which meant innumerable stays in hospital when she lost too much blood to walk, let alone work. Because she attended a Catholic hospital and she was so young, the doctors held off giving her the hysterectomy that she so obviously needed. It made me want to cry to see her in pain, but I tried to be as strong as I could and not let her see me suffering. That would only make her feel worse, I knew.

Thankfully, Mum was not totally alone. Her two younger brothers Tommy and Tony stepped in to help and would take me off her hands as much as they could. In doing so they became my surrogate father figures. Being the youngest of her family, they had the energy to get me out and about on a regular basis. Often we would visit Mum's two elder brothers, Wally and Bert. These two always seemed a little scary to me, and to visit them involved taking long, exciting bus journeys to exotic places like Putney, where Uncle Wally lived. He was a large, white-haired but powerfully set man, the eldest brother, whose resemblance to his father (Granddad Smith) was remarkable. Wally was cut off from the rest of the family after World War II because he had married an Indian woman named Ruth. At the time this was an unthinkable scandal, but Wally told the moral majority where to stick it, and love and right prevailed. My Aunt Ruth was a tiny though dynamic woman of striking beauty, and had the darkest eyes I'd ever seen. Her wonderfully aggressive nature was a delight to behold as she bossed her giant husband and two grown-up sons around. They lived in an immaculate flat on an estate that would take what seemed like hours to reach on a 74 bus.

Sadly, Ruth was addicted to cigarettes, which eventually whittled her already tiny frame down to a pitiful six stone. At one time her habit got so bad that my uncle had a cigarette vending machine fitted in the kitchen, in order that she wouldn't have to tax her lungs with the walk down to the shop to buy them. She still had to put the shillings in the machine to get them out – Uncle Wally didn't want her buying her fags in bulk – and he thought that with the machine she might at least be regulated in her smoking. The heart-breaking image of her with heavy black circles under her eyes as cancer ate away at her, fighting for breath as she coughed up huge chunks of phlegm from her tiny chest, still remains with me.

If Ruth wasn't enough to put me off, I had never been impressed with smoking. When I was ten, I asked my mother for a puff of her cigarette and she obliged. Calmly she gave me one, and then another, 'Just like the big boys do,' she said. Midway through the third Rothmans I felt so dizzy and nauseous that my career as a smoker terminated there and then.

Wally was eventually reunited with the rest of the extended family, although sadly not until after Ruth's death. I know it meant the world to my granddad to have his eldest boy back again.

Uncle Bert was without doubt the black sheep of the family. The most gypsy-like in temperament, he'd always gone very much his own way in life. Quiet, and with something of a mysterious air about him, he was tall and lean, with a shock of black Laurence Harvey-like hair. He was married to an attractive Welsh woman whom he seemed to dominate without a word. Just a look would silence her. The only memorable event of visits to Uncle Bert for me was getting my hands on a small banjo-type instrument that he would let me play. As with my earlier experiences with the piano, I thought the songs would come miraculously from nowhere when I played it. At some point during my childhood the trips to see Uncle Bert stopped. Mum told me that he and his wife had upped and split for Australia, where he got a job as a bank dick in Melbourne.

I'll always love my uncles Tony and Tom for the way they helped Mum and me. Tony was already a bit of a veteran, having first taken me out as an infant to the local parks at weekends. This, he later informed me, had not been an altogether unselfish act on his part. 'You got me laid many a time, son,' he assured me. His technique was slick, easy and effective. His uncanny resemblance to Michael Caine helps to explain his success rate with the flood of French au pair girls that hit London in the late fifties and early sixties. Tony would send me over to play with the dogs or children that these girls would be innocently taking out for a walk.

'Now come away, Stuart!' Uncle Tony would falsely protest, moving over to the unsuspecting blonde goddess usually named Heidi or Brigitte. 'I must apologise for my nephew, he's such a nosy little pickle,' Tony would laugh.

Nine times out of ten the au pair would reply, 'Oh no. Eet is not iz fault. I sink 'ee is a gorgeous leetil chap . . .'

And they were gone, hook, line and sinker. Tony's *Alfie*-like charm, baby-blue eyes and the filthiest laugh known to mankind would do the rest.

Uncle Tom had spent much of his childhood undergoing terrible operations on his legs as a result of an air raid during the Blitz when a bomb fell on the house and my grandfather dived on top of him to protect him from the blast. In doing so, he crushed Tom's legs. Metal plates were put into him to replace smashed bones. As he grew, he was trained as a cobbler, a profession that would allow him to stand up all day and help his legs. His courage was a great inspiration to me as I grew up, as he never let any of it get in his way, and never mentioned it. And should the subject ever come up, he was always the first to joke about it.

Uncle Tom lived at home with Granddad, who was still working for Broads when he was well into his sixties. When he reached sixty-five they retired him and gave him a clock and leaving do. The next day he got up at five a.m., went to work, took a medical exam, which confirmed he was stronger and fitter than anyone there, and resumed work till he'd decided he'd had enough. Even then he started another job the next day.

Uncle Tom was a brilliant snooker player – he could stand up and play, of course. He taught me, and I became quite good at it, though I say it myself.

One day Uncle Tom brought home his sweetheart, June. She was a very pretty girl and was always very kind to me. I therefore felt no threat from her, but saw less of Uncle Tom as he was always 'off having a talk with June'. Their courting was not helped along by my grandfather, who made no effort to put on any graces or act thoughtfully towards Tom's 'Precious', as he fondly nicknamed her. Granddad would sit there at the end of the sofa, slap-bang in front of the TV smoking his Boar's Head roll-ups one after another, oblivious to the foul odour that filled every crevice of the front room. Then there was his cough, which churned up lumps of phlegm. Here he did make one small concession. He had mastered the art of spitting a wad over the top of the evening newspaper as he read the results.

My uncles assure me that he never missed the fire – they'd wait for the sizzle and then cheer. When June arrived, though, he settled for a big red plastic bucket and a box of Kleenex extra strong tissues. It should be noted that this act was not so great a concession, as around then the fireplace was blocked in and an electric bar heater installed. (I do, however, remember the occasional sizzle. Old habits die hard.)

Whenever I stayed there, I slept with Granddad. The bedroom was always freezing cold because the window was kept wide open. He preferred it that way. The room smelled of old times past. The sheets were clean and heavily starched, and I'd slip in on the far side of the bed, quiet as a mouse, and not move a muscle all night. Then, at five a.m., when it was still dark outside, his coughing and tea ritual began. Granddad would let out with his morning chorus of 'Ooh, this cough. It's a bastard!', then follow it with five or so minutes of tea stirring, ending with a seven-tap melody on the side of his mug. He was as tough as old boots, with white stubble on his Desperate Dan chin and fine white hair . . . oh, how I loved him, and miss him as I write this.

Uncle Tom and June were married at St John's Wood church in the early 1960s. The reception was held at Cicely Davis Hall, just down the road from Granddad's flat. I felt well hard and trendy in my first suit, even though it featured short trousers. My hair was combed forward in true Beatles style, although it was always too wavy to get it quite like theirs.

Both families came to a big stand-off inside the hall, June's relations on the left, the Smith brood on the right. The atmosphere was polite and, as with all English weddings, a bit awkward until everybody got tipsy enough to meet each other for real. The room fell silent as the round of speeches was about to begin, but before they could, my grandfather did three things. First, he drank the water from his finger bowl with the usual slurp that came with drinking from a saucer, as if cooling down his tea. Second, he let go with a hefty chorus of coughs. And third, he blew his nose on the crisp white serviette, shaped like a swan, that stood in front of him. This caused endless amusement to our side of the hall, but a great deal of embarrassment to the poor bride's loved ones. Again there was a long silence, broken once more by Granddad, who discreetly deposited the wad he'd just brought up into the serviette, and, out of habit, sighed the usual, 'Oh this cough, it's a bastard!' He received a round of applause, and the proceedings continued splendidly from that moment.

•

By the time I reached my last two years at Barrow Hill, 1963–64, the Beatles had arrived, big time. They were Merseyside gods with their haircuts, matching suits, immaculate pop records and droll accents. Too young to be teenagers, we nine-year-olds bopped along in the shadows, wishing we were one of the Fab Four. It didn't matter which one, any would do. At Barrow Hill an era of tennis racket Beatles impersonators had begun and was in full swing. Usually made up of a four-piece of older boys with painted cardboard cut-out guitars taped to the fronts of tennis rackets, they would mime in the main hall to 'Twist And Shout' or 'She Loves You'. They'd shake their heads on the falsetto 'woo's just like John, Paul and George. To nobody's real surprise, the reaction from the girls was the same as if these four boy impersonators were the Beatles themselves, as they screamed and wept and attacked the group members before, during and after each song.

How us smaller boys envied those boys as they signed their autographs on the swooning girls' exercise books or pencil cases. So convinced was I that the ability to play, or even pretend to play, an instrument was the key to a perfect social life that I headed straight for the school music teacher demanding to be taught how to play an instrument. I would learn the hard way that this was not the case.

The choice of instrument made available to me was less

than inspiring – violin, viola or cello. Nevertheless, I would not be put off – at least all three had strings, a shaped body and a neck, and with imagination weren't that far away from the guitar in appearance. The music teacher said I was too small for my first choice, the cello, and handed me instead a shiny new viola. Fair enough, I thought, well impressed with the beautiful varnished wood finish, neck cushion and bow.

We began with simple enough tunes revolving around half a dozen notes. I loved it, but, alas, it didn't love me. After a month of trying, the screeching noise I produced sounded like a tom cat being castrated with a blunt pair of nail scissors. Patient as the mistress had tried to be, she was only human, and one afternoon she grabbed the viola from beneath my chin in mid-performance and announced that class was ending early. She felt bad about it, she said, as she admired my undoubted enthusiasm, and would find something else for me to play, perhaps something a little more in my line of things.

I was transferred to 'percussion'. But the triangle didn't capture my imagination, as I'm sure she hoped it wouldn't, and I returned to enviously watching the ranks of screaming young things watching the Beatles-boys. I'd go straight for the guitar next time.

Equally inauspicious was my debut as an actor, which also took place around this time. My first production was a project put together for UNICEF (United Nations International Children's Emergency Fund) Year, with members of the class wearing the different national costumes of the countries involved. In front of the school, parents and teachers we stepped forward in turn and said who we were and what country we came from. What a splendid Ukrainian yokel farmer I made, complete with frock shirt, knee-breeches, hat, shepherd's stick and a piece of straw hanging from my lips to add a touch of authenticity. It wasn't the line, I thought, so much as the way I said it. I was hooked by the drama, the excitement and the tights I got to wear. I wanted more, more, more of this.

Soon enough my prayers were answered. So impressive was (I believed) my UNICEF performance that I was immediately rocketed into the big school production of 'Persephone in the Underworld'. As a spearholder. With one line. Still, the costume was great. When my moment came I savoured it, rushing forward and grandly throwing back my red cape to reveal the shiny bronze plastic Roman breastplate and matching helmet my gran had bought me for Christmas.

I looked at the audience for a second or two, before telling Zeus: 'Persephone has been abducted and taken to the Underworld!'

Then I took a step back, wrapping my cape over my shoulder, threw another look at the audience and walked off. Twenty years would pass before I would be invited to take to the boards again.

•

One fine spring afternoon in the mid-1960s, on the way back from Barrow Hill school, I quite suddenly became aware of the most irritable itching sensation on my lower back and waist. I hitched up my shirt and had a bloody good scratch. Then I noticed the rash. That moment of pure ecstasy you get as you scratch an itch soon passed and made way for a rather nasty stinging sensation, as if I was being stabbed with a hundred little pins. When I got home the itching grew worse. I stood in front of Mum's dressing-table mirror and positioned a hand mirror at the necessary angle to discover a large colony of scarlet, angry-looking spots. I'd had measles, mumps and chickenpox and believed it was impossible to get them again. After a couple of sleepless nights I decided to show it to Mum, 'not that it's anything serious,' I assured her. She took one look, told me off for not telling her earlier, and whisked me straight up to Dr Gilbert for the diagnosis.

'Shingles, a severe case too, contagious as hell,' he told Mum firmly.

It seems that shingles is a nervous disease, and despite all my attempts to hide my rash, I now stood helpless as the strain I'd grown up with (Les, my hallucinations, my mum's health) and accepted as normal turned me into a grotesquely spotty, contagious outsider. I could see the guilt in Mum's eyes as the doctor asked if I'd been under any strain or if anything was worrying me. We both denied it vehemently. All this had come at a very inopportune moment, as my mother was finally about to go into hospital for a hysterectomy and would be there for three weeks or so. Once out of hospital, it would still be weeks before she was fully recovered. Since I was contagious, there was no way Auntie June or Uncle Tom could look after me, as it could seriously endanger Granddad. Les was in no fit state to look after me, not that my mother would ever have allowed him to do so even if he could have, so strong was her hatred for him at the time. There was only one thing left – the Local Authority.

The next day the council took over, assigning me first to a state orphanage hospital and then to a proper foster home, where I would stay until I was fully recovered. No time limits or dates were given, and they made no bones about the fact that I was now in their care and would be returned only after meeting their stringent standards of health. I kept thinking about Dickens's Oliver Twist. I took it rather well, bravely even, helped no doubt by the fact that none of it seemed to be really happening. And who knows, I thought, it might even be an adventure.

I was taken to a large orphanage outside Slough. At least, that's where I think it was. It was like a military barracks of red-bricked houses formed in a square, with a perfectly mown lawn at its centre. At the far corner of this square was the hospital wing. Here I spent my first month in relative peace and quiet. Each day one of the nurses would spray me with a translucent plastic skin, to prevent me from scratching my irritable spots, and thus curb their spreading any further. After three days or so this plastic skin had to be removed. As they peeled it off I began to realise how sick I was. The pain was overwhelming, as dead tissue and muck from the sores came away with the plastic skin. I was told that if my rash joined entirely around my middle I could die, and that was why they had to spray me. This knowledge stopped a large amount of idle scratching and helped me deal with the inevitable pain every three days.

This was the first time I'd truly been away from home, or slept in a room by myself, and I found the privacy and the peace and quiet very soothing. It was a relief, almost, from the havoc that had been going on all around me. One might even say a comfort. I welcomed especially the cup of hot cocoa they gave me before I went to bed and the little kiss the on-duty nurse would give me while tucking me in. This was the only affectionate gesture allowed to members of staff, who were instructed not to show preference to any particular child. But there in the dark, in secret, how I clung on to that kiss, trying to fall asleep as quickly as possible with it fixed in my heart and mind, cocooned in its warm glow.

The place was clean, not too run-down and the food, I thought, was very good. It wasn't so bad, this being ill lark, after all. What did upset me, though, were the real orphans who lived there. I felt great compassion for them, coupled with guilt for having a real parent to go home to. This was the only thing that made me cry during my stay there, and for perhaps the first time in my life, I was not crying for myself. All the kids wore old, ill-fitting, oversized clothes, usually threadbare and patched. They were always so grateful for any privilege or treat that might come their way. They were all looking for love, parents and a home. One boy sat in a corner all the time and didn't speak or join in. But others would show great affection to the nurses and staff, hugging and kissing them whenever and wherever possible. They called everyone 'Auntie' this or 'Uncle' that. There was no 'Mum' or 'Dad' here.

During my time as a part-time orphan, the song 'Concrete And Clay' by the group Unit Four Plus Two was played on the radio all the time (which makes it early summer 1965 and me ten years old). To this day the dislike I have for that song makes the hairs on the back of my neck stand up whenever I hear it. I think of Slough on a hot summer day, missing my mum and wondering if my exile was going to last for ever.

Because my mum still wasn't strong enough to look after me, when I got over my shingles I was sent to a foster home a few miles away, just outside Maidenhead. It was a typically faceless suburban two-up, two-down, with a sizeable garden at the back. Not unpleasant, and at the time I suppose rather sought-after. The names and faces of my foster parents entirely escape me, but their attitude and manner don't. They were experienced, cold and professional. They had a child of their own and three of us foster kids. There were 'no-go areas' in the house we were to steer clear of, unless invited, which actually left us with only the lavatory, our beds, and the garden to roam freely in. I shared a room with the two other kids who at first hardly spoke to me, not out of unfriendliness, it seemed, but a kind of fear. The first, a black kid about my age and on the tubby side, became a bit friendlier towards me as time went by, but never let himself go. Perhaps he didn't want to be abandoned any more by anyone he got close to. The other boy was a bit of a strange one. Older than us, in his early teens, he was tall and thin with short black greasy hair. He didn't like to wash much and consequently was a bit whiffy. This was not helped by his perpetual bed-wetting. He said very little, and if he did it was laced with anger and frustration, usually in defence of his few belongings or 'things' as he called them. He was very territorial, especially about his duties, given to him by 'Auntie Vicki and Uncle Ken' (let's say). Instinct, as well as my nose, told me to stay well away from him, as on one or two occasions we'd seen him have a type of fit in the bedroom, after some tiny thing had sent him into a rage.

I began to miss the hospital and to wish I could have had the shingles for a bit longer. But just as I was becoming miserable in Maidenhead, the strangest thing happened. My miscreant father was granted permission to take me away with him for long weekends, leaving on Friday evening and returning on Sunday evening.

As fate would have it, and by an enormous stroke of luck, he was living with my Great-Aunt Mary and Uncle Charlie in nearby Cookham. How I'd welcome the sight of Dad driving up to the foster home in his cherry red Ford Anglia, registration number FGP 131C (easily remembered by me as standing for 'Fat Gutted Pig 131C'). He would even turn up on time! Then we'd drive for a half-hour or so across the beautiful open Berkshire fields by the river to a heaven on earth. The tiny village and my Aunt Mary and Uncle Charlie would save me more than once in times of great need. As a result of this weekly escape, the rest of my time as a part-time orphan flew by, and in discovering the sanctuary of Cookham some good came out of the experience, as well as the fact that I now valued my parents more than I had ever before had cause to. Les, for all his faults, had come through when the chips were down. For all his faults, weaknesses and the distance between us, he was, when it came to it, my father.

•

Back at De Walden Buildings, Mum and I made the best of our surroundings when we were back together. My folding Z-bed was now a permanent fixture at the foot of her bed, in the corner by the window. On the wall above my headboard I pinned the two full-colour team shots of Chelsea and Manchester United that I'd sent off to the Typhoo tea company for. Next to these, on the adjacent wall, Mum let me draw 365 neat vertical lines on the wallpaper, one of which I would cross out each night with an equally neat diagonal line. I had a nightly ritual during which I'd kneel by my bed and whisper a prayer, 'God bless his flock. Amen', with the occasional P.S., '. . . and please let me grow a bit taller', then I'd cross myself, scratch out a line on my calendar and hit the sack.

Every Sunday I would be picked up by my dad to spend the day with him. Or rather, with his car. Come rain or shine, hell or high water, at eleven a.m. on Sunday morning I would be out in the street waiting for Goddard. And wait I did. All I did was wait. Very rarely was he on time, confirming my belief that he had no desire to see me at all, and only did so to spite my mum and enforce his 'rights' as a father.

Never before 11.45, and often as late as two p.m. he would roll up in his or his boss's car, throw open the door and order me to get in. There was always some excuse about the terrible traffic hold-ups, or how the alarm clock had let him down yet again. But he never fooled me. I knew that swollen, red face of his. The sour stink of stale beer on his breath as I dutifully leaned over to kiss the cheek he so dutifully offered gave him away every time.

I was picked up either pre or post pub hours. On the rare occasions that he did turn up on time we would often visit the Imperial War Museum in Lambeth. Then it was straight off for a beer. A large proportion of my Sunday was spent waiting outside pubs, sipping at countless glasses of warm Coca Cola and munching bags of crisps with little blue bags of salt inside. Sometimes Les would be so long in the pub that the amount of coke made me feel quite sick. Never once did he come out before that one drink too many. And never before they threw him out. Then it was off to Gran's house, where he lived. By the time we arrived the dinner would be ruined, and another dreadful argument would ensue.

Nothing had changed, just the time, place and target of Les's filthy mouth. Again I'd try and shut out the aggressive, piss-fuelled abuse that streamed from his foul mouth. Although slightly toned down (this was, after all, his mother) and never ending in physical violence, the effect on me was still the same.

Eventually we would sit down to eat, which for me was always a comfort and joy. Les would eat only the meat and then stumble to the couch and fall asleep. From that moment onwards, my Sunday would take a turn for the better. Gran and I would sit watching the Sunday film or chat over a cup of tea. There was always a book I could look at, or some old photo annuals lying around. And all the while Les would snore like a bastard.

There were occasional nice outings with him, such as one Christmas when we went to Hamleys toy store on Regent Street and I met former boxing champion Freddie Mills. He was a giant of a man in a huge pale grey suit with padded shoulders and looked like a gangster but had the wrong accent. He had a shock of black curly hair and a Desperate Dan chin. He knelt down, put up his fists and invited me to 'thump me as 'ard as you like'. So I did, and he toppled over backwards, moaning as he lay spreadeagled on the floor. He was there to sell a branded punchbag, which we didn't buy, but I thanked him for his kindness in giving me a truly exciting moment.

Other Christmases Les took me to Selfridges on Oxford Street to visit Santa. That was until I was rudely awakened to the fact that Santa didn't exist by my father and his drunken mates one sad Christmas Eve. I think we were at my grandparents' home in Bravington Road. Les, who was well pissed, of course, was playing Santa and tiptoed his way into my room. There was much giggling and energetic 'Shh'-ing, as drunks are prone to do. An almighty crash woke me up screaming. Les, en route to the foot of the bed, had slipped and dropped the lot. There he sat, surrounded by gifts, pathetic and glassy-eyed. He looked at me and said with a belch, 'Son, I think you're old enough to know, there's no such thing as Santa.' Outside the door, silhouetted by the landing light, his audience laughed and sniggered. It was all great fun to them. Arseholes.

My father had a passion for aeroplane modelling, and on rare Sundays our beeline for the pub would be diverted by way of a model shop or two. As a result I became interested, and between us we knocked up a rather fine two-stroke-engined Messerschmidt 109 and a decent torpedo boat, which we lacquered red after hours of sanding with finer and finer grades of sandpaper. Those were the few good times we had together.

•

Mum always referred to our flat as 4 De Walden 'Prison', and true enough, the brickwork did have that Wormwood Scrubs design to it, but I began to enjoy the old place, especially after my time as an orphan. Being home with my mum was great, of course, but there was something else about the place that I liked. If I looked out of the window by my bed, up on to the top balcony opposite, I could see the front door of the first true love of my life: Sonya Palmer.

I had had no real girlfriend before the divine Sonya, if you don't count Harriet under the table at Robinsfield, Kimmy Dumbleton along the hallway, Mrs Saloman and, at a distance, French Vivien.

My knowledge about sex was zero, although I didn't realise this at the time. Les had assured me that I knew 'all I needed to know' after his birds and bees lecture given one afternoon as he dropped me off at the flat. He'd made a big enough deal about it, after all, when he took me into the bedroom, at Mum's insistence, and awkwardly asked me if I knew anything about 'the birds and the bees'. Some friends at school had told me about similar lectures from their dads, and out of embarrassment I'd always nod, wink and say I had received the same. But now I was getting the mystery talk. I couldn't wait. It went like this.

'Daddy loves Mummy. Daddy kisses Mummy and, if they *really* love each other, a seed passes out of Daddy's mouth and Mummy swallows it. This seed drops into Mummy's tummy, and grows into a baby. Nine months later, the baby pops out.'

And there it was. The facts of life according to Les.

Still, this was a vast improvement on his previous 'baby shop' explanation, which up until then had me believing that I had been purchased some nine years earlier.

By a strange coincidence, my first real education in sex took place, on two separate occasions, in the same place: the St John's Wood burial ground in Wellington Place, right opposite Lord's cricket ground. This quaint little garden housed old bleached headstones, long neglected by family and friends. There was a great playground on the south side with swings, roundabouts, seesaws and an enormous slide. Close by stood a headstone that for some reason fascinated me. It had a military coat of arms at the top and was the grave of a lancer in the legendary 8th Hussars who had survived the infamous Charge of the Light Brigade in 1854. The grounds around it were well kept, with splendid rows of tulips everywhere, hedges neatly trimmed and trees were full of blossom. It was here, on a glorious summer afternoon shortly after my little chat with Les, that I found a rather grubby brown paper envelope at the foot of a mulberry tree. Inside was a discarded porno mag. Rather heavy stuff, too, with three kinds of intercourse on display. The bodies were presented in vivid pinks and reds, bloated and desperate as if they were in agony (which, given some of the positions, they were in, I suspect they were). I wasn't shocked or disgusted, but rather confused. I had nothing to compare it with. There didn't seem to be any kissing going on, not mouth to mouth, anyway, so I doubted that this was baby-making in process. I had no opinion of it other than that this was not something I'd take home and show my mum. It would, however, require further investigation, so I returned to De Walden and hid the magazine behind a loose brick at the far end of the playground by the bins. In the day or two it took for me to pluck up enough courage to have a more detailed look, my sordid treasure had disappeared. Not being entirely stupid, I began to put two and two together, and although always coming up with five, it must have become clear to Mum at least that I was not convinced that I had been told the whole story. Maybe it was the sudden attention I began paying to newspaper photos of young lovelies with their miniskirts, thigh-length boots, false eyelashes and plenty of attitude.

At the Saturday morning picture shows we boys had always been too busy stamping our feet and shouting whenever anything lovey-dovey came on screen. Now I began to watch and take it all in.

Into this mess stepped my Uncle Tony, who proved to be my saviour and the only one willing to tell me the truth, the whole truth, and nothing but the truth about sex. One afternoon he took me to that very same burial ground and told me the facts of life. Straight and with no frills. He didn't talk down to me, as a child, but on equal terms, like the big brother I so longed to have. He covered all the main points of sexual intercourse, putting great emphasis on the use of contraception, to both avoid unwanted pregnancies and contracting a disease known as VD, which was where he lost me. This sounded more like something to do with a German World War II rocket. He smiled a most comforting smile and told me not to worry. Then, out of his wallet he produced a strange square packet, which he tore open carefully, pulling out a little round rubbery thing.

'Do you know what this is, son?'

'No, Uncle.'

'It's what we call a Durex, or Johnnie.'

He then unrolled it for me. It looked like a big, oily, transparent snake, or sock, possibly best employed for drainage of some kind. Very medical, it made me think of hospitals. The idea of pulling this article over my cock seemed highly unlikely, and most awkward.

'Now, if you ever get any discharge or soreness down there after you've had a bit,' Tony continued, pointing at my privates, 'you just go to a VD clinic, you don't give your name or anything, they give you a number, and they'll take care of you. OK, son?'

I nodded and suddenly felt very much more grown-up than I had before our little chat. I doubt that Uncle Tony ever realised that my pecker had been used solely for pissing at this time. I hadn't even enjoyed my first trip down Ejaculation Street, premature or otherwise. Which brings me back to Sonya Palmer.

Although I must have known her for most of my life, we had hardly ever exchanged a single word, only the occasional glance. Her mother forbade Sonya – or François, her younger brother – to play down in the yard with us plebeians.

At this point in my life, armed with all the grown-up information I'd just received, I had noticed how beautiful Sonya had become. No longer a scrawny, shy little kid, she suddenly took on a radiant teenage aura. François was always peeking over the top balcony outside their flat. Although banned by his mother, he would always wave at me if by chance I happened to look his way. He'd smile that great big gummy smile of his (his front teeth had not grown through), and invariably Sonya would appear from behind and remove him. It was while doing this that our eyes first met. She lifted François down from the balcony, and instead of moving off she looked down, right at me. A moment passed and then she smiled and managed a little wave. I responded in kind, but before I could speak she was gone. I didn't sleep a wink that night. I just lay in my bed looking up at her balcony opposite. Hours were spent cooking up plans to get up there. Should I throw a tennis ball and go up to find it? Or wait until she pulled François away again? During the next two days I ate very little, tasting none of the food I did swallow, and sat at my window. I wanted to be alone. With Sonya, preferably. Then, on the morning of the third day, I decided to brave the big, cold stairs leading up to her door, and knocked.

Her mum opened the door, looking big, dark and severe. She looked me up and down and asked, 'Yez, zo vot too you vont?'

'I'd like to play with Sonya and Frankie, please.'

'Hiz name iz François!' she corrected me.

'Oh, sorry. But, er, I've er, seen them both up here and just wanted to be their friend.'

A good ten seconds passed, during which time I was convinced I might just be grabbed and thrown over the balcony.

She looked over her shoulder and saw her two children looking out nervously at me. Then she turned, gave a huge warm smile and, stepping aside, ordered, without turning round, 'François, Zonya, come out here, plees!'

And so it began. That first great adventure in that funny little place called Love. François, however, was not to have so happy a time. Younger than both of us, his desire to 'play games' seemed dull and childish. The poor little sod – toothless and alone, his every move was subject to our instant disapproval and ridicule.

'Don't be so stupid, François.' (Ha, ha.)

'You are such a baby, François!' (Ha, ha, ha.)

'Did you hear what he said?!' (Titter, titter.)

Or worse, our pièce de resistance: 'Put your teeth in, François!' (Guffaw!)

Sonya had fine, dark blonde hair, parted in the middle and combed into plaits on either side. She was radiant and always looked tanned, all year round. Her mother dressed her immaculately in simple cotton dresses with bright floral designs, white lace socks and brown Clarks sandals. On her teeth were fixed two rows of vicious-looking metal braces, hinged and sprung, it seemed, by an elastic band. The braces embarrassed her enormously, so I simply ignored them. The subject was never brought up. On the cold landing steps we held hands and had an occasional cuddle. Suddenly, the prospect of playing with all the other kids seemed so unattractively childish and beneath us. We preferred any quiet and remote parts of the block we could find. In the safety of the shadows we sat all by ourselves.

One afternoon, while Mum was out shopping, Sonya came to our flat. She looked at the posters on the bedroom wall, smiled, and, drawing the back of her pleated skirt beneath her, sat down on my Z-bed.

I'd seen a lot of kissing at the Saturday morning picture show, and a voice seemed to whisper to me, 'Kiss her.' In very grand, stiff movements I leaned over and kissed her on the cheek, with feeling. Eyes shut. Before I could withdraw, she grabbed me with both hands round the neck and planted a big, full kiss right on my lips with those beautifully soft, moist lips of hers. It seemed to last for ever. It was like trying to hold your breath for a minute, and ended in a gasp from both of us.

Within minutes we were lying outstretched on the bed, snogging away for all we were worth. No tongues touched, though; we were just enveloped in each other's arms. It was heaven.

Things were never the same after that. As she left for home I stood and watched her from my window. She never looked up or back at me, but I knew she had a delightful smile on her face, one I'd never seen before. It was the same as the one on mine at that moment. Her braces had left my gums sore and bleeding, but I didn't feel a thing and couldn't have cared less anyhow. My insides were shaking and throbbing in a most peculiar fashion, and I knew I either had a sudden case of pneumonia, or I was in love. Now we were a couple. I was her boyfriend and she was my girlfriend, and we didn't care who knew about it. Our love was fresh, innocent and true.

During the year that followed, her plaits went, her braces went, and she blossomed into a beautiful young woman before my eyes. The feeling we had between us never went away. I'll always treasure this first love, as it never got messy or too physical. The kissing and cuddling was the be-all and end-all of our treasured times together. And because soon after she moved away with her family to a council maisonette in Victoria, it never ended. We never ended it, we never said goodbye, so it was never over. And soon I too would leave De Walden.

3

NINE PLAN FAILED

ST MARYLEBONE GRAMMAR SCHOOL FOR BOYS had been founded in 1792 by a bunch of local businessmen who wanted to help the poor boys of the area. By the time I arrived in 1965 the old school was only just surviving. It was still a place for bright, working-class boys – you had to pass the eleven-plus exam to get in – but had only just managed to keep itself from becoming a comprehensive school. Instead the governors gained voluntary controlled status and kept its old traditions in place, among them the practice of administering corporal punishment to unruly boys.

Besides passing the eleven-plus in order to get into St Marylebone I had to pass an interview with the headmaster. On walking into his office he pushed a series of photographs of former masters of the school at me, across his desk. Did I recognise any? Luckily I did. I had been reading about William Wilberforce, the great anti-slavery politician, at home and there he was in front of me. That answer was enough to get me a place. The head stood up in his gown and mortarboard and said, 'Very well done, Stuart.'

On the first day of term, all the new boys, myself included, had their heads shoved down the toilet and flushed by the sixth formers. I tried to take it in my stride, knowing it would be worse if I fought them. Better to get it over with, I thought, and soon. The education at St Marylebone was archaic, with Latin and Greek force-fed by a terrifying master, Mr Barker. He had a head of white cropped hair, bad teeth, and was rumoured to have been a commando during World War II. He carried a large knife, which he would throw onto his table while reciting verbs, or use to clean his nails. He knew that his pupils were all a waste of time, especially one troublemaker whom he dragged by the hair to the headmaster's office for six of the best in the first week. After a short time, I made no attempt to understand Latin and I think he knew that and just left me to it. Or he didn't notice that I was copying homework from my new best friend, Dave Pash, almost word for word. In return I would protect Dave as much as I could in the gym, and from other boys who thought he was an easy option to push about.

The school seemed to be populated by mildly eccentric teachers. The history master, Mr Hookway, for instance, would climb around the classroom using the rafters like some crazed mountaineer as he taught. I enjoyed history anyway, but he made it more entertaining. The main problem with St Marylebone's was the homework. Every night we were given loads of the stuff. Once home, changed and full of tea, I'd be looking at three to four hours of it, which I dutifully did while kneeling at a small bedside table in De Walden. My eyesight definitely suffered as a result.

Then there was the sport. No more football; instead there was plenty of rugby, cricket and gymnastics. I had foolishly picked up a rugby ball during a games lesson early in my first year and scored a try, thus impressing the sports master and earning myself countless bruises, aches and pains as I played every Saturday morning for the school team. I was signed up as the hooker, which meant even less time off. Being the smallest in the team, I was usually pummelled in the scrums. However, we did become the best team in the school leagues. Regardless of freezing blizzards, heavy rain or bright sunshine, and despite being head-butted by some psycho from another team, I had to play. A note from Mum asking, 'Would you please excuse Stuart from games,' didn't cut it at St Marylebone's. Cricket was more civilised, thankfully, and I became house captain. The responsibility didn't try me too hard, though by now I was wearing glasses, which helped enormously with my game. So with the help of Dave Pash in the classroom and my sporting ability on the playing fields, I did settle into a kind of steady pattern at school.

In choosing to attend the Grammar, I had lost almost all of my mates – the ones I used to play football with, anyway. They went to the local secondary modern comprehensive school, with its blinding emphasis on woodwork, technical drawing and football (the lucky bastards). That most of the boys at Marylebone were from better-off families didn't bother me; while at Barrow Hill I had become friendly with posh boys. One of them was Andrew Gorrara, the son of a sculptress, the first bohemian artist I had ever met. Mary Gorrara wore black, thick, roll-neck jumpers, slacks or faded jeans, and sandals. Her long wavy black hair was swept back off her face into a ponytail. She looked a lot like Picasso's wife, Jacqueline, with the same strong features and prominent eyebrows, nose and mouth. Her brown eyes looked right into you. She was always covered in white powdery clay and plaster from her work, and chain-smoked Gitane cigarettes.

Mary Gorrara introduced me to the world of art, and gave me a chance to do something a little bit constructive and imaginative. She'd give me huge lumps of mouth-watering wet clay to do what I pleased with. My efforts, though no doubt awful, seemed to impress Mrs G, which in turn impressed me. She was never patronising or overdemonstrative as she encouraged me to see the job through, so I often took home ugly, lopsided bowls, cups, or mugs, all painted and fired in the oven at her house in Hampstead. She also gave me large sheets of coarse, cheap paper, which I merrily covered with pictures of all shapes, sizes and description. Pencils, charcoal, poster paint and brightly coloured wax crayons were all employed in my efforts. I had been taken under the wing of someone I respected and admired, and who took the time to encourage me to produce something original, in the process teaching me to follow my own instincts.

Mrs G also taught me how to swim, for which I'll always be grateful. I became a pretty competent swimmer, practising with her at the Hampstead lido. However, I didn't discover the true joys of swimming until later with my pals at the now demolished Finchley Road Baths, where I learned to dive, and subsequently 'bomb' other swimmers. (When Les attempted to teach me how to swim, not knowing that I already could, I took great pleasure in conning him into performing a painful belly-flop into the Finchley Road pool in order to impress me. He lost his swimming shorts in the process. I then 'bombed' him, along with half a dozen mates.)

For the first year at St Marylebone Grammar I couldn't and wouldn't invite anybody back to De Walden. It was easier not to have to explain. However, one memorable summer afternoon, the Right Honourable Quintin Hogg, MP, cycled into the courtyard of De Walden Buildings on his trendy small-wheeled bicycle. He removed his bicycle clips and brushed down the lapels of his well-worn camel-hair coat. Photographers from local and national newspapers were there to capture an historic moment.

In a deep resonant voice, this Churchillian figure announced, 'I am here to inspect the living conditions of my constituents, here at . . . er . . . De Lungden Buildings.'

No one corrected him, as the power of the man was quite overwhelming. Ten minutes later, when he came into our very humble abode at number 4, I took a close look at him. He seemed like a giant – fat, distinguished, and tailored into a Savile Row suit crowned in true British fashion with a navy-blue polka-dotted bow tie. His face was set in a permanent frown, as he mumbled gruff, though not unsympathetic, replies to the many complaints from the female residents of De Walden. A fine silver pair of pince-nez looked lost in his huge sea of a face, as they hung on the very tip of his nose.

Mum had me well and truly rehearsed, and I was kneeling down at the white table by her bed doing my homework. Quintin stood above me, clearly horrified by this state of affairs, and further alarmed by the poor quality of light allowed by the bedside lamp, with its handmade frilly lampshade.

'What school do you go to, my lad?' he asked, in the kind of perfect Eton accent that until then I'd only heard on telly in the Sunday film, usually spoken by Laurence Olivier or David Niven.

'St Marylebone G-Grammar, sir.'

'Really?' His breath was thick with the smell of nicotine, probably from a pipe, I guessed.

'Yessir. First year, sir.'

'And is this the only place for you to study in?'

''Fraid so, sir. It's the only place to write in.'

'Well, my lad, I happen to be on the board of governors at St Marylebone, and this will just not do. Not do at all.'

He took out a pencil and pad and scribbled a few notes down, and tutted some more.

'Well, best to you, young man. And don't damage your eyes under that poor light, will you?'

I assured Quintin I would not, but alas I lied. We did not change the light, because we simply didn't have the money.

After a few more poses for the *Marylebone Mercury*, he was gone. The visit had taken twenty minutes. It must have been election time or something.

Perhaps by coincidence, or perhaps it was just that our time was up, a letter arrived from the council not long after offering us a two-bedroomed flat on a nearby and more recently built housing estate. It may have been a plain and faceless old council flat to most people, but to Mum and me it was an honest-to-goodness orange-bricked palace. My life was taking a turn for the better, I realised, when I first walked through the front door. There were so many rooms, or so it seemed, that we couldn't decide which one to look at first, or which one would be the bedroom or dining room. We both burst out laughing and hugged each other as the tears rolled out of us. For the first time we were crying together for joy.

We only had enough furniture to put a couple of token bits in each room, and I spent that first evening carefully pacing each room, measuring its length with my feet. Our one 'carpet', which had looked so huge at De Walden, now became a mere rug, sitting lost in the middle of a sea of cold, brown Marley tile.

That night I slept in my own room for the first time in my life. No one walked through the room or past my bed. At last I could shut my own door.

•

Not long after we moved, Mum got a new and oddly glamorous job as a daily for Beatle Paul McCartney. After school I'd walk down to his huge white Georgian house in Cavendish Avenue, NW8, past the handful of tired, sullen girl fans standing and sitting outside, waiting, waiting, as they always did. How they must have envied me as I pressed the doorbell, looked up into the security camera, and stepped through into the square paved courtyard beyond.

Having one of the Fab Four living in your area was exciting enough, but to have your mum working for one was something else altogether. An Irish couple, the Kellys, ran Paul's house, and they kept a very low profile, providing him with the peace and quiet he no doubt craved after going through three years of Beatlemania. At the time that Mum started working for him, the Beatles had stopped touring and playing live and were working on songs that would be released on *Revolver* and then *Sgt. Pepper's Lonely Hearts Club Band*. Since they always recorded at Abbey Road Studios, which were just around the corner from

Paul's house, he was often at home, usually with someone Mum described as 'a beautiful girlfriend with red hair', which can only have meant the actress Jane Asher.

Mum's tasks were simple enough, being mainly ironing or cleaning up around the house. The hardest part of the job was having to fight her way through the hordes of girls waiting outside, many of whom had come from abroad and camped there for days or weeks at a time. They would beg her for a souvenir, or sometimes just a touch, believing she may have rubbed shoulders with Paul. Mum would sometimes bring some-thing out with her when she left, a bar of his soap, maybe, or an old comb or newspaper. They would grab these bits of trash wide-eyed, unable to control the tears that came flooding out, receiving each item as if they had been given some kind of holy relic.

Occasionally, I would be allowed to take Paul's huge sheep-dog, Martha, for a walk around the block, giving me a sense of purpose and usefulness as well as bags of envy from the fans. Those fans and millions of others would have been overcome with envy had they known that Paul had given me an advanced pressing of the *Revolver* album, together with a note that read:

> To Stuart,
> > Best wishes
> > > Paul McCartney (Beatles)

It was pinned on my bedroom wall next to the Chelsea and Manchester United Typhoo Tea posters until I moved out, six years later.

I was allowed to walk around the upper floors of the early eighteenth century house, which was done out in perfect pop-art style. I think Paul was working on *Magical Mystery Tour* at this time, and his music room was full of instruments painted in psychedelic designs. There was a stand-up piano in the centre of the room, with an assortment of acoustic and electric guitars, and a tambourine. I vividly recall there being two bass guitars, a Rickenbacker stereo, and his famous left-handed Hofner violin bass, leaning against a series of screen doors decorated with Renaissance-style inner panels. These were a gift, or so Mum said, from the Royal College of Art. Elsewhere the room contained some beautiful sculptures by Sir Eduardo Paolozzi, the most striking of which was a huge wrought-iron fireguard, brightly painted, like something from a carnival. (A few years later I would work for Paolozzi and he gave me a couple of beautiful sculptures and a brass plate.)

There was a huge black room on the top floor, with no furniture, just a huge pile of his gold and silver discs and assorted memorabilia which had somehow escaped being given to the fan club for distribution. Also there, still in its box, was his MBE which, unlike John, he had not sent back to the palace.

His bedroom was large and a bit dull to my nearly teenage eyes, only interesting for its step-down sunken bath.

Paul was always friendly to my mother, and always said hello to her whenever he came down for his favourite 'tea and sarnies'. It appeared to me that success had not gone to his head. He was just like he was in *A Hard Day's Night*, apparently. In all the time she worked there, I only ever saw him once, and that was through a crack in the door. He came down the stairs and asked my mum, 'Betty, will my shirt be ready soon?'

I stood transfixed. There was a Beatle, larger than life, with his long ebony hair and Sergeant Pepper moustache. I was surprised by how tall he was, and by the six o'clock shadow on his chin.

As for John, George and Ringo, however, Mum's opinion was quite different. During their many visits to the house she had evaluated and summed them all up, and remained for the most part unimpressed. John she considered 'arrogant and rude', while Ringo was 'very moody'. As for George, who asked Mum to come and work for him after Paul married Linda Eastman and went to live in the Outer Hebrides or some such such place in 1970, Mum refused without giving it a second thought. It was too far away from her home to even consider travelling to George's house, and she wasn't going to move just for a job.

Because my mum worked for Paul McCartney, I, of course, was considered somehow cool to know – at least on the estate where we lived. Which helped, because attending grammar school did not make me many friends round where I lived.

•

The estate we moved to from De Walden was the second to be built in a massive council housing scheme constructed during the 1950s and 60s and dumped right in the heart of St John's Wood, one of London's richest and most select areas. Even today it stands out like a sore thumb, its characterless orange brick dulling the elegant white hues of the Georgian houses that stand around it. I have a theory that the architect made the model with Lego bricks and the construction chief merely duplicated the Lego. At the time that it was being filled up with the working-class poor of the area (and some from further-lying areas, too), the tenants were made to feel about as welcome as a fart in a spacesuit.

It used to be that, when asked where I was brought up, I would answer 'Marylebone', or 'near Edgware Road'. But if I did admit the truth of the matter, I would always qualify the St John's Wood part with, 'On the council estate, you know.' Not that our fourth-floor (of six) flat was ever anything less than a comfortable home. With the help of the tally man (otherwise known as a loan shark), who used to knock at our door every Friday evening to collect his week's interest, Mum was able to buy more furniture on the 'HP'. With us being on welfare, the weekly collections must have been an enormous strain on her.

Not long after we had moved into our new home, my mum started to see a man named Tony. After a short while I realised that he made her happy in a way that I had never seen Les manage. Tony was a true hero, and had been a tank driver during World War II. A little bit older than my mum, he was almost the exact opposite to Les in that he was sober, kind and generous. Maybe the experience of having been in the first wave of Allied soldiers to have liberated Auschwitz had had a humbling effect on him, but it's just as likely that he'd been born that way. I quickly came to love him as a father. (He married my mum when I was sixteen, and I was best man.)

Once we'd moved, I spent every night seated at my desk with a load of homework. My only comfort came from the sounds of the wonderful Tamla Motown hits that floated up from the youth club four flights below and along the road. I never met the DJ of that club, but I thank him now for saving my soul and spirit by providing me with an education in R&B, Stax, Philly, soul and reggae. It was through him that I first heard Marvin Gaye, Tammi Terrell, Smokey Robinson, the Temptations, the Four Tops, Diana Ross and the Supremes, the Jackson Five, Stevie Wonder, Isaac Hayes, James Brown and my personal favourite, Al Green. I must have listened to Freda Payne sing 'Band Of Gold' over a hundred times in 1970. (Little did I imagine that one day I would be invited by Berry Gordy Jnr to perform on the same stage as these giants of soul, as part of the Motown twenty-fifth TV special.)

By my third year at St Marylebone Grammar, the original skinhead craze had begun. It was an entirely macho movement, with violence and racism at its core at worst, but with a brutal, stylish flashiness at its best. It was the logical progression in British working-class street style following on from the mods, who were the younger brothers of the original Teds. There was an acute lack of girls around the scene, though. I had only a rare glimpse of female skinhead beauties when the older lads' girl-friends danced in formation at the youth club – it was rumoured that they would actually do the naughty behind the club house. They took my breath away in their two-toned miniskirted suits, patterned tights and French-crop haircuts. They chewed gum, chain-smoked and looked tougher than their boyfriends. All that us little ones could do was look, dream and fantasise about them in the quiet of our lonely rooms.

For a year or so, I lived a double life. At home, on the estate, I was a football-loving, potentially loutish lad, but at school I was a rugby-playing, grammar school twat with a lot to learn and as much to prove. My inner conflict was eventually expressed in the form of a fifteen-foot mural I was commissioned to paint on the wall of the youth club that played all those great records, by then renamed 'Reflections'. Justin, the leader of the adjacent adventure playground, had asked me to do it, so, next to a shield carrying Captain America I painted a tiny hippy character with thought bubbles floating out of his hairy head, reflecting on being a superhero. The name 'Reflections' had been Justin's idea to move the club into the seventies. It was a bad one. A week after I'd finished the mural, it was painted over with blue emulsion.

Mural painting was not new to me by then. I had started with a five-foot rendition in oils of the Beatles in cartoon form, copied from the cover of Yellow Submarine. (It remains in the toilet still, and my mum proudly giggles when any unsuspecting guest is taken short at her house.) When my bedroom was damp-proofed by the council, I asked them to leave just the white lining paper, and then painted a dozen or so Disney characters on it, as well as the Pink Panther and Captain Haddock, Tintin and Snowy from Hergé's Adventures of Tintin. Later, I would cover the wall behind my bed with a large collage of images cut from newspapers, or any type of gaudy, shiny, silvery psychedelic wrapping paper I could find. Kenneth Halliwell had nothing on me! Even a newly sealed service hatch between the kitchen and parlour could not escape the rampant strokes of my brush. I took the opportunity to paint a moody half-tone portrait of Marlene Dietrich, in all her red enamel glory. I never had the slightest fear of painting on a large scale; on the contrary the boldness and commitment required appealed to me.

With my artistic development taking shape in one part of
my life, my apprenticeship as a junior bonehead progressed
nicely in the other. Memories of being an apprentice suedehead
are mainly of a lot of boredom and time spent hanging around,
acting hard. Then there was the darts.

We played a lot of darts.

One day a very tough Irish skinhead named John Mc-
Gloughlin threw a dart which missed the board and buried itself
in my foot instead. There was no pain – at first. I looked down
incredulously to see it buried deep in my flesh, having pen-
etrated the perfect white canvas upper of my sacred Dunlop red
Flash trainer.

Another memorable occasion was the christening of my new
Levis which, tradition had it, needed to be properly shrunk to
fit. This process usually involved the new owner of the jeans
putting them on and climbing into a bath filled with nice, clean,
warm water and sitting there for a while. (In fact my jeans were
actually Levi Juniors, which were a lot cheaper than the holy
501s with the red tab, and had stupid reinforced knees made of
a square denim patch.) However, my shrink-to-fit process was
not carried out in the usual tradition. I was picked up by my
skinhead 'mates' and thrown into the kids' circular boating pond
in Regent's Park wearing the new jeans. They shrank to fit OK,
but they also always had a shiny, oily finish to them, however
many times my mum washed them.

I only tasted real danger as a lad on two occasions. The first
was during a big local gang fight between our heroic local
shineheads, and 'Roscoe of Willesden' and his boys. Roscoe had
achieved near legendary status around our way by spraying his
name all over the walls of the estate. This particular day, word
had it that he was on the warpath. I was chosen by one of the
big lads to run to the local pub and give the rest of the St John's
Wood lads the urgent message.

How I ran. I was Captain Nolan at Balaclava, with the fate of
an army at stake. I reached the pub exhausted, threw open the

door and blurted 'Roscoe!', pointing to the estate I'd just come from. They jumped up, slammed down their lagers and steamed past me fearlessly into the fray.

I never found out what happened in the fight, but I had at least played my part. Done my duty. I was a fucking hero in my own lunchtime.

The second occasion was one Saturday night when my friends and I – having saved all our cash earned from milk and paper rounds – ventured into the infamous Country Club on Haverstock Hill, which at the time was *the* skinhead hangout in North London.

As we walked down the dark alley to the entrance of the club, we all realised the mistake we had made, despite at least looking the part. We reached the entrance and huddled there in the doorway in our very finest attire, clothes that had cost us virtually every penny we had: black and green Harrington windcheater jackets with red tartan lining, cream Levi Sta-Prest trousers held up with thin elastic braces. Tucked into these were cherished light blue- and pink-striped Ben Sherman buttondown shirts from the Edgware Road. On our feet we wore the all-important pair of highly polished oxblood royals, black brogues or threepenny loafers (with a threepenny bit or, if you wanted to be flash, an American quarter, placed inside the lip at the nape of the shoe). I say all-important, because the fashion called for all trousers to have a small turn-up, so not only did your footwear have to be correct, but it always had to be polished, too.

Once admitted to the Country Club, we had our first big scare. We were herded into a tiny room just behind the box office and interrogated by plain-clothed and uniformed policemen who sat behind a square of impromptu interview tables. There, under an intimidating bright yellow naked light bulb, we were all asked serious questions by serious policemen, none of whom were going to take any bullshit from a bunch of hooligans like us. They wanted our names, addresses, occupations and whereabouts a fortnight ago. Were you at the club that night? they asked. We were all fingerprinted and photographed. This was the real thing, a murder investigation.

Eventually we got inside the club proper, and it was dirty, sweaty, packed and pitch-black apart from some very inadequate red lighting. The music was a deafening combination of heavy ska, reggae and soul, which bounced off the walls. The first song I remember hearing was 'Return Of Django' by the Upsetters, then 'Reggae In Your Jeggae' by Dandy Livingstone, and then the Pioneers' 'Long Shot Kick De Bucket'. This thrilled me, as I knew and loved these songs, which was just as well because all we dared do all night long was stand on the very same spot, pinned against the very same safe piece of wall. All around us the older skinheads with fabulous clothes that none of us could afford danced with their equally tough girlfriends, either up close or in formation. The skin girls wore miniskirted two-tone suits with patterned tights and a lot of eye make-up. But to be honest I didn't get a good look at anyone, and for good reason. As the divine music of Sam and Dave, Otis Redding, Marvin Gaye and Tammi Terrell held me in thrall that night, I and my mates had to concentrate on not grinning too much or looking anyone in the eye for more than a second. Either could easily lead to a shout of, 'Oi! Wanker! Who you fucking screwing?' from some skinhead usually larger than you and capable of inflicting swift amounts of physical violence, more often than not with the help of his mates, while you lay helpless on the ground.

We spent the evening trying to forget the danger and the fear, but when we got home, that was by far another story. We were local heroes for even having set foot in the place, and gained a reputation enhanced by the murder inquiry and even more by our own exaggerated accounts.

Eventually, though, I became bored with all this posturing and let my hair grow and grow and grow. For the next three years, in fact. The longer my hair grew, the further away I moved from the whole suedehead/lad mentality. By the time I was seventeen I had a shock of hair down to my waist, although I would still wear much of the skinhead attire I had come to love. Fortunately for me, St Marylebone Grammar introduced me to a set of new friends, all older than me, and for whom I had a degree of respect, mainly because they seemed interested in things other than clothes and football and pretending to be hard.

•

In order to be able to afford the clothes and records that I so loved, as well as being able to take girls to the movies or gigs, I had two jobs as a teenager. The first I got when I was sixteen, working part-time as a groundsman in the Regent's Park Golf and Tennis School. At six a.m. I'd be there, levelling the clay courts, watering, sanding and finally pushing a huge cast-iron roller up and down in neat rows. After school, at five-thirty p.m. I'd do the same again. On Saturdays I worked in Courtney Chemists in St John's Wood High Street. By the time I was seventeen I had become a stock manager there, a job that allowed me some perks, giving me time to read a book and nibble some healthy biscuits with fruit juice. I always did every-thing that was expected of me, though. I was never a shirker at anything I did.

With the money I managed to save, I bought a Sunburst Fender Precision bass guitar and started a band with Dave Pash (who taught me to play) and Paul, a guitarist. We played mainly Cream and Hendrix songs, which I'd sing and play bass to at the same time.

We learned 'Little Wing', 'Crossroads' and 'Crest Of A Wave' by the late, great, underrated Rory Gallagher. My first amplifier was an Orange, a huge box on castors, with four twelve-inch speakers bolted on to a wooden frame, the amplifier part being powered by huge valves that glowed and burned red hot when the amp was warmed up, but took an age to get to a playable state. The thing weighed a ton. I knew that for a fact, since I would have to push and carry it half a mile to Paul's mum's house and half a mile back again in order to rehearse. We played just one gig, at St Marylebone Grammar School, of course. We stood right at the back of the stage and the audience stood at the back end of the main hall. There was no applause whatsoever after any of our numbers. Not a squeak. 'Fuck 'em' I thought, and decided that being in a band was not going to get me a girlfriend if I only played at boys-only schools.

Being at an all boys' school is a dreadful experience. Other than staring at the teachers' wives at school sports day, girls didn't seem to exist, and those that I did encounter seemed to come from another planet altogether. So when a French teacher called Madame Horrocks came to St Marylebone, the impact on five hundred pubescent, hormonal boys was immense. She was a beautiful woman and very voluptuous. Every time she turned to the blackboard, several boys would drop a rubber or ruler to get a better view of Madame H's anatomy.

By this time I had discovered the delights of orgasm. The first time was almost an accident, and I had no idea what was happening, just that I didn't want to stop whatever it was that I was doing that was so pleasurable.

It was a warm summer evening. Downstairs the youth club disco was blasting away with its Tamla Motown hits. I started to roll gently from side to side, then my groin started to tingle and my dick got hard of its own accord. My first orgasm seemed to go on for ever. All of my senses came together, crashing to a slow throb. It was the most intense experience that I'd had in my short life, and by far the most enjoyable. I'd spend the rest of my life looking for this same experience, I decided. The music that accompanied my erotic awakening contributed to the level of enjoyment, I'm sure, since it was Marvin Gaye and Tammi Terrell singing 'Ain't Nothing Like The Real Thing'.

From that time on, my irregular meetings with girlfriends had more of an objective to them. I had begun to meet girls while working and hanging out with my non-grammar school mates and found, thankfully, that girls seemed to like me almost as much as I liked them. I and a girl either went to the movies on a 'date' and sat in the back row snogging, or would stand in the playground as the night came in, snogging. A few times I had fumbled around with a girl's clothes and she mine, but until I discovered the joys of orgasm, I had no idea what it was that I was supposed to do, or feel. After Marvin and Tammi, though, I knew to place their hands firmly on my dick, and between the ages of fifteen and eighteen enjoyed endless hours of being wanked. Surprisingly, perhaps, it wasn't until I was eighteen and out of St Marylebone that my then girlfriend, Vicki, asked me why we hadn't done it yet. We had been going out for a few months at the time and had just been to visit my dear Uncle Charlie and Aunt Mary at their beautiful cottage in Cookham, which is how we came to be sitting at Cookham station. Vicki asked me if I didn't I think it was a good idea, to go all the way. You bet I did.

The first time was not that good, as we had to use condoms and it was over all too quickly. But we didn't give up. Vicki obviously had more experience in things than I did, and we got better with each try. Vicky was very generous in her lovemaking, and she was a good teacher (even though, or rather perhaps because, she was a hippy chick). After the first time I made love, I made a lifelong decision to give up wanking for good. My eyes were in a bad way as it was. I decided to be patient; so what if you had to wait for weeks or months for sex? I had ceased to be a wanker.

At the time I lost my virginity, I was studying for three A levels. I had six O levels and was taking A level Art, History and English. I was the only A level Art student at the place, having studied under the wonderful Artie for five years, taking his sarcastic asides to heart, finding things to love and hate about all kinds of different art. Despite the headmaster at St Marylebone and other teachers trying to dissuade me from taking Art, Artie had truly supported me, going as far as to organise a trip to the Tate to see the Andy Warhol exhibition in 1971, despite his personal disdain for him. The show was an eye-opener for me and included a lot of the now classic material, including the Elvis gunslinger, Marilyn, Brillo boxes and screen-printed Elizabeth Taylors.

Artie had been an enormous inspiration to me. Obviously gay and more than a little camp, he would often smell of booze as he talked to me about Turner or Picasso or Van Gogh, but he always made great sense. He also claimed to be impressed by my having seen the great English artist Stanley Spencer when I was a young kid. I was about four at the time and visiting my Uncle Charlie and Aunt Mary in Cookham for a family picnic on Cookham Common, when my cousin Paul and I spotted a grumpy-looking old tramp pushing a decrepit wire pram with an old umbrella sticking out of it. The man was tiny, with a shock of straight white hair and thin plastic-framed National Health spectacles, which had a strip of plaster holding them together at the bridge of his nose. He seemed irritated and mumbled to himself as he rushed to wherever it was he was going. We found him very amusing until he came close to us, and we ducked down into a bank of grass below his path. This was quite definitely the Bogeyman as far as we were concerned. We clung to each other in fear while he passed us by, before returning to our family, pointing the weird man out to them as he made his way up towards the High Street. 'Oh, that's only old Spencer,' we were assured by everyone. 'You don't want to worry about him. Dirty old bugger.'

It turned out that my family, like all families in Cookham at the time, had played a small part in creating the Spencer legend. However distasteful they may have found the scandalous, bigamous behaviour of this tiny man, they still had the utmost respect and awe for his genius as an artist. I discovered, much to my joy, that my family had more than one connection with him. He had sketched my Auntie Pamela, along with some of her friends, incorporating them in some of his local religious work, in which he depicted heaven as the normal everyday life and people of his home village. My aunts Mary and Pamela describe how they would watch him paint the – by now priceless – views of Cookham, honouring the silence that he requested via a hand-painted sign perched in his old pram.

In the early 1950s my Aunt Mary's daughter Anne, who was a teacher, together with her artist husband Anthony, invited Spencer to the local school to encourage the children to paint. They also had him round for supper on a few occasions. These visits were not well received by my great-grandmother. When she ran her own laundry shop a generation before, she had refused to take Spencer's laundry in due to 'the indescribable state of his sheets'.

It was some years before I found my way to the wonderful Spencer Trust Museum Gallery on Cookham High Street, which houses the finest collection of Spencer's work. It was there, in the middle of that tiny church hall-style gallery that I first set eyes on a Spencer painting which to this day remains my favourite. It is the enormous unfinished work, *Christ Preaching at Cookham Regatta* (1956–59). Despite being unfinished, it gives you an insight into the workings of Spencer's painting. There is a fantastic richness and detail to the finished areas, which perfectly complements the bare bold lines and symmetrical grids of the unfinished canvas. There is a great confidence and grace to the pencil lines.

That one large unfinished canvas left me in such awe, such envy of the skill and talent of this man that it inspired me to attend Art School. After passing my A levels, I applied to and was accepted by the then notorious Hornsey College of Art.

4

JORDAN (SEND A LETTER TO)

THERE WAS A FINE TRADITION in Britain during the 1960s and early 1970s for working-class boys to go to art college and then drop out in order to concentrate on making music. Keith Richards of the Rolling Stones was probably the most famous art school drop-out. I didn't get into art school so that I could muck about until a career in pop music took off, though. I worked hard at my art and passionately believed that I would finish my degree and become a working artist. I was eager to make the right kind of impact on my first day at Hornsey and felt a little nervous as I walked up the Seven Sisters Road towards the college on a cool, grey September day in 1973. I didn't know much about the place except that the guy that I wanted to teach me, Peter Webb, had written a great book titled *The Erotic Arts*, which was a set text at the time. And that Hornsey had a bit of a reputation as a progressive, politically active college.

In 1968 Hornsey became one of the first places in England where a student sit-in brought the place to a standstill. Classes were cancelled and self-elected members of the student body entered discussions with the governing body about how lessons should be run. The sit-in was partly in support of the same kind of student protest taking place in universities in Paris and America. There was some discussion about stopping the war in Vietnam, but mostly it was all about revolution for revolution's sake. As the alternative newspaper of the time, the *International Times*, put it in an article about the sit-in entitled 'Hornsey – The Flower Breaks the Concrete', 'Revolution of thought and feeling is the only revolution that matters'. It didn't include the exclamation 'Maaaan!', but it might as well have.

Of course the sit-in made no difference to anything, except that the place gained a reputation for being exciting and 'revolutionary'. It did launch the political career of future Labour education minister Kim Howells, though. He planned the sit-in and remained proud of the fact that he had told the principal of the college to leave. Soon after the sit-in Howells gave up art, claiming that it was 'bourgeois individualism'.

But Hornsey College didn't look at all revolutionary to me as I walked about on my first day – in fact it seemed that Howells had been right. Most of the students looked as if it was still 1968, with their long, lank hair, flared jeans and sloppy sweaters. As I walked around the campus, though, I spotted a very splendid looking bloke with serious apache-style hair to his waist, dressed all in black. He, like me, was wearing some black brothel creepers. We nodded a sense of approval at each other but passed each other without a word. A few days later I discovered that he was Danny Kleinman, the leader of Bazooka Joe, who at the time were a well-known rock 'n' roll revival band. He was soon to become my best friend.

The immediately impressive thing about Hornsey for me was the wonderful array of girls around. There were beatnik types and some Laura Ashley-wearing hippies thrown in, too. I was looking forward to getting to know as many of them as possible from my first day there. During my foundation year, before the three-year vocational course, I decided that I would do graphic design, typography and photography.

I soon got to know Peter Webb. He was a friend of an English artist who I had a little knowledge of, but was to come to know much better through him: Allen Jones. His work was primarily about sex, and what was considered at the time to be perverse sex, too. Jones's erotic paintings and photographs often featured women in bondage, being whipped or spanked, blindfolded or masked. Sadomasochism was beginning to interest me. Ever eager to get myself noticed (without throwing bricks through windows), I felt attracted to Jones's imagery because of its shock value as well as the aesthetic. I began dressing in a Jones-inspired way, getting myself black leather trousers made and so on.

After attending classes for a few weeks, it soon became clear that I couldn't live at Mum's flat and make the journey every day from there to Crouch End where the college buildings were, and so, for the first time, I left home and moved into a room in Southgate. Back then Southgate seemed even further outside London than it does today. There was a tube station, but that was about the only thing that reminded you that you were in a large, exciting, sprawling and cosmopolitan city. Southgate was suburbia, the kind of place where people lived out their lives of quiet desperation, the kind of place that George Orwell wrote about in *Keep the Aspidistra Flying*.

I had a large, sunny room to myself, although I had to share everything else in the house, like the kitchen and bathroom. Most importantly, it was cheap. In the tiny room next to me was another new best friend, Dave Gibb, a Scotsman studying sculpture at Hornsey with Anish Kapoor. I had told Dave that the room was great – a bit small but with very good vibes – and he'd bought it.

We lived a short bus ride away from Muswell Hill and Crouch End, the two places where there was any kind of local night life or places to eat out. Not that there was much choice – just the Wimpy bar where the plastic-coated photographs of the food available always looked far more appetising than the mush that arrived on your plate. Yet at the age of nineteen, living away from home, everything seemed possible and within reach to me. The lack of any kind of rigid structure to the teaching at Hornsey began to play havoc with my lifestyle, though. Since I had no reason to get up early, I would stay up as late as I could, sometimes drinking vodka with Dave and sometimes going out to gigs with Danny (Roxy Music at the Hammersmith Odeon in 1971 was a particularly memorable night), and watching Bazooka Joe perform. After a while, Danny asked me to become their bass player so I started playing the gigs and singing with them instead.

We used to rehearse at Danny's parents' house in Stanmore. The music we played was as diverse as the band members. Bill Smith, the keyboard player, wrote songs with names like 'Rock In A-Flat' and 'Clerical Officer', while Danny's songs had titles such as 'Spaghetti', and 'Bike'. After a few months we also began to play a few of my early efforts, which included 'Cardiac Baby'. Bazooka Joe had backing singers led by Arabella Weir (now a best-selling author and former comedic actress), a good friend of Danny. She and two other girls were known as the Absorbing Lillets, and they'd stand at the side of the stage in flashy 1950s-style dresses with long gloves and croon 'Oooo-Wah' in tune, while performing little dance steps.

Bazooka Joe were excellent at playing old 1960s instrumental numbers like the Shadows' 'Apache' and 'Walk Don't Run'. Both these little gems served us well (and possibly saved our lives) when we turned up at a hard Ted hangout, such as the Bobby Sox Club. At our first performance there it was clear from early on that the hard nuts, dressed in drape jackets and with enough oil in their hair to keep a Norton motorbike running for a year, wanted no part of us. Or maybe they'd like a scalp or two. When we played our own material they stood and stared at us without moving, cigarettes burning slowly in their mouths, the smoke never creating a tear as it curled up their squat and square heads. We learned that night that at times like this, the best thing to do was play the old instrumentals and get out asap.

Around this time there was something of a Teddy boy revival going on in England. Glam pop acts like Wizzard, Mud and the

Rubettes wore extravagant Ted outfits along with their bizarre make-up (in Wizzard's case) and long, non-DA hair. The Rubettes even dared to take Gene Vincent's old blue cap and make it into a far more floppy, camp affair, which was brave of them. Brave because the old, that is, original, Teds, many of whom were still around, since most of them were only in their forties at that time, meant business. Which for them was cracking skulls with a bike chain. To those guys, anyone under forty years old on stage was cruising for a bruising. One night during 1974 at the Camden Town Hall, I recall Joe Strummer with his band the 101ers playing a very speedy set before getting the hell off stage. As we were the headline act, it was harder for us to get away as fast.

'Good luck with it,' said Joe.

'I'm gonna fuckin' need it,' I replied.

The next time we would meet would be at a Sex Pistols gig at the Nashville in Earls Court, he with the Clash and me with Adam and the Ants.

•

For the first year or so at Hornsey, I played bass with Bazooka Joe (which meant meeting lots of women, at least), worked hard at college and began to feel as if my life was changing. Or that it needed to change. And then I spotted Carol.

She was the cutest little blonde at college. She was wearing satin hot pants, suede knee-length boots and had truly great legs. Maybe it was looking at Allen Jones's art that did it, but I always found myself appreciating a woman's legs before any other part of her. If Carol had only had great legs, that would have meant some serious sex. But since she was also beautiful, kind, generous and understanding, that meant something altogether different.

I was in love. Just like with Sonya back at De Walden Buildings, my heart skipped a beat when I saw her and I could spend for ever just kissing her, lying with her, being with her. Unlike with Sonya, though, there was also the sex. With Carol I experienced 'puresex' for the first time.

Sex was a dirty word in the Britain of the 1970s. Saying it out loud could still cause a fuss in public places. Repression was the norm in much the same way it had been during Victorian times. There was a huge market for pornography, Carry On films were popular, and double entendres were the stock of most television comedians – all of which seemed designed to make sex either a joke or dangerous. I didn't get it. To me sex was the greatest experience possible, particularly when desire was equally strong between two people. To me such desire felt pure, not dirty, furtive or wrong, and so I began to think of the act between Carol and I as 'puresex'.

That was enough; I was a romantic and wanted Carol for myself only and for ever. There was only one way, I thought, of making sure of that, and so I asked her to marry me. She said yes, my mum and my stepdad Tony heartily approved, and her parents would do anything to make their only daughter happy. So they agreed that we could and should live with them in Muswell Hill. (Which turned out to be a great mistake, of course.) At a white wedding in St John's Wood in 1975 we exchanged rings.

I have often asked myself why we married and struggle to come up with a sensible answer. I had no right getting married at that time. I had no income and no idea of what it would mean. Neither of us was ready for marriage, but we were carried away by our romance and everyone seemed supportive of the idea. Carol's mum was a social worker and her father a lens maker and seemed to me to be in control of their lives and smart enough to know if it was a good idea or not. I certainly thought at the time that it was the right thing to do.

In the autumn of that year, Carol switched to St Martin's College to study fashion, and was to excel in knitwear. For a few brief months, with me feeling high, restless and full of energy, we had a great time together. But then things started to change.

I began to feel the pressure of living with my in-laws, felt enormous pangs of jealousy if Carol as much as spoke to other guys, and couldn't manage to both work at college and make music, which I was increasingly driven to do.

Then, one night in November 1975, I saw the Sex Pistols play their first gig.

They were the support act to Bazooka Joe at St Martin's Art School. It wasn't obvious to me at first – there was no blinding flash of realisation (not like other people who saw the Pistols in the early days claimed) – but at the Pistols' first gig, the idea of Adam Ant came to me.

The Pistols had got the gig because their bassist Glen Matlock was a student there, and they used to rehearse across the road from the college in Charing Cross Road. So they carried their (mostly stolen) gear across the road that night and set up in the early evening. They didn't even ask about a sound check. When they kicked off, it was clear that Johnny Rotten was not your usual front man. He didn't try to entertain or really even sing. He stood back from the microphone with his hands in his dirty, oversized trousers and spat out his version of the lyrics to the Small Faces' 'What You Gonna Do About It'. He changed the words, of course, to, 'I want you to know that I HATE you baby, I want you to know that I DON'T care'.

The Pistols were loud and raw, but they could play, and the energy they generated was hair-raising. That the long-haired, polite students didn't get it made the Pistols' performance althe more exciting and confusing to me. Danny didn't think that they were very good, and he even had a go at Rotten when he came off stage for sneering, 'Now for some real music,' at us in that sarcastic whine of his. Johnny was wearing a T-shirt that had Pink Floyd printed on the back, over which he'd painted I HATE. It was ripped and covered in safety pins and paint splatters. Danny was wearing one of the silver glitter jackets that we'd had made a few months before. The contrast between them couldn't have been sharper. Danny grabbed Johnny and threw him against a wall. The Pistols' manager Malcolm Mc-Laren watched and didn't do anything, just smiled.

After the Pistols' twenty-minute performance, which was greeted with silence by the students, we played our usual set, but it didn't feel right to me. The anger and the don't-give-a-shit attitude that the Pistols had shown before our performance made our rock 'n' roll pastiche sound as old and second-hand as it was. I felt annoyed and frustrated. They'd spoilt it for me.

•

After seeing the Pistols, I wanted to do something different, be someone else, but couldn't work out what and who. I knew that I didn't want to be Johnny Rotten although we had a lot in common, not least the fact that we had both had a rough time with our dads. I called Danny and told him that I wanted to leave Bazooka Joe and start my own band. He was fine about it and we remained friends.

I named my new band the B-Sides because we only played the B-sides of 1960s singles that hadn't been a hit. It was my first real band in the sense that I formed it. Lester Square (whose real name was Tom Hardy and who would go on to become part of the Monochrome Set) was my first co-band member. He joined when I told him that we were going to be a losers' band, which is also what we told bassist Andy Warren (whose sound was as sharp as an ice pick with an edgy bottom end), when he joined us after answering an ad in *Melody Maker*, which read, 'Beat on the bass with the B-Sides'. We called ourselves losers because at that time punk didn't really exist as a genre, and the term wasn't used by the press as a term of insult for bands like the Pistols, X-Ray Spex, the Clash, the Damned or Chelsea until well into 1976. We didn't want to be plastic pop stars like the

Electric Light Orchestra or prog rock stars like Pink Floyd, both of whom were enormous at the time. If that was what being winners meant, then we wanted to be the opposite.

With the B-Sides I was still singing other people's songs, at first. Then I began to write my own. As we rehearsed through Christmas 1975 and into the early part of 1976, I could feel Adam growing stronger. I could hear the music that I wanted to make forming in my mind, but I felt that it was being stunted by the B-Sides, so I took a break from them while I worked on my own songs, some of which would later become Ant songs, including 'Fat Fun', 'B-Side Baby', 'Fall In' and 'Puerto Rican'. As I was getting my stuff together the B-Sides continued to rehearse, with an old mate of Andy's singing, but they didn't get anywhere; they were not ready to gig.

It was around then that I decided college had to go, too. There was no way I could carry on and finish my BA because music was going to take all of my time. I'd told Peter Webb, the head of my course, that I was going to give up and he'd told me not to, but seemed to accept that I had taken as much from him and the course as I could. I'd always be grateful to Webb for introducing me to the work of Allen Jones and his S&M art, of course. A lot of what I'd learned at Hornsey would become a part of Adam Ant's stage show.

But while I was trying to get Jones's imagery and my own dark thoughts into the form of songs, I was barely sleeping and eating only occasionally. In the few weeks before I killed Stuart, I wasn't leaving my in-laws' house very often. That little house was getting to feel pretty claustrophobic. Inevitably perhaps, as the long, hot summer of 1976 began, I started to suffer hallucinations and depressions as bad as they'd ever been when I was a kid. I had no idea why it was happening, since they'd stopped when Les had left De Walden Buildings, and I didn't know what to do about it.

Carol couldn't make me feel better, alcohol didn't help and I

couldn't create music because I had no energy. I was in a right
state on the night when I knew I couldn't be Stuart Goddard any
more and took the pills.

•

Carol's dad drove both of us back to his house from Friern
Barnet hospital without saying a word. Carol cried quietly as I
lay my head on her shoulder and stared, unblinking, at the neon
lights passing overhead through the windscreen. As each lamp-
post passed I mentally clicked off the countdown to the moment
that I would tell Carol that I was leaving her.

Back in our room in Muswell Hill, Carol tried to get me to
explain why I'd done it. I don't think that I ever properly
managed to. She was scared, of course, and I think possibly
a little bit relieved when I said that I had to leave her and the
house. Because it felt like the end of my 'old' life and the
beginning of a new one, I explained that I had to live somewhere else, at least for a while, to make a new start. We would
still see each other, I hoped, and she agreed. We didn't sleep
much, but the pills that I'd been given on leaving the hospital
(the only thing that they'd done for me was to give me some
sleeping pills) made me feel calm.

When I left Carol's house the morning after I could have
gone to Mum's place. But I didn't. She didn't deserve that, she
deserved time alone in happiness with Tony. They didn't want
a miserable git of a son lying around trying to work out what to
do with his life at the age of twenty-one. Besides, I told myself,
it was going to be impossible to tell her that I'd killed her only
son, Stuart Goddard. I didn't tell her about this episode until
quite a few weeks later.

Instead I went to see my biological father and his second
wife, Doreen. I knew she would get it and not tell me to stop
being so stupid. Les wouldn't understand, but he'd be glad to be
able to tell his drinking buddies that his only son had decided
to come and live with him, rather than go to his mother's. My

being at his place would be a source of pride for him. At least for a while. Long enough for me to get somewhere else to live lined up.

By the time Doreen answered the door to me, my mind felt clearer than it had for months. Whether it was the drugs from the hospital or because I was on a 'high' having made a positive decision about my life, I still don't know.

'Stuart! Bloody hell, love, you look terrible. You've lost so much weight. Have you been ill? What's going on?'

'It's all right, Doreen, I'm fine, but don't call me Stuart any more. I'm Adam, OK?'

'Oh love, you can be whoever you want to be. Come in, I've put the kettle on. Dump your bag in the spare bedroom and come and tell me all about it.'

Doreen and Les lived in the porter's flat of the block that he was supposed to look after. It was in Westminster, not far from Mum's place in St John's Wood, but far enough away that I knew how to avoid seeing her for a while. Les was still drinking heavily and he and Doreen would often fight, loudly and violently. He'd married a woman who could and did give him as much grief as he had given Mum. Doreen wasn't well, though. She would, over the next few years, be in and out of mental hospital. A victim of severe depression and manic fits, she was bipolar and would be sectioned in order to protect her from herself and other people. When in a settled mood, though, she was great to me and very understanding. So much so that I started to call her 'Adamum'. Doreen was completely accepting of Adam and defended me against my old man's occasional moans about 'who the bloody hell I thought I was'.

Having decided that I wanted to be Adam and concentrate on making music, I set about getting to know one of the most incredible-looking women I'd ever seen. She worked in a shop called Sex in the King's Road run by Malcolm McLaren and her name was Jordan. She had been at the St Martin's gig looking fantastic with her hair in a pointed beehive and a Bowie-type black zig-zag of make-up across half her face when I first saw her. In her tight pencil skirt, vicious-looking stiletto-heeled shoes and a pink mohair cardigan, she reminded me of two women that I'd known as a very small boy, Brenda Hill and French Vivien. I was so impressed by her that not long after the Pistols' gig, I'd started writing to her. She'd never replied, of course.

Soon after moving into Doreen and Les's place, I started to visit Sex regularly.

The shop used to be called Too Fast to Live, Too Young to Die when it sold Ted and rocker gear, but McLaren renamed it and started to sell vibrators, rubber suits, bondage and leather S&M gear as well as the Ted stuff. Most of the gear in the shop that didn't come from wholesale outfits in Holland was made by McLaren's partner, Vivienne Westwood, who created glam-influenced Ted trousers in pink and mohair jumpers in bright colours. I kept going there partly to look at and buy the clothes – hand-painted T-shirts, leather trousers, and suede and patent boots – but mostly in order to work up the nerve to talk to Jordan, who could kill you with a look. Finally, one day, after wandering around the shop, I picked up a Destroy T-shirt and nervously approached the counter.

I couldn't help but sneak peeks at Jordan, trying to get her to serve me so that I could talk to her. Probably unnerved by the looks she was getting from me, Jordan slipped into the back of the shop with another assistant, Sue (Catwoman). I could hear them giggling together as I stood with my T-shirt, waiting to pay.

As Simon, the only male assistant in the shop, took my money, he asked if I lived in Muswell Hill. I stammered that I used to, and Jordan and Sue strangled a scream. The postmark on the letters I'd sent (which I later turned into the song, 'Jordan [Send A Letter To]') had given me away. I decided to front it out and ask Jordan if she would ever come to see my band play. She didn't say no, just that she'd have to see. I left Sex that afternoon happy and determined that my band would play live as soon as possible.

Because of a lack of money, and because Carol, who had decided to change her name to Eve to show the world that she was my wife, wanted to see me, Lester, Andy and I rehearsed at her parents' house. We were no longer the B-Sides and had begun playing songs that I was writing and I changed the name to the 'Ants'. I'd chosen the name because it went with Adam very well and because ants were incredibly hard working, tough and communal – they worked for each other. I wanted my band to be all those things and hoped that the fans would also consider themselves 'Ants'. The music we were making wasn't outright punk as it was being played by the Pistols *et al.*, but it was still raw – and loud. God knows what Carol's parents or their neighbours thought of the racket we made, but there was never any complaint, as far as I recall.

Making music was occupying me full-time that summer of punk, and the energy that I put into our rehearsals was sapping, but it made me happy. My hallucinations had stopped and my depression had gone. I was hyper a lot of the time, and always active. I felt as if I could do anything I wanted.

In the weeks that followed my making contact with Jordan, I kept going back to Sex and we began to make friends, spending each visit talking together for longer periods. Soon we were going to see bands together at the various new punk clubs as they opened up – the Roxy, the 100 Club, the Nashville Rooms – and hanging out together. I had put myself in the eye of the punk storm, standing alongside Jordan, and yet it didn't seem odd or unusual. It didn't feel like anything other than 'normal', at the time. But then, what's normal?

5

JUBILEE

JORDAN DIDN'T HESITATE. She took the razor blade from me, and I lay face down on the floor in her bedroom. She slashed a hole in the back of my black T-shirt, spread the fabric away from the small of my back and then carved the word FUCK in my flesh. I'd thought it might be a suitable name for the band, but I changed my mind when the cutting took place. I had been looking at a lot of tribal books when the idea came to me (particularly *People of Kau* by Leni Riefenstahl). Cutting was a rite of passage for the warrior, and I had decided that I wanted to be one. I didn't feel a thing while Jordan wrote, but I jumped up after she'd finished a bit too quickly and had to sit straight down again, feeling faint. Jordan washed the blood away and put an old T-shirt on to my first bit of body decoration to soak up the blood. Then she put the kettle on.

After a cup of tea, I stood and admired Jordan's handwriting in a mirror, complimenting her on it. She shrugged and said, 'See you later.' With my leather jacket slung over a shoulder, I decided to go for a walk down the King's Road with the fresh air stinging my wound and the shock of the people I passed increasing my mood of growing euphoria. A few part-time punks with their safety-pin-splattered school blazers and home-made bondage trousers looked suitably impressed when I threw them a look over my shoulder.

• Grandad
Tom Goddard in
army uniform.
(Author's collection)

• Grandad
Walter Smith
in navy uniform.
(Author's collection)

• Les Goddard in
army uniform, doing
what he did best.
(Author's collection)

- My mum Betty and me in a photo booth.
- Me aged three at home, in the De Walden Buildings.
- In the garden of my aunt and uncle's house in Cookham. Left to right: me, Grandma Bill, my great grandmother, Aunt Mary and Uncle Charlie.

(Author's collection)

Danny Kleinman and me performing as part of Bazooka Joe.
My leopard-print jacket was a tribute to Bryan Ferry.

(Author's collection)

Jordan singing her part in 'Lou' on stage, 1977.

(Ray Stevenson / Rex Features)

Inside: Close Encounters of the Third Kind   march 1978   60p

films and filming

ADAM ANT in Jubilee

• An early front cover
to promote *Jubilee*, 1977.

• Me and Siouxsie Sioux, 1977.

(Ray Stevenson / Rex Features)

An early studio portrait, 1977.

(Pat Booth)

A rare photo of me
without make up and
wearing glasses,
with Eve, 1977.
(Ray Stevenson / Rex Features)

I 'relax' on the laps
of the Ants in the
recording studio while
making *Kings of
the Wild Frontier*.
Left to right:
Terry Lee Miall,
Kevin Mooney,
Marco Pirroni
and Chris Hughes.
(Author's collection)

On stage during the 'Kings of the Wild Frontier' tour, 1980.

(Author's collection)

A few hundred yards down the road a very bubbly character ran up to me. He had short-cropped black hair, piercing eyes and a cut-glass upper-class accent. He said he was a director and would I like to be in his film entitled *Jubilee*, all the while beaming a cheeky smile at me. This became bigger when I told him I had a band and that he should talk to Jordan, too. He told me that he had already cast Jordan in the leading role.

A couple of hours later she telephoned me and asked if I wanted to be in a film with her. 'Derek said he'd met this great-looking kid walking along the street who looked perfect for the part of the pop star in the film,' she laughed. 'He said you had what he was looking for, the way you moved, the attitude in your face.'

Jarman hadn't realised that FUCK was written in blood until Jordan told him. (Jarman later wrote a scene into the film in which one of the central characters uses a razor to write 'fuck' into another's back.) Would I like to be in the film? Of course I would. At the time, June 1977, this was the kind of break, I thought, that could take the band into the big time. In fact it had the opposite effect.

•

Derek Jarman always claimed that he was 'inspired' to make *Jubilee* after seeing Jordan walking towards him on a London street in late 1975 dressed in a miniskirt covered in white 'GB' car stickers, fishnet stockings and with her hair in a strawberry-coloured beehive. I knew just what he meant, since I'd been in awe of her ever since I'd first seen her. But Derek was braver than I'd been and had gone straight up and asked to get to know her. His reaction was highly unusual at the time, though. The major effect of punk in England in the mid-1970s was one of shock and most definitely not of admiration.

It's hard to believe today that the sight of a woman wearing a mask of make-up with black eyes, ripped fishnet tights and madly coloured hair in a messy style could cause such a commotion. But back then it was front-page news, quite literally.

Britain in the mid-1970s was a very different place from the one we know now. The social revolution that had taken place in America and parts of Europe in the wake of the student riots of the 1960s had not happened in the UK. The country was still run by men who had either fought in World War II or gone into Parliament in the aftermath of the war and so were very definitely of a different mindset to me. They had grown up in a world run along Victorian lines and believed that class and status were fundamental issues in their country – just as long as the upper class ruled and everyone else did as they were told then things would be fine. By the 1970s, though, the working class and the trade unions had begun to rebel. Strikes and industrial action turned into three-day working weeks and power cuts in order to save the nation's fuel in England during 1973. These had led to the re-election, after only four years under Ted Heath's Conservatives, of a Labour government under Harold Wilson. Not that anything got much better under them. In fact, Labour's inability to deal with the unions led to the election of Margaret Thatcher and a Conservative government which lasted from 1979 until 1997.

Britain was an unhappy place in the mid-1970s. Most of the country used to close down well before midnight. Television, all three channels of it, ended at the same time pubs chucked people on to the streets, at eleven p.m. The only 'after hours' clubs open at the time were either for members only, or discos which charged an entrance fee for the privilege of drinking watered-down beer and spirits and watching secretaries from the suburbs dance around their handbags. Nightclubs had strict dress codes and age policies (usually over twenty-one). London had a few discos, but most British cities of any size would be lucky to have one. Live music went on at a handful of pubs, which closed at ten-thirty or eleven p.m., or at venues that were controlled by professional promoters. They usually put on a regular bunch of jobbing R&B acts, pub-rock bands and heavy metal wannabes playing Deep Purple and Led Zeppelin cover versions. Two or three times a year a major rock act might play the mega venues around the country. Pink Floyd, for instance, would play a few nights at Earls Court to promote a new album, Rod Stewart or the Who would fill football grounds, while the Stones, Yes, Led Zep or Genesis would top the bill at outdoor summer 'festivals'.

For the most part it seemed that the great British public was racist, despite large numbers of Asian and Afro-Caribbean families living in most cities since the 1950s. There were clearly defined ghettos divided along racial lines in places like Birmingham, Bristol, Liverpool and London, and all erupted into racially motivated violent riots between 1976 and 1983. Sexism was also common, and, like racism, apparently acceptable; the Sun newspaper had carried topless Page 3 girls since 1969. Television 'comedy' shows like On the Buses, Love Thy Neighbour, Mind Your Language, Please Sir, The Black And White Minstrel Show and The Benny Hill Show joked about black people and had semi-naked girls in them, just like the Carry On series of films had since the early 1960s.

For a generation of people who had grown up with mates who were not white and with women who didn't want to be housewives, Britain was a dull place to live. We wanted to change the world.

Punk was the way we thought we could change things. We wanted to shock Britain out of its small-minded, cosy complacency. The music was deliberately loud and simple in direct contrast to the overproduced, far too clever musical rubbish coming from the mega-rich rock stars who had nothing in common with us. We didn't want twenty-minute drum solos or pathetic, self-obsessed rubbish offered up as lyrics.

Punk fashion was all about sex, revealing and trashy in direct contrast to the smart casual dress of the day. Because everyone wore flared trousers, punks wore straight-legged trousers. Because men and boys still wore ties, punks wore ties, but studded them with safety pins and wore them more like a noose than a necktie. Because men and women wore their hair neat and styled, punks wore theirs deliberately messy, badly cut and brightly coloured. Because sex was still an activity that took place in private in Britain, between two (married) people, punks acted provocatively and perversely. Because a glimpse of stockings was still regarded, as the song says, as something shocking, punks wore them without a skirt over the top. Female punks made their sexuality so clear and obvious that they ceased to be sexually alluring to 'straight' men who preferred their women to be sedate, obedient and in the missionary position. Punk was incredibly arousing.

•

By the spring of 1977 I had moved into a freshly painted (black, of course), sparsely furnished room on the top floor of an Edwardian villa-style house in Redcliffe Gardens, SW10. The house was split into separate bedsits, each with its own lock. The kitchen and bathroom were shared by everyone – Donny, a hard-drinking American actor who also lived on the top floor and would appear in *Jubilee* too, a Sloane Ranger-style junkie and a couple of other people I didn't see too often. I spent Christmas 1976 with Doreen and Les at their porter's flat in Chelsea, and was still visiting and occasionally staying over with Carol (now Eve) at her parents' place in Muswell Hill. Carol had declared that she was completely behind me in whatever I wanted to do, which was great of her. My marriage to Eve might not have been what most people thought of as 'normal', but we still cared greatly for each other. We seemed to understand one another enough that we could live apart and be happy.

Having my own place to live made me feel totally free for probably the first time in my life. Apart from that brief period in the hospital wing of the kids' home when I had shingles, I had never really spent time alone, living by myself. Even in Southgate, before meeting Carol/Eve, I shared everything in the house with Dave Gibb and others, except my bedroom. At Redcliffe Gardens I could lead my life as I wanted to without worrying about anyone else. Which was just as well.

Redcliffe Gardens was perfectly located for me. It was a walk away from the King's Road (and Sex, now called Seditionaries) or Doreen and Les' place. My mum's was a brief bus ride (or tube journey) away. I could get into the West End quickly and easily and, if necessary, even walk back home from the Roxy, Marquee and any number of other places in the West End if I missed the last bus. There were no night buses and I couldn't afford a taxi anywhere.

Having made a good friend in Jordan, I became part of the punk scene that was based around the Pistols, Malcolm McLaren and Chelsea. London was like a great big playground to us in 1977. We were the odd gang of kids who hung around together not mixing with the 'normal' kids who did their boring, straight thing while we plotted, giggled, poked fun and made mischief on the fringes. Clubs like the Roxy, 100 Club and Marquee were the equivalent to us of 'messing about behind the bike sheds' – being 'different' in the middle of all that stultifying normality.

A couple of miles away there was another punk gang, centred around Ladbroke Grove and the Clash, managed by Bernie Rhodes, who had been Malcolm McLaren's partner until early 1976, but whom I never spoke to. The Clash scene was more political and sloganeering than the King's Road scene, and the only real link between the two at that time was Johnny Rotten, who had been 'discovered' by Bernie and introduced to the Pistols. Rotten, like Bernie Rhodes, was interested in changing the world, not just selling T-shirts and being 'a pop star'. Rotten hung out with Don Letts, the Rastafarian DJ at the Roxy and a good pal of the Clash. After the Roxy closed at eleven p.m., Don and various W10-based punks would return to his flat in Harlesden to smoke dope, listen to reggae and argue about any- and everything. If Cook, Jones, Matlock or any of the other Pistols

ever went along to Don's place after closing time, it was purely
for the smoke. They didn't care about politics or 'the kids'.

Pistols manager Malcolm McLaren didn't approve of 'his'
band hanging out with what he saw, in the Clash, as the
opposition, which was good enough reason for John Rotten and
his mate John Ritchie (soon to become better known as Sid
Vicious) to hang with them. Johnny would take any chance to
stick two fingers up at Malcolm. Because I didn't take drugs and
at that time didn't drink, I wasn't a regular visitor at Don's place.
I usually went to places with Jordan and people who were not
part of that scene – the Sombrero mostly, a tiny after-hours club
in Kensington High Street. Jordan preferred a lesbian club called
Louise's in Soho, which Johnny Rotten also liked, but I only went
there a couple of times. Most often we'd hang out at a great big
posh flat near the Houses of Parliament which was a brothel.
It was run by Linda, a tart with a heart who loved us punks. I
never saw any of the W10 punks there, though.

All of which might be confusing for people who were not
part of the original punk movement in 1976 and 1977. Punk is
usually referred to as if it was one big happy family affair
centred around Seditionaries, the Roxy, the 100 Club and Vortex.
The truth is, that was only partly true. Although it was a very
small, if hugely influential, movement, there was a lot of personal loathing between the original punks. Most of the journalists who wrote about punk for the national music press were
not part of the real scene and so didn't know who was mates
with who and which bands were not considered to be 'real'
punks. Those writers who were actually to be seen (and heard)
at punk gigs and parties, like co-founders of Sniffin' Glue fanzine
Mark Perry and Danny Baker, would write about who was 'real'
and who wasn't, but they'd be pontificating just as much as
their hippy counterparts on the NME, Sounds or Melody Maker. To
anyone who didn't know better, which was most of the world,
punks were all part of the same scene.

There was at least one obvious parallel between the two West London punk factions, though: in Bernie Rhodes the Clash had as colourful and powerful a personality for a manager as the Pistols had in McLaren. It was hardly surprising that the two men could not keep their management partnership together, since both had different and very definite opinions about how things should be done. (Although Malcolm had been in Paris during the 1968 student riots and had seen the sloganeering of the Situationists who had spray-painted walls across the city with stupid proclamations, it was Bernie who put the practice into effect first, with the Clash. He got them to spray slogans on their clothes and amps.)

Because punk was as much about how you looked as anything else, clothes shops played a major part in kick-starting the scene. The Pistols' Glen Matlock was the Saturday boy at Sex (working with Jordan, Sue Catwoman and even occasionally Chrissie Hynde), and Don Letts had a day job working in Acme Attractions, another King's Road shop selling vintage rockers' clothing, which reinvented itself in 1977 as Boy! To those brave few who had been the first to appear in public wearing clothes and make-up that provoked ridicule among the general population, there were some distinct dividing lines between different punk scenes made clear by what you wore. You either thought punk was political (with a small 'p') or you thought punk was about fashion and was the biggest joke to be played on the music industry since Elvis Presley had shaken his pelvis on national television in America. To put it another way, you either hung around Ladbroke Grove and Camden wearing army combat fatigues with slogans sprayed on them, or you hung around the King's Road and Camden in brightly coloured and expensive clothes (usually shoplifted from McLaren's shop). Everyone went to the same clubs, but there was usually an invisible line drawn between the separate factions, home-made punks on one side and Seditionaries-clothed punks on the other.

The Damned and other bands signed to Stiff Records caused a bit more confusion when they appeared in their theatrical outfits. The Damned were a caricature of punk in the same way that Screaming Lord Sutch was a caricature rock 'n' roller in the 1960s. Damned drummer Rat Scabies was a kind of end-of-the-pier Sid Vicious, their singer Dave Vanian looked like an extra from *The Munsters* and their bassist Captain Sensible seemed to believe everything that the tabloid newspapers were writing about punk. Yet they managed to get their singles and album out before either the Pistols or the Clash, and were touring the UK before bands like Siouxsie and the Banshees or Adam and the Ants could persuade promoters to put us on anywhere outside the usual punk venues in London.

I, of course, stood firmly on the Seditionaries side, with Jordan and the punks for whom the look was the most important statement, and for whom the fact that it marked us as outsiders, as different from everyone else, meant we had to believe in ourselves. When you dressed the way we did, there was no hiding from the moronic beer-bellied boot boys who thought that we were their natural enemies and that they had to attack us whenever they could. When Rotten started wearing Teddy-boy drape jackets and styling his hair in a quiff in the summer of 1977, he had what was left of an ageing Dad's army of Teds after his blood. By association, that meant that all punks were considered the enemies of Teddy boys (and their sons, who all seemed to own copies of their dads' gear).

The tabloid newspapers of the day made as much of the Teds versus punks 'battles' taking place on the King's Road that summer as they had of the mods versus rockers battles that had taken place on the beach at Brighton in 1964. There were instances of punks being cornered and beaten, slashed or maimed by gangs of Teds (including Rotten, who ended up in hospital getting stitches for a knife wound), but it certainly wasn't as bad as the 1960s pitched battles.

One sunny day I found myself cornered by six rough-looking

Teds as I came out of Sloane Square tube station. I was dressed all in black leather, with my face white, one eye covered in black kohl, and split-toed Chinese wedge slippers on my feet.

'What are you, then?' snarled one of them.

My pulse raced and so did my brain. 'I'm, er, a Gene Vincent fan, mate,' I stammered.

Six neanderthal brains topped by greasy quiffs churned. 'Whatchoo mean?' asked another.

'Well, er, he wore leather all the time, didn't he?' I answered, continuing, 'You know, er "Be Bop A Lula", "Wild Cat", "Cruisin'"', "Pink Thunderbird" . . .' I ran through as many Gene Vincent song titles as I could and they started adding their own titles. It worked. They let me go without smacking me or breaking any of my limbs, which was unusual at the time. I was on my way to Seditionaries to see Jordan and knew that, as in previous weeks, and as would continue to happen for a few more, Teds would come to the shop and kick in the window. I'd help Jordan to sweep up the glass and keep her as calm as I could.

Unfortunately the rest of Britain seemed to think that the Great British Way of Life was under more threat from us – the handful of punks with our ripped clothing and heavy make-up – than it had been from Hitler's Luftwaffe. The 'Anarchy in the UK' tour of late 1976 featuring the Pistols, the Clash and the Heartbreakers collapsed as different venues around Britain were banned by their local councils from putting the gig on. It didn't help that the Pistols and the Clash had fallen out on the bus, nor that the Heartbreakers – made up of former New York Dolls Jerry Nolan and Johnny Thunders – spent the 'tour' stoned out of their heads on heroin at the back of the bus. A tabloid frenzy around the tour turned punks into Public Enemies No. 1 and fuelled an anger towards us from people who didn't understand what we were about and felt threatened because of their ignorance. In some quarters that anger was inevitably vented at us through violence. They didn't get the irony of trying to hurt people who were clearly hurting themselves far more effectively than a boot or fist ever could, of course. Self-mutilation was common among punks. Whether it was pushing a safety pin through an earlobe or lip, carving words into our bodies, taking drugs, getting drunk or pogo-ing into each other, punks damaged themselves constantly.

The common adoption of a false name by punks was not intended simply to be 'colourful' or 'different', or to fool the Social Security, it was more than that – it was a statement of rejection of identity, of our past, a clue to the damage done to us when we were kids. It wasn't that surprising to find that some of the original punks later told of having been abused as kids or of having had a miserable and poor childhood.

The original punks were all born into working-class and deprived families. Later, posh, middle-class kids who had been deprived only of being deprived, and who thought that being a punk was 'romantic', became punks. Unsurprisingly, they didn't slash their chests with broken bottles, squat wrecked houses or have to sleep on the floor of scummy, unheated places because there was nowhere else to go. A few of the posh punks became junkies, but then Mummy and Daddy would pay for an expensive cure for them before giving them money to go off and start their lives again.

Punk was still a very small thing in 1976, and remained so for most of 1977. We all knew who everybody was, but we were not all mates. Not at all.

•

By May 1977 Malcolm McLaren and Vivienne Westwood couldn't fail to know who I was since I had begun to hang out in the shop fairly regularly, but neither of them spoke to me that often.

Malcolm was busy 'masterminding' the Sex Pistols' career at the time, of course, and so wasn't in the shop as much as he had been before he'd signed the band first to A&M, then EMI records. He had become almost as much written-about as the Pistols were in the music press, the *NME*, *Sounds* and assorted punk fanzines that had sprung up since summer 1976, and was clearly enjoying being a media star. At the time, I thought that Malcolm was a genius, and one of my ambitions was to get him to manage the Ants. It was – like my appearance in *Jubilee* – one that would be realised, but not with quite the result that I wanted.

Vivienne was always in the back of the shop, which had been renamed Seditionaries early in 1977, cutting and designing clothes. She had begun to gain a reputation as a gifted clothes designer. Her T-shirt designs with overlong sleeves made of muslin or cheesecloth, tartan bondage trousers, leather trousers covered in zips and logo-sprayed shirts had become the official 'look' of the punk movement. Unfortunately most punks couldn't afford the prices of Vivienne's clothes, so a lot of stock was shoplifted from Seditionaries and a lot of cheap imitations of her designs started to appear on various market stalls in Kensington, Beaufort Market and Camden.

I got to know a lot of 'customers' in Seditionaries. Among the self-proclaimed Bromley contingent, I became friendly with Siouxsie and Steve Severin who, along with drummer Kenny Morris, would eventually form Siouxsie and the Banshees. I had seen their first ever gig at the 100 Club Punk Festival in September 1976, when they had performed with a great guitarist called Marco Pirroni. Like me, they were really into Roxy Music, Bowie, Iggy Pop and shock tactics. Siouxsie Sioux appeared at early gigs wearing a swastika armband, thigh-length leather boots and with her breasts bare but her face covered in the sort of kabuki white-face make-up that I had begun to use. By the middle of 1977 the Banshees had dropped many of their original members and their swastika obsession. Siouxsie was still into using her sexuality in a creative way, though. She, like Jordan and a handful of other punks, had helped create a demand for clothes from Sex and Seditionaries.

Punk was the first youth movement in which women played as big a part as men. For the first time bands had female members who were not there solely as sex objects. Patti Smith was the first poet of punk, an almost asexual skinny New Yorker full of no-shit attitude. The Adverts had Gaye Advert playing bass at the back of the stage, her playing rudimentary but essential, her 'look' non-sexual, just a leather jacket and ripped jeans. X-Ray Spex had the wonderful Poly Styrene as lead singer, and she'd often appear on stage with rollers in her hair, braces on her teeth and a 1950s wool two-piece suit bought from Oxfam worn over leggings and men's shoes. The Slits were an all-female band who were confrontational and unsexy in any conventional way (there's a clue in the name), but powerfully sexual in performance. And of course there was Jordan. She had attracted me to punk almost as much as the Pistols and Johnny's attitude.

The Ants 'officially' came into existence at the last night of the Roxy on 23 April 1977. The Banshees had played the last ever set in the basement club that had been running for less than six months but had become the greatest punk venue. Inspired by the gig and the feeling that things had to happen soon, I asked Andrew Czezowski, the Roxy's manager, if he would manage my band. He said maybe. We hadn't actually played any gigs at that time and didn't have any booked, so we had to arrange a showcase performance for him. I told him that we'd play for him in a couple of weeks, and then set about getting the band into shape.

On 5 May Adam and the Ants made our world premiere – in Eve's room at her parents' place. I'd asked a few friends along to give us feedback on what we were doing. They were encouraging, of course. The line-up was me singing and playing guitar, Lester Square (whom I named Thomas da Vinci for some now forgotten reason) on guitar, Andy Warren on bass and Paul Flanagan (who'd answered an ad in *Melody Maker* a few weeks earlier) on drums. Among the people watching us was Poly Styrene of X-Ray Spex, who had just signed a deal with Virgin records. The manager of Poly's band, Falcon Stuart, had been encouraging to me whenever I'd mentioned the Ants to him and I had also asked him for professional advice. We were to play a showcase for him the day after the one for Andy Czezowski, at a different rehearsal studio.

The showcase for Andy took place on 6 May at Scarf Studios, and the one for Falcon at Alaska Studios on 7 May. Things didn't go brilliantly at either one, which was bad since I'd managed to con the Institute of Contemporary Art theatre in Chelsea (it later moved to Pall Mall) into giving us a gig in their restaurant by telling them that we were a folk act, and the gig was to be on 10 May. Two days before the gig and the day after the Falcon showcase, Lester told me that he didn't want to be in the band. The next morning I asked Mark Ryan to join and we met at Eve's to go over the set for the gig. Nicknamed the Kid, Mark Ryan (whose real name was Mark Gaumont) borrowed a guitar and we rehearsed until three or four in the morning. We were as ready as we'd ever be.

The staff at the ICA restaurant were a little surprised by the amount of gear we set up in a corner.

'We thought that you were acoustic,' said the manager.

'We won't be loud,' I lied, looking around at the nicely dressed people eating their dinner before going into the theatre to watch a comedy show headlined by John Dowie (the support act being Victoria Wood).

Just before we began, I dodged into the gents' loo to get changed, and a bunch of Chelsea punks noisily made their way to tables in front of our gear. The look of horror on the manager's face when he saw my Cambridge rapist T-shirt, leather trousers and kabuki-style make-up was classic. He spent the first two numbers with his hands over his ears, and after we played 'Beat My Guest' he rushed over and told us to stop immediately.

'Why?' I asked.

'Fuck off!' yelled one of the punks.

Ignoring me, the manager started pulling our plugs out of the wall. The punks jumped up and tried to stop him, someone called security and a fairly typical (for the day) stand-off developed in the restaurant between the forty or so punks who'd come to see us and the ICA staff.

It was clear that we were not going to be able to finish the gig, and, incensed, I stomped off to find John Dowie. He'd been quoted in the NME recently as being a fan of the punks, so I figured that he'd be able to help somehow. He did. We finished our set on the stage of the theatre in the interval between Victoria Wood and his performance. The sound must have been terrible, but the punks in the audience loved it because it was a victory for us. We'd fought the management of the ICA and we'd won. It wouldn't have mattered if the Ants had played a set of the Mamas and the Papas cover versions. As I came off stage, dripping in sweat, Dowie asked me, 'How am I supposed to follow that?'

The next night we were booked to play support to X-Ray Spex at the Man in the Moon pub in the King's Road. Falcon hadn't said that he would manage us, but he was willing to help as much as he could. We went down well enough to be booked for the same slot a week later, and then a week after that – 25 May 1977 – we were booked to headline. In the week leading up to the headline gig I realised that neither Andy nor Falcon were going to become manager of Adam and the Ants. But I'd had another idea.

'Jordan!'

'Yes, Adam.'

We were sitting in the back room of Seditionaries, drinking tea alone.

'Have you ever thought of becoming a manager?'

'What, of a shop like this?'

'No, of a band.'

'What do you mean, a band? Who?'

'Us. Adam and the Ants.'

'Oh. I dunno. Are you any good?'

'Come and find out for yourself. We're playing the Man in the Moon tonight.'

'All right. See you there.'

The audience at the gig that night wasn't huge, probably about forty people, among them friends like Siouxsie, Steve and Kenny from the Banshees, Eve, French Valerie (another Seditionaries punk) and Jordan. I'd told the band that we had to impress Jordan because I wanted her to be the manager. We started with 'Jordan (Send a Letter To)' and I really went for it. I was wearing a black leather mask with a zip mouth and leather pants over the top of black trousers. (The Slits used to wear their knickers over their skirts and trousers which I thought was a great idea.) I leapt around as usual, left the stage and crawled through the audience, grabbing people's ankles. Jordan later recalled that we played the same song three times and then the equipment blew up, by which time everyone had left except her, Siouxsie, Steve and Kenny and the others.

Jordan loved the performance and agreed that night to become manager. We went off after the gig to plot the future for Adam and the Ants over a cup of tea.

A week later we supported a band called Desolation Angels at my old college, Hornsey. Unusually they were led by their drummer, a guy called Dave Barbe. 'He's great,' Jordan said to me as they finished their set. 'We should nick him.' We did. Dave replaced Paul Flanagan a month later and became a mate and an Ant for the next two years.

Jordan's first action as band manager was to find us somewhere to rehearse that wasn't going to cost us a lot of money. She asked her friend Roger, who managed the Screen on the Green cinema in Islington (where the Pistols had famously played in December 1976), if we could use the stage when the cinema was closed. He said yes, but that it would have to be from midnight until dawn. We jumped at the offer, and in June began a very punishing schedule of rehearsal and song-writing there.

•

By this time, Sid Vicious had replaced Glen Matlock as bassist in the Sex Pistols. I knew him through my irregular contact with Rotten, and I have never really believed all the stories of the havoc that Sid is supposed to have wreaked during his tragically short life. Marco Pirroni was a friend of his in the early days of punk, and he later told me that Sid would visit him at Marco's parents' place in Harrow and bring an Action Man with him. He was a very immature eighteen.

I did see him throw a couple of bottles into the audience at the Vortex club in Soho during the late summer of 1977, but outside of that he seemed like any other well-turned-out punk rocker. That was, until he met Nancy Spungen, and then things changed as heroin crept into the picture.

Nancy had travelled to Britain with the Heartbreakers late in 1976. She was a junkie groupie who was as dumb as Sid was immature. Rotten claimed that he'd passed her on to Sid in order to get her off his case, which would have been exactly like her – trying to latch on to a famous boyfriend. Once she'd got her hooks into Sid, who had little experience of women, the pair of them became inseparable. They would turn up at a couple of places that I regularly visited at the time, particularly the brothel at Buckingham Gate, run by Linda, who catered for those Members of Parliament who had exotic tastes.

Linda was gay and a dominatrix. Her wealthy and important clients would visit her to be disciplined, insulted and/or hurt. She was a lovely woman, in her late twenties, a proper punk with the hair and make-up that boldly said so. Her flat was large enough to accommodate a couple of her hooker pals and their clients at the same time that she was entertaining members of the punk hierarchy in the living room. Johnny Thunders and the Heartbreakers, Steve Jones, the Banshees, Jordan, Derek and Simon, who both lived there (as did Jordan), were often to be found hanging out there before and after closing time at the pub. Johnny Rotten was often to be found of an evening reclining on Linda's sofa, which is why Sid and Nancy would appear at the door, looking like ghosts and desperate for another fix, trying to borrow money from him. You knew Nancy was coming before you saw her because she smelled so badly, as if she'd pissed herself en route. Unsurprisingly, nobody liked her.

I liked it at Linda's place, and in the summer of 1977 I wrote a lot of songs there, listening to Iggy Pop's *The Idiot* (still my favourite album). Because I had little money, I would sometimes earn cash by painting people's flats, often also sleeping there while doing the job. Linda's was such a place. I didn't sleep very much at the time, and usually just had a pillow on the carpet and a sleeping bag.

One night after painting Linda's kitchen a brilliant white, I took off my clothes and went to sleep in the sleeping bag, exhausted but satisfied at having finished the job. Some time later I felt a whack on my cheek. I woke up to see Sid's face looking down at me.

'You bin talking about me, 'aven't ya, Adam?'

Before I could answer (I was still half asleep), he threw several punches to my face, which I hardly felt, and finished off with one in the groin. Then he was gone. Unzipping the sleeping bag I quickly checked for any wounds. Finding none, I got dressed and rushed out to catch him. But Sid was well gone. I was unhurt, but furious. My pride was at stake. The next day I began a search for Sid with a hammer tucked up the sleeve of my leather jacket.

After a couple of hours visiting the usual cafés and rehearsal rooms where Sid might be found but without any luck, I went to

St John's Wood to seek advice from an old school chum, Stephen Sophocles. He was a black belt in karate and had a great presence and a real air of serenity. He sat patiently as I blurted out my tale of woe, before stopping me mid-sentence.

'So, how badly are you hurt?' he asked. I had forgotten all about any physical injuries that I might have suffered.

'Well, he didn't really hurt me,' I replied.

Stephen shrugged. 'Then why lower yourself to his level?' My concealed hammer felt a lot heavier suddenly, and we both started to laugh.

'He has to look over his shoulder now, doesn't he?' Stephen pointed out.

'Fucking A-right.'

'So calm down, get some rest and maybe you'll run into this chump somewhere in your travels. Then if your fists want to do some talking, so be it. It's better to walk away, but I think this time it will be him doing that.'

That night, backstage at the Marquee club, there they were leaning against a graffiti-covered, black painted wall: Mr and Mrs Stink. I very carefully wrapped a small chain from around my waist (a present from French Valerie, said to have once belonged to veteran rocker Vince Taylor of Brand New Cadillac fame) around my fist. Then I walked up to Sid, muttered, 'So here you are Sidney, I've been looking for you,' and punched the wall to the right side of his head.

'Only thing is,' I continued calmly, 'I'm not naked in my bed, you cunt.' Another punch to the wall just missed his face, which went whiter than usual. He quickly upped and moved off, giving a silent wave and exiting stage left. A whisper from Nancy to turn around and attack me merely prompted Sid to push her away and tell her to fuck right off. I slept very well that night.

Of course, I wanted to know why the whole thing had started, though. What had sent Sid on a bash Adam trip?

I had an idea that it was something to do with the Pistols' Jubilee cruise on the Thames. I had been on board for the trip on 7 June. The Pistols played two or three songs and were truly awful, but by far the worst was Sid on bass; he could not play at all. He looked the part, sure, but he had no idea. I mentioned this to someone, I can't remember who, saying I'd be only too happy to give him a few lessons. Sid must have heard from this mystery person and decided to pay me a visit soon after.

As it happens, the boat trip was stopped because of an incident when a poor little Japanese photographer was kicked to the dance floor, loaded up with gear and helpless, trying to protect his cameras. It was enough to put an end to festivities and turn us back to the Embankment quay, where the police greeted everyone (except Jordan and yours truly) with a kicking – especially Malcolm. The best thing to come out of the evening was the mention we got in the *Sounds* report of the trip, published a couple of weeks later. Jon Savage wrote, 'Meanwhile, Jordan's telling me about this group she's managing, called The Ants'. It was the first mention of the band in the music press.

For Malcolm, the boat trip represented another acre of space in the tabloid papers. For his band it represented the beginning of the end. Sid was about to bring the whole thing crashing down around their ears. When the Pistols kicked Glen Matlock out, the music went out of the window. Glen is an excellent bass player and provided some raw backing vocals, too. Then in walked Sid, the perfect Sex Pistol, who eventually stole the whole scene with his Rock 'n' Roll Suicide act and his rendition of 'My Way', made a hit courtesy of the video directed by Julian Temple.

The last time I saw Sid and Nancy alive was outside Camden Lock's Dingwalls in Autumn 1977. They were sitting in a Morris Minor. Sid's face was all beaten-up, especially his right eye. I asked what had happened, and Nancy answered that some asshole was staring at her in Dingwalls, and Sid had gone up to tell him to stop or else. It turned out that the guy was a marine and dealt with Sid quite viciously. Sid looked exhausted. 'I'll get him next time,' he muttered pathetically.

At the end of January 1978 the Pistols imploded in America.

Eight months later Sid stabbed Nancy to death at the Chelsea Hotel in New York, and in February 1979 he died himself of a heroin overdose in Greenwich Village.

•

Three days after the boat trip, I began to keep a diary. It was not an ordinary diary, by which I mean that it was not a book of nice, clean, white pages, all ready to receive the secrets of the life of a 22-year-old punk rocker named Adam Ant. No. It was actually a paperback edition of William Burroughs' *The Naked Lunch* (Corgi, 1976, cost 95p). At the top of the inside cover I wrote '9.6.77. 3.10pm. Have just bought this book, hope it's good.' I went on to write,

> Didn't mean to tell anybody about this writing, but I'm so
> enthusiastic! Why not? Sitting in greasy Italian, tea no money.
> Got to ask my stepdad Tony (who I now *love* and respect as a
> man of the world who has more courage than I will ever
> experience or hope to have) for maybe £30 cash for my
> delightful room at Redcliffe Gardens.

Needless to say, I didn't finish *Naked Lunch*, and instead wrote over the printed pages of the entire book in black ink.

Originally I began to keep a diary to record a period of my life that was full of activity, and writing it filled the rare times when I was alone. At that time, if I was not playing music with the band, I was writing songs. If I was not doing that, I was either painting walls for money (during the day) or going to gigs (at night). And then there was sex. I now understand that sex and music, particularly the performance of music, playing live and rehearsing, were helping me to contain my then undiag-nosed bipolar illness. My manic phases were spent having sex or working as a painter and decorator, or making music. My depressive phases were spent crying, writing in my diary and then, to raise myself out of them, having sex.

Sex was my panacea. Puresex was my salvation.

Puresex was usually at its most enjoyable when the relationship between us was new, but there were several women in my life with whom every time we made love it was puresex – at least for a while. During the writing of my first diary, for instance, I was still seeing Eve but had begun relationships with a number of other women. Among them was Nell, my co-star in *Jubilee*, and a woman who had seen me perform at the Marquee and written me a letter telling me what she would do with me if she had the chance. (She got it.)

The diary also served as my confidante in troubled times, as the following example from November 1977 shows.

Dear book, console Adam, he is not having a very good time. I know work is the answer. Work so that I can show those critical, mirror-loving poseurs (I mean your London 'Punk' public) that as there is nobody else with any credibility at least there is Adam & The Ants and the lovely Jordan willing to take them all on.

Sex has to be coped with, you see, book. I am on an unlucky streak, for despite the fact that I can get the commodity – sex – from any of a number of girl friends, that is unfair to them and me and is not Puresex. I have to be in the mood for friends because I like to treat them like friends, to talk and enjoy each other's company. Fucking is the logical, lovely conclusion to this kind of meeting. But Puresex by sure, mutual agreement and chance is what I want and need. I need to meet new women so that I can start a new relationship and even if it lasts for a whole week, like Louise* and myself, it is still so valuable and I for one, value it. I know this in my very being and when things are on a downer (as now) I can't make any concessions. All I know is that I have been indulging in the greatest of all crimes – sleeping in, in the mornings – for the last few days.

•

---

* The names of some people have been changed.

The making of *Jubilee* in the summer of 1977 was as chaotic as the finished film looks. Derek Jarman was making it up as he went along. He wanted the film to be a true reflection of the self-inflicted pain and mayhem of the punk scene and went to any lengths in order to ensure that he got realistic scenes on film, although, since the film included scenes that had Queen Elizabeth I travelling through time to a post-punk and post-Thatcher London and walking along streets filled with burning rubbish and marauding girl biker gangs, the concept of 'realism' was subjective. Buckingham Palace is a recording studio and England is run by a music business mogul who selects my character as a future star. Meanwhile my character, simply called 'Kid', becomes friends with a girl gang led by Jordan and Jenny Runacre and who like to murder men at will. It didn't make much sense, but it was an 'art film' so that didn't matter.

Our drummer Paul Flanagan soon became bored with the filming and failed to turn up for our first big scene, of us playing 'Plastic Surgery' in a white room. Kenny, the drummer with the Banshees, stood in. Jordan told Paul not to bother turning up again and contacted Dave Barbe, who was on the drummer's stool three days later when we played at the artist Andrew Logan's party at his warehouse studio in East London. Logan was a friend of Jarman, and the party was full of the arty, upper-class lot who had begun to regard punk as a rather interesting movement. Logan later started the Alternative Miss Universe competition for transvestites, and became a darling of the New Romantics, who were much more into the idea of being upper class than I was.

That party served as a good warm-up for what was an important gig for us. On 11 July we played the first night at a new club, the Vortex (along with the Slits and Banshees). The Vortex filled the gap in punk's live circuit that had appeared when the Roxy had closed its doors for the last time three months earlier. Just along the road from the Marquee, like the Roxy it was a basement and became just as big a part of the punk legend. My diary tells me that I thought that we were only 'average' that night.

Three days later we recorded our very first single, 'Plastic Surgery', and then four days after that we were let into the Drury Lane Theatre to film the Ants performing 'Plastic Surgery' for *Jubilee*. The theatre had been loaned to Jarman for an afternoon only and didn't include the use of any of the lighting or sets, which was a shame because it looked fantastic when we arrived. However, Jarman set up a bunch of arc lights, and after a rudimentary sound check we started to play as the camera moved around us on the enormous stage. Being wired for performance, I threw myself about with the usual abandon – and dislocated my knee. It really hurt, but no one except Jordan seemed to take my pain seriously. She helped me back to Redcliffe Gardens after filming, where I lay for a few days, unable to walk, let alone perform. Despite Jarman and the lovely Nell visiting me, bringing food and affection, a letter arrived after a couple of days from the film production company's offices, telling me that I had to be back at work that day or else. 'Fuck off' was my short reply.

It wasn't the last time I was injured when filming, either. There are two fight scenes in the finished film involving me. One is at a party, filmed in Jarman's own warehouse flat at Butler's Wharf in the East End. The dancer Lindsay Kemp and his troupe are performing as Christ and his disciples while the punks dance in another room. Also on the dance floor are the two coppers who later chase and kill me. One of the actors playing a cop was an American, Donny Dunham. Jarman decided that he wanted Don drunk so that when he attacked me it was more than just acting. 'I don't care if you break his leg,' he told Donny before we started, 'it's got to go on celluloid.' Jarman had decided not to tell me about it, though. Donny took a swing at my head and I ducked what was a hard right hook. I grabbed him, caught him off balance and knocked him over. Jarman loved it and screamed, 'Again! Do it again!' Donny jumped up and lunged at me, trying to break my jaw. If you look at my face you can tell how pissed off I am, and it's a good job that Jordan was there to calm things down. She and Eve (who's also in the party scene) pulled Donny off by the hair and pushed us apart.

I wanted to walk away from the film altogether at that point, but was persuaded to finish it by Jordan. My last scene was the one in which I end up drenched in blood. Again, some of the 'acting' by the cops was a little overenthusiastic and I ended up with bruised ribs and an uneasy feeling that the film was not going to be as good as I'd hoped. It gave Les a bit of a shock that night when he opened the door to see me on his doorstep drenched in fake blood. I'd gone straight there after the filming and forgotten about how I must have looked.

The ending that appears in the film (in which the police beat me to death behind a rubbish bin) was an alternative to the one that Jarman had first asked me to do. That had involved me being raped by the coppers in a photo booth as the machine popped off pics. No way was I going to be stuck in a small space with a possibly pissed Don Dunham 'pretending' to beat me up, so I refused. I was glad when it was all over, to be honest. Not that it was, entirely. Although the filming was finished, the finished product wouldn't appear until 1978. And my life was to continue to be affected by it for some time. As a director, Derek had been truly selfless, I guess, sinking everything into the film. Everyone else was talking about making punk films at the time, but Derek actually got it done. He gave me the part of Kid, and then beefed it up into something larger. He got together a great cast which included, as well as Toyah Willcox and Little Nell, Jenny Runacre, the Slits, Chelsea and Wayne County. He commissioned Brian Eno's first original film score for it, too. But the film was seen in some circles as a cop-out, for which the Ants took most blame since we were the only punk band involved with it all the way through. After being filmed, Siouxsie and the Banshees had withdrawn their involvement, slating it as 'hippy trash'. *Jubilee* was not a documentary, though many of the reviewers seemed to think it was, or that it should have been. It was an art film, and what Jarman did was make art films which asked questions and challenged convention. Because of the artiness of *Jubilee*, I was derided as not being a 'true punk' by various music papers and punk fanzines. Whatever that meant.

But I have to say that Derek Jarman inspired his actors to go for it under any circumstances. He was a kind of gay film terrorist, and the fact that he never stopped working, right up until his death from Aids, was a testament to his courage. The last time I saw him, he was sitting in Maison Bertaux in Soho, surrounded by young film people, all focused on one of Derek's sketchbooks. He looked completely happy.

RIP, Derek.

•

During filming I had begun to see Nell off set. She was a fantastically positive person and it made me happy to be with her, which was just as well, since the strain of making the film had begun to take its toll on my health. Unhappy at how things were going, at times I found myself slipping into something resembling a hallucinatory state. As I described in my diary, one episode happened as I was sitting outside Redcliffe Gardens, waiting for Nell to visit.

> I looked up at my window, which had a blue haze on it, and felt strange and ever so sleepy. I saw a couple of men pass by on the other side of the street and got the strange sensation of slowness that I used to get as a bambino lying up in bed during a nightmare. It's like a record which should be played at 45 rpm being forcibly played at 33 rpm. A forced slow – slurred, slow thought and vision.

It passed as soon as Nell arrived, but it left me a little shaken. Maybe she noticed that something was wrong with me, because she began to visit me fairly often – and I didn't discourage her. Usually she was alone and would stay the night, but on one visit she arrived with Derek and, as usual, brought food and drink. After chatting for a while they both started to discuss Jordan, specifically her ability – and deficiencies – as a manager. Later I realised that they were trying to make way for an approach by a couple of *Jubilee*'s producers, Howard Malin and James Whaley, to manage me.

Malin and Whaley had started a company that they called Megalovision in order to become media moguls. They'd put up some of the cost of *Jubilee* (the total cost of which was £50,000; I got about £40 for my performance), and were always looking for new business. Howard was a street-smart, wide-boy type with a glint in his eye. I thought he'd make a great manager, but I was a bit scared of him. James was quieter but just as determined.

I got to know both men during the making of the movie. Howie (as I then called him) invited me to his flat a couple of times, and I even painted a few walls for him (possibly for more money than I was paid to be in his film). James tagged along a couple of times when I went out with people from the cast. Just as filming was winding up, I decided to ask Malin if he'd like to be my business manager and Jordan my personal manager. I always had big ideas, even then, when the Ants were playing support to the Buzzcocks and Generation X, as we did occasionally through the autumn of 1977 at the Marquee and numerous London colleges. Megalovision readily agreed to manage me.

It was true that, despite getting gigs around the capital, Jordan wasn't moving things forward as fast as I'd hoped in 1977. We'd been courted by CBS (the Ants played a company party at the Vortex in July) and RCA, but nothing had come of it. In fact RCA blew themselves out of the water with me when they gave Jordan and me tickets to see Iggy Pop live. After the show, when I was asked if I wanted to go and meet Iggy, I said sure, as long as Jordan could come too. The camp guy from RCA who'd invited us said, 'No, just you,' and gave me a hard, meaningful stare. I again said no, and he laughed. So I told him to fuck off and we left for another party. I didn't get to meet Iggy Pop and RCA didn't get to sign Adam and The Ants.

A week later, in August, the Ants managed to play our first date outside London when we were booked with the Banshees at Rebecca's in Birmingham (three weeks after that we supported the Models, featuring one Marco Pirroni on guitar in Crayford). We almost didn't make the gig, since no one had thought about how to actually get there. The gear went with the Banshees in their van, but there was no room for us. Eventually a mate of Jordan's who worked for Haringey council turned up with a council van. Halfway up the M1 we ran out of petrol and had to walk over fields to get some. The van then managed a few more miles before its engine blew up, leaving us at least twenty miles from the gig. There was nothing else for it. Our dauntless manager (who should have made the travel arrangements in the first place, of course) got us all out and we marched along the motorway, Jordan with her thumb out. Amazingly a lorry stopped and we all crammed in, making it to Rebecca's with ten minutes to spare for a sound check.

The gig was great. We were becoming a really tight live unit. I pushed the band through four-hour rehearsals which, in September 1977, took place at the offices of Megalovision, who were putting up money for us to get to gigs. They bought us a van and handed money to Jordan when we made our first trip in it, to Plymouth's Top Rank club. Malin insisted that Jordan bring back receipts, of course, which was a new experience for all of us. Malin and Whaley knew nothing about the music business, so they were happy for Jordan to run the everyday side of things.

I also asked a guy named Don Hawkins, who'd worked on *Jubilee* and used to be a member of Vince Taylor's Playboys in the 1960s, if he'd be our road manager. He agreed after seeing us at the Marquee with Generation X on 4 October where we gave a debut to our new guitarist, Johnny Bivouac (Mark Ryan had decided to start his own band) and the Ants Mk III. He told me that he'd once walked into a Hamburg bar and seen a similarly leather-clad band rocking the place and that the Ants had reminded him of that time, and that we'd rocked him as much as the Beatles had done in 1962. I wondered if either John Lennon or Paul McCartney had jumped into the audience as I'd done, and received a kicking for their enthusiasm? Having said that, the place was full and we got an encore, which was very satisfying – even if I was in pain.

Don joined us for the trip to Plymouth on 7 October. Mind you, his experience didn't help us with route planning and it took twelve hours to get from London to the West Country, simply because we went due south to the coast and then turned right, driving along B-roads and doing no more than 40 or 50 m.p.h. The gig was then cut short when I leapt up in the air in my usual exuberant manner and promptly split my head open on a low beam. It didn't register straight away, but as the warm, sticky blood trickled down my face, I started to feel very faint. Jordan and Don had to carry me off stage, straight into the van and make off for the hospital. We sat in A&E, me feeling dazed and confused, while the nurses kept coming up for a look, amused and confused by the sight of me. There I was with my white pancake face mask, streaked with blood, wearing black leather trousers and a Seditionaries T-shirt.

'Who's this?' asked the doctor when I was called into a cubicle.

'Mr Ant,' sniggered a nurse.

The doctor wasn't as amused by my name as his staff were, and was clearly offended by my (and my friends') appearance, so he savagely worked stitches into my head after claiming that there was no anaesthetic for such an occasion. It hurt like hell for days after and hurt even more a week later when, performing at Eric's, a tiny Liverpool venue that saw the debut gigs of, among others, the Teardrop Explodes and Echo and The Bunnymen, I leapt up and split the stitches open again.

However, splitting my head open (or dislocating a knee) was always preferable to me than not being able to perform, as happened in Brighton, at the Regency. The usual bunch of neanderthal bouncers gave us constant lip and hassle, while the management demanded £90 for 'microphone hire'. That was ridiculous, given that our whole fee for the gig was £50, so Jordan got into a slanging match with them, which culminated in her pushing the DJ off his stool, grabbing the mic and telling everyone that we weren't performing and that they should ask for their money back because it was the management's fault. Which is exactly what the audience – well over two hundred people – did. For possibly the first time, I realised that we had fans, real ones, not fashion-led Chelsea punks. Instead of being pissed off, kids helped us pack up our equipment and stuck around chatting, getting photos taken with us. Antmusic was starting to catch on, and the music industry was at last starting to pay attention to what we were doing.

We played the Marquee three times before Christmas in 1977 and did well enough to earn a residency booking at the famous old place. We were booked to play the first four Sundays of January 1978. In the middle of the month I had percentage talks with Megalovision, and they assured me that the Ants were their priority. 'I do not want to be side-tracked nor concerned with anything other than The Ants and Antmusic,' I wrote in my diary after the meeting. 'Everybody has to realise that I am not a dreamer, there are no risks involved at all. The only thing that can stop me is my death.'

•

As 1977 drew to an end, the Ants played two sets at a party that Derek Jarman held at his warehouse flat. The place was full and everyone seemed to really enjoy us, which was good because it had been bloody dangerous to play, since there was no electrical earth in the place, and we all kept getting shocks. On Boxing Day we played at Camden's Music Machine with the Banshees and again went down really well, even getting a positive review in *Sounds*, which was highly unusual for the time. There was so much for Adam and the Ants to look forward to, including getting a record contract, of course, to keep me occupied and determined. By the end of 1977 we were attracting the attention of several major record companies plus a couple of smaller independents who would definitely suit me. As much as I wanted to be successful, it had to be achieved on my own terms, and I knew that a smaller label – such as EG, for whom we'd played a showcase in late December and who would release the *Jubilee* soundtrack – would allow me to do that. Christmas 1977 should then have been a happy one. Yet I was not eating and spent too much time in bed. All through the year there had been many nights and the occasional day when loneliness and despair got the better of me. One particularly desperate night in December, my diary records, I awoke from a sleep that was:

> Unpleasant – I dreamed I was lost, had no confidence and had lost heart. Like the first stages in my illness / before the death of Stuart. It was awful, a painful, terrifying calm.

At the time it seemed that only by keeping really busy and having as much sex as possible would I keep the awful depression at bay. And so that became the big idea for Adam Ant – work and sex for a healthy life.

6

THE IDEA

MANDY WAS SWEET SIXTEEN when we first met, but she had a lot of front. She and a friend approached me at the 100 Club at the end of January 1978 asking if they might come and visit me some time. I was in a fucked-up mood that night, sitting backstage after what I felt was a very mixed performance. We had not been as tight as I'd have liked. I was sitting with Steph (who had 'played' the bass in Toyah's band in *Jubilee*), thinking about how she and I had enjoyed a glorious weekend, when I saw Eve through a crack in the door. She was kissing – really kissing – a guy that lived in the squat that she had just been evicted from. She'd asked to stay at Redcliffe Gardens, and I had let her. We'd made sweet love only a couple of nights earlier, and now she was almost devouring this guy, Mickey, in front of me. I stood outside the door and stared at them.

'Don't fucking do it, lady,' I thought, and then said loudly, 'Be less conspicuous, can't you?'

Despite my busy and varied sex life, I would not and had never flaunted any of my amorous affairs in front of her, and never would in public. In fact lovers often commented that I seemed to be cold and distant with them in public, never holding hands and barely even talking to them when with other people.

Eve and Mickey backed away from each other and looked at

me. Mickey immediately tried to 'explain'. I just looked at him and he shut up. He'd obviously been told about the previous occasion, last year, when I had smacked a guy that I found kissing Eve.

'Don't mind, Adam,' Eve pleaded, 'I was just giving Mickey a goodbye kiss.'

'Yeah, sure.'

I walked away and bumped into Mandy and her friend. I gave them an address in Chelsea and said to call by next week. I was staying there on and off while I painted it and figured that, after what had just happened, I was more likely to be there than at Redcliffe Gardens.

Despite my reaction, though, I realised that I wasn't actually that pissed off. I had not felt the urge to smack Mickey in the head and so was clearly getting over my jealousy concerning Eve. What had annoyed me was that I had tidied up the room for her before she came to stay and within a couple of days she'd turned it into a pigsty. I hated mess around me, didn't have much in the room and preferred it to be as sparse and minimal as possible. Now there was stuff spread everywhere.

I knew that to be jealous was hypocritical, even if I couldn't help it. My love life was as complicated at that time as it would ever be. That day I had had a call from an older woman that I'd enjoyed a brief couple of weeks with before she'd become ridiculously possessive of me. I was incapable of having an exclusive relationship with any woman at the time, and that one ended as acrimoniously as others had before and would in future. She had cried and screamed at me and I couldn't think of anything nice or comforting to say to her. A few hours after we'd parted she telephoned me to say that 'it' was 'over'. I felt only relief.

It was a couple of days after that episode when Amanda ('though I prefer Mandy') Donahoe came to visit me in Chelsea. It was difficult to believe that she was only sixteen – certainly to look at. She was beautiful, with black hair and a perfectly formed woman's body. She was also very intelligent and sharp-tongued, with a wicked sense of humour. After an hour of chatting and laughing about all and everything, it seemed, on the sofa in the front room of the mid-terraced house, I was made speechless by her suddenly kissing me and biting my lip. I didn't expect her to be experienced and had no intention of going any further with things until we knew each other better. We went upstairs and lay on the bed. I couldn't believe that this was happening; she was so beautiful, so relaxed and happy. As I gazed down at her, though, she said, 'We can't . . . I'm not on the pill.'

Oddly, I wasn't disappointed. The next few hours were spent in the most incredible state of delightful, sweet, sexual longing.

It would be more than a month before we could finally make love, but when we did it was so good, I recorded in my diary that 'it was life-enriching.'

•

John Peel was the DJ for the coolest radio show in the UK in 1978, and he had the power to break a new band with one play of an independently recorded vinyl single or even demo cassette. Despite having been a leading figure in the hippy movement of the 1960s, Peel had retained a level of street credibility that none of his colleagues at Radio One, the only national pop and rock music radio station in existence at the time, could ever hope to have. Peel had managed this by being totally unpretentious and committed to playing music that he liked and thought worth hearing. He had impeccable taste for the most part, and had been a champion, for example, of Marc Bolan in the early days of his recording career, when T. Rex were still known as Tyrannosaurus Rex. Peel also championed David Bowie before he became famous, and played Roxy Music and Iggy Pop material on his radio show when mainstream radio wouldn't touch them. There were few 'pirate' radio DJs, even, who'd managed to play the same kind of underground and challenging music as Peel. It was amazing that his bosses at the BBC hadn't sacked him for playing some of the early punk and now post-punk stuff that he did. It must have helped that Peel's show went out after nine p.m. when the BBC governors were either firmly ensconced in their opera boxes or tucked up in bed. His was unarguably the only radio show to be heard on when we got our first Peel Session booked. These Sessions were given to unsigned bands, or ones without a vast release output, anyway. We would be given a BBC recording studio in which to record four songs that would then be played, exclusively, over the course of a three-hour John Peel Show on Radio One.

Peel's producer at the time, and the only man capable of bestowing the next best thing to the Peel stamp of approval, was John Walters. A large, bearded, sardonic man of eclectic tastes, Walters would go to the gigs that Peel couldn't make (because the DJ was either spinning records at his infrequent personal appearances or attending other gigs). He had become known to the Sex Pistols crowd in the early days of punk and so knew Jordan well. When Walters heard that she was managing and performing with a band (she'd always sing 'Lou' on stage with me whenever we played live), he decided to find out himself if we were any good.

Which is how we had come to find him and Jordan accidentally locked in our dressing room after a December gig at the Royal College of Art. That Walters and Jordan were both in the dressing room meant that they'd gone there after only our fourth song, and so he had not actually seen most of our performance, which annoyed me a bit. But it turned out that after they had agreed that the Ants should record a Peel Session on 23 January 1978, they'd found themselves locked in, unable to see the rest of the show. They'd had to sit there for the best part of forty-five minutes until we came in.

We recorded 'Deutscher Girls', 'Lou' (with Jordan), 'It Doesn't Matter' and 'Puerto Rican' for Peel. The next day we recorded 'Deutscher Girl' again, this time at Air Studio for the *Jubilee* soundtrack album. We also recorded 'Plastic Surgery' and 'Catch A Falling Star'. I, at least, intended 'Deutscher Girls' and 'Catch A Falling Star' to be the first Adam and the Ants single release. Exactly who would release said single was another matter, of course.

The soundtrack album for *Jubilee* was being released by EG Records. Although apparently an independent label, it was actually a subsidiary of Virgin and had been formed by EG management – David Enthoven and John Gaydon – to allow one of their clients, Brian Eno, to release his Ambient albums (since no major would touch them at the time). EG had also managed T. Rex, Emerson, Lake and Palmer and King Crimson, among others.

EG had shown an interest in signing us and would continue to show interest for the next six months. They had paid for the recording of our two songs (and a third on the album, 'Nine To Five', which Toyah recorded), so it seemed natural that they'd release 'Deutscher Girls' as a single. Plus, of course, they were the only record company that Howard Malin actually knew, which made it easier for him to keep on at them to give us a deal. I had enjoyed such a surge of pride on seeing my name and those of my songs on the cover of a record for the first time when *Jubilee* was released that I felt well disposed towards them.

However, while EG dicked about, other record labels were sending A&R men to watch us perform. We were playing regularly and to enthusiastic crowds, at venues as far apart as Nottingham and Bristol. Yet the music press continued to make snide remarks about the Ants. In the NME Nick Kent sulkily wrote, 'unfortunately this lot [The Ants] look like being the next big punk thing,' but not until he'd also accused me of hero-worshipping Nazis and deserving to get my balls fried. At least he'd had the best part of two-thirds of a page to write about us and used two pictures, which was good. A week or so later someone else at the NME wrote, in reference to another band altogether, 'Well, if Adam Ant can get mileage out of cheap S/M references there's hope for this awful group, too.'

'Fuck you, NME,' I thought. 'I will have you all on your knees in a year's time, dying for exclusive interviews.'

Then Jubilee opened and Malin demanded that I be 'seen' out at parties with Jordan. I managed a couple, but hated everything about them. When I was asked to go to France to promote the film I refused, so Jordan went alone. The music press hated the film and used it as another weapon with which to bash me in print. I took both my mum and nan to the premier, though, and despite people hissing and booing through it, they thought that it – and especially I, of course – was good. I felt embarrassed by the film, to be honest. It seemed like a complete mess on first viewing. Today I think it's an amazing achievement and a testament to Derek Jarman's persistence and ingenuity, given how little money he had to make it with. But after the screening I cringed when Mum and Nan started calling me a star, because I knew that I wasn't. Not yet, at least.

•

Towards the end of March 1978, a couple of weeks after MCA had passed on the chance to sign us, Howard Malin told me that EG had said 'yes' to signing the Ants – but only on various conditions. They were, one, that I change and lose my heavy image – which meant no more rapist mask and S/M outfits; two, that I think of the deal as a long-term option – I had previously said only two singles and an album; three, 'think à la Adamant, and not Adam and the Ants', as they put it, which meant be a solo act, not the front man for a band; four, I was to come up with some new songs.

At the time, desperate for action, for the chance to get records out, I felt that none of their 'conditions' were any kind of problem. I had been considering a change of image for a long time, could easily face the idea of a long-term deal and already had a bunch of new songs. The only slight problem might have been the idea of being a solo act, except that things had started to unravel in the band by this time. Jordan and Andy had begun to bug me about doing things the way the Pistols had (i.e. being deliberately confrontational to everyone, getting banned everywhere they played and so on), which I didn't want, not at all. I had my own way and needed everyone to believe in that.

Barely a month later, Dave Barbe played me a demo of songs by the Kid (Mark Ryan), our former guitarist. It was OK, nothing out of the ordinary, I thought, and said so, which was when Andy told me that the Ants – Andy and Johnny – were playing on it. That really pissed me off.

'They can play with whoever they want,' I told Dave, 'but they should have told me. Though that's not the real problem. This is substandard stuff they're playing and they've shown that without me there to show them how, they're useless.'

I ranted a bit more, threatening to split the band and find a better bassist and a guitarist who was ten times better than Johnny Bivouac. I even blamed them for the lack of a contract, which, a month after the original offer from EG, was still not forthcoming. Mind you, Howard Malin had seemingly disappeared; I hadn't seen him for three weeks. He was in Europe, promoting *Jubilee*. All of this, combined with a bout of flu, made me miserable and angry.

A week later, in mid-May, after a meeting with Dave and Andy, things were sorted between us. We decided that there would be no more keeping quiet about how we were feeling the band was doing, and that we would be like the Three Musketeers, all for one and one for all. We also agreed that both Johnny Bivouac and Jordan were no longer to be considered Ants. I wrote down that we'd decided on the following course of action: 1. to record an album; 2. Bivouac to go – he didn't even own his own guitar, which really pissed off Andy and me; 3, Jordan to have no more say; 4. I was to do all of the guitar on the album; 5. All moves were to be reported between the three of us, no more arguments.

Jordan felt more than mutual about the split and said that she'd been offered another film part anyway. We parted on good terms and knew that we'd be friends for a long time.

Feeling happier, and with EG promising that they'd give us a definitive answer in two days, I started to plan the debut album, putting the running order of songs together and even planning cover design. A day later I got to meet Iggy Pop at a rehearsal studio, where he was getting ready for a UK tour. We were introduced.

'Jimmy, this is Adam Ant.'

'Ants Adam?' Iggy smiled and said, 'Later, in a break.'

I squatted at the back of the room watching as he ran through a few numbers, and he was terrific. In his usual off-white T-shirt, too-tight jeans and white sneakers, he wasn't at that time as muscled-up as he later became, and his hair was not as long as it had been (or would be), but he gave everything to the set, despite it being in a rehearsal room. When the band took a break he came to the back of the room and squatted next to me, and I told him how good I thought it was – better than the gig I'd seen at the Rainbow Theatre last year, even. He smiled and we talked some more. When I left I had the definite feeling that he liked me, which made me smile all the way home.

The smile stayed on my face for a week.

And then EG declined the chance to sign Adam Ant.

What could I do? We played the Roundhouse in Camden with X-Ray Spex (whose debut album was about to come out on Virgin), and Jordan and Bivouac made their last appearance with us. I wore a kilt and felt restrained, didn't leap around or into the audience. It felt like the death of something. For me, it was. It was the death of the Ants Mk III and the death of punk.

The next day we went into Virtual Earth Studios and recorded 'Young Parisians' (as a possible A-side to a single), 'I Saw A Lady' and a slow version of 'Catch A Falling Star'. I'd used the gig money to pay for the studio, and now, I thought, I had something to sell. Two days later we played our first gig without Bivouac and Jordan, just me on guitar, at the Chelsea College of Art.

An entry in my diary made on a Sunday night not long after the Roundhouse gig in May 1978 reads,

> I remember my illness. I am frightened. I hit myself on the jaw to remind myself.
>
> I want to cry but can't.
>
> I have a talent. I have a right to portray my art in my way.
>
> I will win. Even at this dire moment when I have £1.14p to my name I believe that.

A week later Matthew Ashman joined the Ants Mk IV as guitarist, but despite that, my mood swung between feeling empty and lost, and more determined than ever that Adam and the Ants would succeed. I also craved sex almost constantly and sometimes would fuck with different women on the same day, at different places and times. That summer Mandy was in Germany for five weeks and I missed her badly. She was visiting her mother's family, who were German, and, still being at school, was not given the choice to stay or go on the visit. Mandy's parents hadn't really taken to me, unsurprisingly. Her father would simply ignore me when I was at their nice big house in Golders Green, although her mum would make small talk. She wasn't exactly encouraging to me, though. I'm sure some of the attraction that Mandy had for me came from knowing that her parents wouldn't approve, and she'd often ask me round for 'tea'. On those afternoons I would feel uncomfortable in the living room, chatting with Mrs D, but Mandy seemed to enjoy it.

Even when Mandy returned to England, my sexual desire could not be and was not satisfied solely by her. After receiving any kind of bad news – about the band or contracts, for instance – I had to have sex. The need was too great, I couldn't resist, and when, on rare occasions, I couldn't find anyone to fuck or even talk with, I would not be able to sleep, feeling speedy and needy. My diary is littered with the contents of my mind on each of those lonely nights. I refer constantly to Mandy as being my girl, and to various other women as being friends, sex friends. Some of them knew that I was not 'faithful' to them, although Mandy certainly didn't at that time. She thought that I was her boyfriend and she was my girlfriend and that, naturally, meant that we were faithful to one another. In my mind, I was. I cared deeply about her and wanted her to be happy. But in the flesh I couldn't be faithful to anyone (whatever that meant). I had to have sex with new, different women whenever I could. The sex distracted me, kept me kind of sane.

•

Not long after Matthew Ashman agreed to join the band as guitarist, he had his live debut at a debutantes' ball held in the Hard Rock Café in June 1978. At that time, he was eighteen going on twelve, and a great addition to the band, not least because he always managed to keep us all in stitches, especially with his impersonation of comedian Les Dawson's piano technique. When excited, his voice would rocket up a few octaves to give us an impersonation of Norman Wisdom shouting, 'Mr Grimsdale!!' He reminded me of the *Beano* comic's Dennis the Menace. Matthew once claimed that he had put Marmite on his dick and let his dog lick it off. He was what we British like to call 'a character'.

It didn't take long before we got into an argument over what 'professional' meant – an argument that would be repeated at regular intervals.

'Well, it means turning up on time,' I'd tell him.

'Yeah, but what is professional?' Mathew would persist.

'It means to play the songs together as best you can.'

'Yeah, but that doesn't make it professional . . .' and so on and so on.

Two days after the debs' ball – full of posh girls in posh frocks and their chinless boyfriends in bow ties – we were asked to perform at two benefits for the Rock Against Racism organisation. The contrast couldn't have been greater.

RAR had been set up in 1976 to help counter the growing racism among Britain's white youth. At the time the right-wing National Front organisation had been gaining more support than was ever thought possible, and a vicious, stupid, NF-supporting thug element had infiltrated punk. Perhaps they thought that the use of the swastika by numerous punks was a gesture of support for fascism, but it invariably wasn't. It was worn, naively, to shock. I had suffered a few idiots taking my interest in pre-World War II Berlin decadence and the S&M imagery as featured in *The Night Porter* (starring my personal hero Dirk Bogarde and Charlotte Rampling) as a sign of support for Nazis. It wasn't and never had been.

Figuring that music, and punk in particular, was a good way to get an anti-racism message across, RAR had been organising gigs since early in 1977. Their biggest event so far had taken place in April 1978, when 100,000 people had marched from Trafalgar Square to Victoria Park in Hackney – then something of a stronghold for the NF – where X-Ray Spex, Birmingham reggae band Steel Pulse and the Clash had performed. The gig had been marred by fascist skinheads attempting to rush the stage, something that also happened at smaller RAR gigs, particularly by bands such as Sham 69 and Cockney Rejects. We agreed to play RAR benefits at Ealing College on 10 June and a week later at the South Bank Polytechnic.

The first went off without any trouble, but the second was

almost a disaster. When we arrived there were police everywhere, yet skinheads were wrecking the changing rooms. I was
only concerned about getting the guitars in tune, despite thinking that I should be scared. We went on to a fantastic roar,
which was a surprise, and got through 'Plastic Surgery', 'Puerto
Rican' and 'Physical' before the smell of smoke became overpowering. Someone had set fire to the PA. Naturally we stopped,
but the place erupted and the situation became terrifying. Windows and everything else that could be was smashed and then
the lights went out. The PA didn't work, but the amps and drum
kit could still be played. Everyone started shouting and I lost my
temper. Right, I told the band, let's play it anyway. So we did. I
sang as loud as I could, but doubted anyone could hear me. As
we played, I genuinely began to wonder if it was really happening or if it was a dream. The organisers came on towards the
end of the set and told me that the police would bust the place
at midnight and asked if I could tell everyone to leave quietly
before then. So I stopped all the noise in the hall and shouted,
'Look, the police will bust us at twelve o'clock, and if you leave
in a riot, they've won. If you leave now, quietly, then you've
won.' We finished with 'Lady' and everyone filed quietly out.

After the gig some prick told me off for not telling the
audience about RAR. I flew at him.

'You try and talk to seven hundred kids making a noise with
no PA! I am nobody's politician, I am a singer.' The place went
quiet for a few seconds and then Vivienne Goldman, a writer for
Sounds, came up and said she thought that it was the most
amazing sight she'd ever seen and asked, 'Do you get riots
wherever you go?'

Howard Malin in the meantime had managed to get interest
in the Ants from Mike Smith, an A&R man at Decca. Although it
had once been one of the UK's biggest and most interesting
labels, having signed the Rolling Stones among others in the
early 1960s, Decca had been in decline ever since the early
1970s. The company was headed by a septuagenarian and

staffed mostly by people who'd never worked anywhere else. It must have been surviving on re-releasing past hits for at least five years before they hired Smith.

He was a nice guy and liked the band. There were a few others in the company who also understood what the Ants were about, but I didn't expect much, which is why my diary for Monday, 26 June 1978 reads as follows: 'Decca have made the offer. A record deal. Can this be true?!?!?!?!?!?'

It was, and we signed initially for two singles only a month after the offer.

Two weeks before the signing we had recorded our second Peel Session – 'Physical', 'Xerox', 'Friends' and 'Cleopatra' – which went pretty well. Two days after the signing, we played consecutive nights at West Hampstead's Moonlight Club. I was on a high after the first night, feeling that the new songs had gone down really well with the audience, who took to them as if they'd known them for ages. The next day, however, I had a meeting, which didn't go so well, with Decca's PR and marketing team to discuss the cover of the first single, which was to be 'Young Parisians'. I'd chosen the song deliberately to confuse those people who thought that we were a punk band: it sounds like a 1920s Parisian jazz song – there's not a buzzing guitar in earshot. I'd made a pen sketch for the front of the sleeve of me wearing a leather jacket and make-up in black and white, with the band lined up to one side behind each other, also wearing leather jackets, but my design was not greeted with great joy. It seemed that the 75-year-old who ran the company would be consulted about everything, including single bag designs, and he probably wouldn't like my work. Naturally, I demanded that it be released how I wanted it and, with the support of the art department, it was. That night, the second gig at the Moonlight went as well as the first, and despite feeling that I was back at square one with regards to a record label, I was fairly happy.

But the next day I got a letter from Megalovision.

At the top, scrawled in black felt pen were the words, 'Adam Ant's School Report'. Beneath it, badly typed, was a letter from Howard Malin and James Whaley. It began, 'From the desk of JPW and HDM – ex-managers.' It went on to say that they were embarrassed to be at the previous night's gig. They didn't see any improvement in the band and couldn't see how I could ever hope to play to the kind of audiences that went to see Fleetwood Mac, for instance. I was only appealing to fourteen-year olds, according to them, and they wanted more from me. They claimed that they had overheard fans leaving the gig slagging me off.

The letter went on to a second side of A4, pulling apart my songs and performance in what they obviously thought was a constructive manner, occasionally breaking into an explanation of why they'd written the letter and why now.

They went on to suggest that I take advice from them, instead of thinking that they only criticised me, and in this they had something of a point. Without knowing it, they did make one very good suggestion – that I should find a songwriting partner, a McCartney to my Lennon, a Taupin to my John. While their examples were woefully inappropriate, that was exactly what I would do, though it would take some time. The letter was signed in the same black felt pen, 'Your headmaster', and added to it in blue biro were the words, 'Most of your teachers hope you'll do better next term.'

After I'd got over my shock and disbelief, I felt relief. It was over with Megalovision. Great. It was a new beginning.

•

In September 1978 the Ants began our first European tour, in Belgium. The sound at the first two gigs was terrible, but the reception we got from the fans was fantastic. In fact they got a bit carried away at the second gig, in Ninove. The venue was an old, woodworm-riddled theatre with decaying curtains at the side of the stage and no earth to the electric sockets that we plugged into. By the end of the gig the theatre was unsafe for any kind of performance, the kids in the audience having pulled lumps out of the place, torn down the curtains and removed what little gilt edging had been left on the ornate light fittings.

We still had the VW van that Megalovision had given us, and we put a lot of miles on it over the next two months. After Belgium we returned to Britain and played Margate and Salisbury; the latter gig was ruined by a knife fight started by rockers who had surrounded the technical college where we played, delaying the start.

During two weeks in England before returning to the Continent, I delivered finished artwork to Decca for 'Parisians' and met Wad and Clare, a couple of artists with whom I began a working relationship that was to prove both fruitful and exciting. Clare set about designing me a new stage look based on the Futurists and Japanese samurai. I researched as much as I could about the Japanese element at the V&A before we had to get on the ferry at Dover again to begin a tour of Germany.

We started in Cologne before driving on to Berlin, down the 'corridor' motorway linking the West with the city where Iggy Pop and David Bowie had so recently recorded great albums. Bowie particularly seemed to love Berlin at that time, and incorporated a German electronica element to his work, as can be heard on 'Low', 'Heroes' and 'Lodger'. Our journey was staggered by stops and searches by bored East German guards. At each one we'd see a road sign filled with bullet holes, shot by the guards, I assumed.

In anticipation of Clare's new design, I decided that my look for the first Berlin date would be light blue shirt, black leather tie, black leather peg-leg trousers and matching jacket, light blue shoes with black laces, with a white face make-up and single red rose in my lapel. The second night at the SO.36 Club, I switched to a black shirt, light blue tie, black trousers, black shoes and white flower.

I loved Berlin. It seemed like the realisation of my dream

city. It was decaying but modern, the Wall carving an enormous scar across the city with the ultra-new architecture of the East staring sullenly at the daring grandeur of the West. The club we played was neon-lit and stark, with black and white being the only shades of colour. We managed three encores at the end of the second night and left feeling triumphant.

The next night we played in Bonn and then Lagensfeld, where I cut the fingers of my right hand badly, when I hit the PA in frustration because it was inadequate for the huge hall we were playing.

We then spent a week in London recuperating before setting off for Italy. During the week I managed to meet Dirk Bogarde, which was a truly momentous occasion for me. He was signing copies of his new novel (*Snakes and Ladders*) in Harrods, and I queued for half an hour before meeting him. He signed both the novel and a copy of *Films of Dirk Bogarde*, 'To Adam', and I left feeling elated.

Italy was an incredible experience. Despite having a promoter who didn't seem to know whether we were actually booked to play at a couple of places or not, the Italian media and the kids seemed to know who we were and gave us a great reception. I had done a few radio interviews in France on the drive through to the Mediterranean (the single was called 'Young Parisians', after all), but in Milan we not only had radio and press interviews lined up, but also our first television appearance. Jordan, who had come along for the Italian tour, told me that she thought that the first night in Milan, where I'd had to work really hard to get the three hundred kids going, was 'blinking great', which was as effusive as she ever got. It put me in a great mood for the TV recording and we went over fantastically. I particularly liked the fact that my make-up made my face look slightly green on TV.

Rome was harder work than Milan, and I felt tired and dirty after eight days of travel and performance. I had not had sex for eight days either, which was perhaps the biggest strain of all.

After two days of PR in the city, one of which involved another television show, I was ready to leave, but first we had to play two shows on successive nights. Both of them went well, but I was glad to be on my way back to London when they were over.

Besides a handful of gigs in familiar surroundings (the Marquee and Moonlight) plus a couple of out-of-town dates, the rest of 1978 was spent promoting the single and working on material for the album. *Sounds* phoned me and requested an interview, which I did, and they put me on the cover. My mum was a bit upset by a statement I made in it that I'd had a fucked-up childhood, though.

We recorded 'Kick' at Mickey Most's RAK studios around the corner from my old school in St John's Wood. It was becoming clear that Decca wouldn't release anything else by us, though. 'Young Parisians' hadn't sold well, Decca hadn't pushed it and the boss of the company just didn't 'get' what we were trying to do. Which didn't upset me at all. I went on planning for the UK tour that would begin in January and felt calm and in control.

I was living in a new place in Earl's Court, having given Redcliffe Gardens over to Eve. The entry for 9 November 1978 in my diary reads,

> And so it's Sunday: I am 24. I am front page (*Sounds* + 3-page interview). I work on a tour lyric programme. I have completed the Ant manifesto [a statement of what it meant to be an Ant, designed to go inside the next single release] + press release and today is the third day of my self-inflicted fast. I feel cleaner inside as each minute goes by.

The calm was not to last, though. By Christmas Eve 1978 I was miserable. Decca were unwilling to release 'Zerox', and a planned gig at the Rainbow Theatre had been cancelled just before opening: we were set up and ready to play when the promoter cancelled, citing too few tickets sold. I had hoped to be in Berlin for the holiday season, but that had been cancelled, too. A couple of days after Christmas the central heating in my flat stopped working and the ceiling in my bedroom collapsed.

Because we didn't have a manager, I had to push the promoter to confirm that everything for the tour, which began on 11 January in Leeds, was in order. I spent Christmas feeling sad, stressed and dying to get out on the road and play Antmusic. I hardly saw Mandy, as she spent the holiday with her family, and was longing for a new sexual adventure, which I knew would lift my mood and make me feel strong again.

•

Writing in my diary the morning after the first night of the 1979 UK tour on 11 January (which had culminated in sex with a sweet Leeds girl), I attempted to put into words my sexual philosophy.

> It is not the number of girls I make love to or who make love to me, but the quality + lust value of each relationship as a single element, to be judged purely on its own. Not judged on any past experiences with someone else. All are to be protected by secrecy. Not a secrecy to protect my reputation as 'Mr Nice' but as a lover of women. I need this love for I am sure it moulds the character of my work. When girls call me a gigolo I am offended, because I am not proud of my conquests, not proud at all. I do not consider girls as lumps of meat, nor inferior emotionally or intellectually – quite the opposite, in fact. I try to strike up a relationship (if they want) as I am that kind of human.

Three days later, Mandy travelled to Middlesbrough to see us perform and I realised how much I had missed her, and even felt bad about my selfish behaviour. It was great to have her back, cracking jokes with me, verbally sparring together – and otherwise being physically close. However, later in the tour, which took in Bradford, Northampton, York, Blackpool, Manchester, Liverpool, Swansea, Gwent, Huddersfield, Chelmsford,

High Wycombe, Chester, Nottingham, Norwich, Retford, Reading and Bishop's Stortford, other girlfriends made long journeys to see me. Sex was the least painful activity of my manic phases and helped me to maintain a level of calm while all the time performing, travelling and often getting sick on tour.

At the end of February, Mike Smith of Decca told me that the contract with them could and should be terminated, which I had no problem with. I also had the great pleasure of refusing the NME an interview (because I could) and turning down an appearance in a play that would have paid me £500 a week, plus expenses, in order to concentrate on my music.

At the end of March we recorded 'Ligotage', 'Tabletalk', 'Animals And Men', and 'Never Trust A Man With Egg On His Face' for our third Peel Session. Falcon Stuart reappeared and we talked managerial contracts together, although with no firm commitment from either side. He agreed to give me advice whenever I wanted it, which was good of him. I had already sent demos of the album to seven major labels and been tentatively approached by both EMI and Virgin about buying publishing rights to my songs. Not that there were any offers of contracts forthcoming.

At the end of April we played our biggest headline gig to date, at the Lyceum in London. During the after-show party I was approached by a northern guy named Ian, who asked me what was happening with my album. I told him it was still on the drawing board waiting for a label to record it. He told me he and his brother Max ran a small record label out of an office in Camden Town. It was called Do It Records, and had originally been started by Robin Scott, who had then decided that he wanted to be a pop star, and, after renaming himself M, had had a massive hit with the single 'Pop Muzik', so he'd passed the company to the brothers.

I met Ian and Max a few days later, and after some discussion we agreed a £40-a-week wage for everyone and recording time at Olympus Studios in Primrose Hill in order to finish *Dirk*

Wears White Sox, the first Adam and the Ants LP. Before that, though, I wanted to get 'Zerox' out as a single, and within only three days I had the cover made up while Do It took out ads in the music press and made up press kits ready to promote it.

'Zerox', backed with 'Whip In My Valise', was released on 6 July 1979. A week later the Mael brothers, Russell and Ron (otherwise known as Sparks), reviewed 'Whip' on Radio One's 'Roundtable' show. They liked it. Predictably, the music press didn't.

By now I had moved to a ten foot by five foot 'room' in Earl's Court (rent £7 a week). There I and Dave Barbe talked about the future and decided together that after the album had been released and we'd completed two tours, I would become a solo artist and recruit a new band, based around him on drums. It would be Adam Ant and band, no longer Adam and the Ants. I was doing all the work for the band anyway, so why not be the focal point, we agreed.

•

Our second UK tour of 1979, the Zerox Tour, began on 13 July in Retford. Fifteen dates were spread out across the country, many at venues we'd played on the first tour of the year. It lasted for five weeks and ended with another sold-out night at London's Lyceum. Towards the end of the tour, Polydor made us an offer of an advance of £100,000 for a three-year deal. I declined, believing that they'd triple the offer in time. Instead they withdrew it. Since it had never seemed like a real offer anyway, I didn't feel disappointed. I still believed that they'd be back with a bigger one.

By the last week of the tour, after spending time cramped up on a bus and in shitty hotels with them, I had become determined that Andy and Matthew had to leave the band. Their playing was too loose on stage, their attitude too boorish. But I also had to be pragmatic – I needed to get the tour finished and the album recorded before anything could change so drastically. I talked things over with Dave Barbe and controlled the urge to fire them immediately. Oddly, despite my feeling that we were sounding like some heavy metal act on stage, the NME gave Adam and the Ants their first favourable live review.

The rest of August was spent recording and then mixing Dirk Wears White Sox. I continued to be concerned about the quality of the playing from Andy and Matthew, and was still unsure whether it was as good as it could be a month later when we played two sold-out nights at the Electric Ballroom in Camden. As far as I was concerned the show was dire, and on 1 October, I split the Ants Mk IV and decided that the time had come to be just Adam Ant.

Dave and I rehearsed together from mid-October, auditioning bass players and guitarists as we wrote new songs. I was optimistic that something good was going to happen. And then something did.

On 27 October 1979 I went to a wedding reception with Jordan at the Portobello Hotel. Vivienne Westwood was also there, as was Malcolm. After we'd been seated, Malcolm leaned across the table and asked, 'So, Adam, what's happening with the group?' He knew about the split and seemed genuinely interested in what I was going to do next. For almost three hours he lectured me on the music business in a way that no one else ever had (or could). Among the various bits of rubbish that he offered up as advice, he did hit upon something. Video discs, he said, were the future of rock 'n' roll. The truth of this statement hit home and he had me completely hooked. Here was a man, I thought, who could really get things going for Adam Ant. Not that he would want to. Or so I thought.

We decided between us that the live show was a thing of the past and the future belonged to the artist who could make the best videos. Having said that, though, Malcolm insisted that the only way to break America was by touring constantly. I left the party refreshed, more determined to make things happen for Adam Ant, and also wondering how I could possibly get Malcolm McLaren to manage me.

It was another dream that would come true, but yet another one that would end as a nightmare.

7

KINGS OF THE WILD FRONTIER

'ADAM, I WANT TO LEAVE the band.'

The date was 26 January 1980. Dave Barbe, my longest-serving Ant and one of the 'musketeers', was standing before me in the rehearsal room in the basement of a pub on Camden Road, North London, his head bowed and his voice trembling.

'I've been a good soldier for three years,' he continued, without looking at me. 'And I've put up with a lot of shit from you and I've had enough. I want to do something else. We don't have to listen to you and do everything that you say. Your lyrics are shit and you don't work as hard as we do on getting things right, you just order us about and we don't want that any more. You can't work in a band and be democratic.'

I felt a bit stunned and foolish. Malcolm McLaren was sitting in a corner, his chair tilted back against the wall, biting his fingernails. 'We?' I thought.

'OK, Dave,' I said. 'That's fair enough and I wish you the best of luck. Right, guys.' I turned to Matthew and Lee. 'We'll need to find a drummer, then.'

Lee said quickly, 'I'm leaving with Dave.'

'Oh, well, right then, it's me and you, Matthew, right?'

He sat still, his head down, staring at the guitar on his knee. I was beginning to realise that this was all a set-up, engineered by Malcolm.

'I agree with them,' Matthew eventually mumbled.

I could feel anger and tears building up in me. Dave then went on for another ten minutes or so telling me how terrible I was to work with. To hear him tell it, I was worse than Franco, Hitler and Mussolini put together.

'You're not having the name,' I managed to half shout before turning and almost running out of the door. Halfway up the stairs I broke down and cried real tears.

Malcolm came up behind me and said, very sympathetically, 'Are you OK? Come on.' He put an arm round my shoulder and took me around the corner to a cheap café where we had burnt instant coffee and lukewarm minestrone soup (the minimum order allowed). I felt totally disgraced and humiliated.

'Adam, Adam,' Malcolm said, 'it's not that bad. You're OK. Look, just tell them that you'll come back and work democratically with them, as an equal, that they're a band and not Adam and the Ants.'

'Fuck that. I eat shit for no one and will not write with anybody out of duty or team-building duty. Songwriting is a craft and I will find another craftsman who works as I do.'

Malcolm sighed, said that the door was open any time I wanted to return, and went back to the rehearsal room.

How had this happened after only three weeks, I asked myself? Three weeks of indoctrination and ego-building by Malcolm, our new manager, and the Ants had ceased to be.

I headed towards home in a daze, but then for some reason thought about Marco Pirroni and decided to go to Harrow to visit him instead. It was pouring with rain when I reached his place. I'd had to call Jordan to ask Matthew's girlfriend Max, who was playing in a band named Rema Rema with Marco, for the address. Jordan was livid when I told her what had happened and kept swearing about Malcolm.

Marco wasn't at home, so I put a note through his door asking him to call me. Then I went home, met Mandy and spent the night with her. She cried her heart out and wanted to go and throttle the lot of them.

I couldn't sleep, of course, and kept going over the events of the last few weeks. At the end of November, Steph had borrowed a video camera and filmed us performing 'Zerox' and 'Tabletalk' in the garden of a friend of hers. She filmed the whole thing from the roof of the house, looking down on us. We'd shown it to Malcolm who had given us some very constructive criticism. There were too many ideas in my music, he'd said. I needed to be simpler and more direct. I played him *Dirk Wears White Sox* and he said that the album was not well produced, and it might sell 20,000 copies and was OK, but I needed a hit single to sell 250,000. I should write something that used my phrase 'antmusic for sex people'.

He went on to ask me what my lyrics were about, taking each song line by line, which was exhausting for me, but useful. Finally he said that I should steer clear of disco, because 'it's dying on its arse'.

By the end of the first week in December Malcolm and I had agreed a management deal for me as a solo act. He called it an Elvis/Colonel Tom Parker deal where we got 50/50 each. I had to do as he said for a month in order to get everything right, and then we'd be ready to take the world. Meanwhile Matthew had agreed to rejoin the Ants, but Andy Warren, who had also left the band back in October, fed up with my mood swings and determination to work the band as hard as I could, had refused the chance to rejoin when Malcolm agreed to help us. After a couple of weeks of auditions Leigh Gorman joined the Ants as the new bassist.

On 10 December, I'd set off on a personal appearance tour to promote *Dirk* in Leeds, York, Middlesbrough, Newcastle and Liverpool. The Ants were to rehearse under the guidance of Malcolm while I was gone. On the train out of King's Cross train station I wrote in my diary that,

I must trust him [Malcolm]. Matthew is a large problem/doubt in my mind, though. I feel Malcolm may even take him on and leave me to my fate – paranoia, eh? If I wasn't already a full paranoiac, I am now.

For my trip Malcolm had made me a tape of songs to listen to and learn from. Some of them I knew already, such as Gary Glitter's 'Hello! I'm Back Again', but there were some that I hadn't heard. The full playlist was:

'Wipe Out' by the Surfaris
No Problem by Chet Baker
'He's The Fatman' by the Hawks
'Mystery Train' by Elvis Presley
'Blue Moon' by Elvis Presley
'YMCA' by the Village People
'Hot Dog' by Taps Miller
'Cast Iron Arm' by Peanuts Wilson
'Tear It Up' by Johnny Burnette
'Hello! I'm Back Again' by Gary Glitter
'Where Were You (On Our Wedding Day?)' by Lloyd Price
'Broadway Jungle' by the Flames
'Got To Pick A Pocket' by Ron Moody from the *Oliver!* soundtrack
'I'm not Tired' by Cliff Bennett and the Rebel Rousers
'Rave On' by Buddy Holly
Belly dance music by Farid El Atrache
Burundi Black by Burundi Black

The object was to understand the construction and interpretation of songs, which would help me in seeking a style and sound which would eventually evolve as Antmusic.

Throughout my five days away I called Dave Barbe and he kept me informed of their progress. By the time I returned to London they knew a dozen numbers whose lyrics I had been working on. We set about putting the lot together and adding to our repertoire ready for a gig at Camden's Electric Ballroom on 1 January. We needed to get £1,000 cash for Malcolm. (He and

Vivienne were opening a new shop and were short of money.) I knew we were owed about that much from the gig – it just had to be collected from a very tough promoter. I felt no fear as I marched into John Curd's office and asked for my fee.

'And who the hell are you, pal?' he snarled at me.

'I'm Adam Ant.'

I think it was the national health glasses I had on, but Curd laughed. 'I like you, son, you've got some balls coming here.'

He gave me the money and I went back to Malcolm to tell him he was hired.

A couple of weeks later things were going well, I thought, between the Ants and me. We even all went to singing lessons together. We'd spend evenings sitting with Malcolm at Dave's place while he played us all kinds of music – jazz, classical, opera, African and more rock 'n' roll. Every day in the last two weeks of January, Malcolm came down to the rehearsal rooms. He was often there, when I arrived, with the band. Admittedly, I was finding it hard to sing to the sound that the band was producing, but I gave it a good shot. I could see the cracks between us beginning to appear, though. They'd all be sitting on the floor with an African music 'expert' named Simon who helped them with beats and timing, hitting sticks together, and chanting while I tried to write lyrics to go with the music.

I had taken to reading books on American Indians and African tribes and became fascinated with the whole idea and culture of the warrior, going deeper into the philosophy than I had in 1977. Malcolm kept trying to get me to read stuff about pirates (it was going to be Vivienne's new look, he said), but it was the warrior mindset that intrigued me.

By 23 January I had a number of new songs coming together, among them 'Kings Of The Wild Frontier', 'Shade To White' and a song about Blackbeard (for Malcolm) set to a Burundi-style beat which I thought I might call Antmusic. I wasn't the first person to see the possibilities of this kind of music. On Joni Mitchell's 1975 album, *The Hissing of Summer Lawns*, she 'sampled' the Burundi beat from an old album for her 'Jungle Line' song. You can even hear chants and shouts from the drummers in the background.

Because of the change in how we worked in the rehearsal room – the band supposedly coming up with the music for me to write lyrics to – up to that point they hadn't managed a single song between them. I wished they'd hurry up so that I could get on with performing and losing a few pounds in weight.

Meanwhile, I concentrated on a new look for the stage, deciding that I would go for an Apache/gypsy warrior look, with knee bells to make my moves percussive, kilt flying and a white stripe across my nose. Malcolm tried to get me to model Vivienne's new pirate clothes, but I preferred my own look.

At the same time, I had been asked to submit work for the Milan Triennale exhibition and came up with the idea of a series of T-shirts titled 'My Influences'. They would include one printed with a Lenny Bruce quote, another with a quote from Joe Orton and another with a Dirk Bogarde quote. Jordan told me that Vivienne was considering doing an Ant T-shirt, too, which was flattering.

So I was relatively happy with life even if I had decided that Malcolm was a bit weird, because of his constant 1950s-style London spiv act, always trying to get the band off with 'tarts', as he called them. It was as if Malcolm had studied Laurence Harvey in *Expresso Bongo* (the 1959 film about the beginnings of the British rock 'n' roll scene starring Cliff Richard) and believed that was how managers had to behave. He'd always be talking out of the side of his mouth with a mockney accent, giving it, 'Cor boys, what about 'er?' and almost physically nudging Matthew or Dave as a woman walked past us. He seemed to think that being young men they were only interested in sex. Maybe working with Paul Cook of the Pistols had made him certain of that, and I found it funny at first, but it soon became

annoying. So I ignored his *Carry On*-style leering after a while
and tried to get him to concentrate on business.

He and I had been to see a couple of record companies,
having decided not to sign another contract with Do It. I needed
£5,000 to buy a release from Decca for the demos I'd recorded
for them. We went to see Spartan, who would go on to have
success with UB40 and had originally signed the Police. The
Spartan boss was trying to impress Malcolm and went on for
ages about how good the company was, but Malcolm refused to
be impressed and just told them that now other labels had their
acts and they were laughing all the way to the bank. What did
Spartan have?

Next we visited Decca to ask about getting the rights to the
demos. We were shown into Tracy Bennett's office (he was then
head of the Deram label and later went on to start the dance
label ffrr and to run London Records in the 1990s). While Frank
Rogers, who had been in A&R when I signed with them, went
off to get clearance to release the tracks to us, Malcolm sifted
through the Decca singles cupboard, loading himself up with
records. I looked out of the window, bored, until Tracy got a call
saying that Frank had just been sacked by their new parent
company, Polygram. So I left empty-handed and Malcolm,
clutching his free records, gave me a short lecture about how
the music biz was going through a decline and that selling
20,000 albums in the 1980s would be a big deal. (He was only
twenty years out, but that is now the case.) According to Malcolm, he was going to shake up the music biz and teach them
all how to do it. He was positive about that and so was I.

Malcolm needed a new band because by this time there was
no more Sex Pistols. Lydon had quit the band after the last US
gig in January 1978 and was now fronting Public Image Ltd.
Sid Vicious was dead. He'd overdosed on heroin bought for him by
his mum while he was on bail accused of killing Nancy Spun-
geon. If Malcolm was ever going to take the music biz by storm

again, he had to do it soon, and I thought that he would, with Adam and the Ants. So what went wrong?

I had finally realised a few months back that Malcolm was scouting for a band to back the fourteen-year-old Annabella Lwin, and had settled on the Ants. I think he would have been perfectly happy for me to be part of the backing band, but Annabella was always going to be the singer out front. He must have cottoned on quite early that I wouldn't stand for that, which was why he worked on building the confidence and musical capability of the Ants until they got to where they were on 26 January and blew me out.

Although I knew I should, I didn't despise or even dislike Malcolm at all after it happened once I'd got over the initial shock. I thought he'd made a mistake – which was what Jordan kept telling him in the days after the split. I genuinely wished him and the boys luck. It made me more determined than ever to get Antmusic out there, and I knew that I had to do it before they managed it. Also, the split led me into the longest-lasting and most fruitful working relationship of my adult life – with Marco Pirroni.

•

Marco telephoned me a few days after I'd left the note in his letterbox. 'Adam? It's Marco. You wanted to talk to me?'

'Yeah. Do you want to write songs with me?'

'Yeah, OK. Let's meet in Covent Garden.'

It was as simple as that. We met and agreed that everything would be split 50/50 and that it was to be Ant/Marco. The timing was right. Marco had decided not to continue with Rema Rema and so wasn't playing with a band. He'd only ever seen Adam and the Ants play live once and that was a long time ago, but he liked me and had heard enough to think that it would be a good idea to work with me. I still don't know why I went to see him originally. I'd only spoken to him about three times before, and then it had been brief. I'd say dumb things along the lines of, 'Nice trousers' (he used to work at Johnson's in the King's Road, which specialised in 1950s and 60s clothing), or, 'I've got a guitar like yours.' Marco was scary when he was a punk. He was big, unapproachable and self-contained. It was that self-contained air that impressed me, I think. Marco had declined many offers to join various punk bands, always wanting to do something different. He'd even left the Models after they'd had a minor hit in 1978. And he was the best guitarist I'd ever seen.

Like me, Marco was an only child. He'd grown up a lot happier than I had, even if he had been left alone at home at an early age because both his parents worked. No one beat him up when he was a kid, though. He was loved by both his parents and had a self-assured, couldn't-give-a-shit attitude and gave off a sense of calm and control. It was probably that which made me both in awe and a bit scared of him.

From the first day of making music together, I knew that we had something. We didn't necessarily like all the same stuff, but we both knew and agreed on what we didn't like. He was organised and methodical, and would make me decide early on how many lines were in a verse, how many times a line was repeated for a chorus. I'd ask him how things should be and he'd say, 'How do you want them to be?' Marco gave me confidence in my songwriting because I knew that he was creating a structure that worked properly. I asked him if he thought Dirk sounded right. 'How did you want it to sound?' he asked. Marco was always answering my questions with a question in order to get to the point of everything.

We were both fans of Roxy Music and Glam Rock. We both agreed that the Glitter Band's use of two drummers was worth trying again. In the early 1970s lots of bands had used two drummers, including Wizzard and Showaddywaddy, to make a big-beat, vaguely 1950s rock 'n' roll kind of sound. That was what we decided to base Antmusic on. Add the Burundi idea and we had a great, percussive sound to start with. Marco's big guitar sound and reverb on my voice were the added ingredients needed to make the sound truly ours.

For two weeks we met every day at Marco's place in Harrow to write. Then we'd travel into Notting Hill and sit in Tootsies, admiring the waitresses and planning the future of Adam and the Ants. Because Falcon Stuart had been calling me ever since first hearing that Malcolm was managing me, I'd called him and told him about the split. He agreed to work with Marco and me (without a contract), and soon, without ever playing a note to anyone, we had Beggars Banquet and Polygram interested in signing us.

In order to fulfil the last obligation to Do It, Marco and I went into Rockfield Studios to re-record 'Car Trouble' as a single for them (and 'Kick') on 18 February 1980. Marco had suggested using a guy named Chris Hughes to produce. He was great and also happened to be a drummer, so we asked him to join the band. He agreed and adopted the name Merrick for the role. Marco suggested that we also ask Terry Lee Miall, who'd been in the Models with him, to join as second drummer, and so we had our first two band members. All we needed was a bassist. Surprisingly, a couple of weeks after finishing 'Car Trouble', I found one, living with Eve. Kevin Mooney was her new boyfriend, and beside the fact that it didn't bother me at all, I found that I liked the guy enough to suggest that he come to a rehearsal and try out.

In a brave or foolish gesture a couple of weeks later, I accepted an offer from a new promoter, Noel D'Abo, to join his agency (Action Star) and asked him to organise a tour for Adam and the Ants, to begin as soon as possible. The first date was fixed for six weeks away, in late May. Falcon thought that it was a good idea and advanced me £500 to pay for our expenses, at the same time letting me know that EMI Publishing were about to make an offer for the rights to publish our songs.

Meanwhile the *NME* (Nick Kent, writer) had 'broken' the story that Malcolm McLaren had sacked Adam from the Ants. The *News of the World* asked if I'd be interviewed about it. I considered it seriously, deciding that Malcolm would be disappointed if I didn't do it. So I didn't. Malcolm was getting ready to launch his band, now called Bow Wow Wow, and according to Jordan, who'd heard them, they were using Burundi-style drums, making warrior sounds and wearing pirate gear. We had to get moving on recording and releasing our sound so that the world knew that Antmusic had come from us and not Malcolm.

On Saturday 19 April we recorded 'Kings Of The Wild Frontier' at Matrix Studios. It was the first of the Ant/Marco songs to be put on tape, and was in complete contrast to all the recordings I'd made previously. It took a long time to get right, but we did, and I felt elated on hearing the finished track. I knew we had cracked it. The drums sounded like ten thousand Zulus banging their shields. Terry Lee proved most useful in that part of the recording, banging drum cases and lumps of wood of all shapes and sizes with abandon.

I couldn't wait to get the band on the road. It had been four months since I'd last played a gig and I felt incredibly restless and physically bored.

I'd been spending increasing amounts of time with Mandy alone since the split with Malcolm and the Ants. We'd spend several nights in perfect harmony and then we'd argue non-stop for a couple of days. I was convinced that she wanted to be part of the new Blitz/New Romantic scene that was just starting in London, and I really did not want anything to do with them.

Mandy was unsure about what she should do for a career, and I suggested that she become an actress, so she applied to the Central School of Speech and Drama at Swiss Cottage. At times I felt that the seven-year age gap between us and my selfish obsession with getting Antmusic together was bad for her and that she should start seeing other people. But if I got any idea that she was seeing someone else, I'd have a jealous fit of rage.

By the time the new tour started on 22 May, I had spent the best part of five months with only Marco and the Ants or Mandy. Getting back on the road was a relief and delight. Before the Ants Invasion Tour 1980 (as we called it) began, we played a showcase at John Henry's PA Co. sound stage for some record company people. I thought it was too low-key and relaxed, and that whoever had seen us (Falcon claimed that people from MCA, EMI and CBS had been there) would run a mile.

The opening night of the tour, at London's Electric Ballroom, was a sell-out, despite there having been little advertising for the gig. At one point Malcolm had suggested that the next Ants tour be 'clandestine' and that we build by word of mouth. It looked like the Ants Invasion Tour was going to be just that, since the music press were ignoring us and the promoter hadn't put too many ads out there. I began to miss Malcolm, thinking that at least he would have got us lots of press coverage. 'Car Trouble' had gone into the Top 10 independent singles chart, however, and I heard that Malcolm thought that it was 'the best thing [I'd] done', which cheered me up.

Mandy came along on the tour and acted as 'wardrobe' mistress, painting feathers with stripes and sewing ribbons into hair extensions for me. Everything was going well until the third date, in Manchester. I had left our hotel room early while Mandy was still in bed. When I came back, she was running down the road towards the train station, crying.

'I hate you,' she screamed at me when I caught up with her. 'I don't ever want to see you again. You're a liar.'

I kept asking why and tried to get her to go back to the hotel. Eventually she told me that she had found and read my diary. She felt bad not only because of what she'd read, but also because she'd read it. She was close to being hysterical, and I tried vainly to calm her down. At the time I was sorry that she'd read my diary because she didn't deserve to be hurt in that way, and I cried real tears of regret. After a couple of hours of fighting, shouting and then both lying exhausted in my hotel room, Mandy left for London, saying that she didn't want to end things like this. I felt indescribably bad. I felt I was not reacting like the kind of person that I wanted to be, but like the person that I had to fight every day. That was the bad Adam who had black thoughts, temper tantrums when things weren't going well for him and forced people away from him when they tried to make him feel better.

I argued with myself that Mandy had known about the other women, but she hadn't, at least not in the kind of detail that I had put into my diary. It occurred to me that perhaps by reading it Mandy was looking for a reason to end things between us. Yet when it came to it, neither of us could end the relationship. Not yet, anyway.

If it hadn't been for the gigs and the fact that the band was tight, both musically and personally, on that tour, I knew that I would have been in a very bad way indeed. But instead of dwelling on Mandy, I could perform and talk with Marco and write new songs. I dedicated the Manchester gig to Ian Curtis, the Joy Division singer who had committed suicide a week earlier. Two nights later, in Bournemouth, a girl named Janet Hayworth died during the gig, from an asthma attack. I felt awful.

The next gig, in Bristol, was good and I went to my hotel room alone but only managed to sleep off and on. Between bouts of sleep I planned the next tour, to promote our next LP, *Kings of the Wild Frontier*. The next night, Mandy reappeared at my door. We talked all day and agreed that things would be different between us, that they'd be better. She stayed the night and then returned to London.

The tour went to Edinburgh, where a bunch of Glasgow punks got into our hotel and started in on me for never playing their home town. I got angry with one of them and the police, embarrassingly, stepped in to stop a full-scale fight erupting.

The next night we played an old school hall in Dundee, which was fun. In Sheffield I was visited by the 1960s pop star Dave Berry, which was a great honour for me, since I'd been a fan in the 60s. We agreed that he'd play support for us at our final London date, at the Empire Ballroom on 8 June. After a violent gig in Huddersfield but a great one in Leicester, we returned to London ready for that date full of energy and hope.

All through the tour I had worn a nineteenth-century British military jacket on stage. I had hired it from Dave Whiteing, who worked at theatrical costumiers Berman's and Nathan's in Covent Garden. It had originally been made for David Hemmings to wear in the film *The Charge of the Light Brigade*, Dave told me. An expert in military dress and a really interesting guy, Dave and I became friends (later I got him to star in quite a few of the Ant videos). By the time we played the final date at the Empire Ballroom there were kids in the audience who were also wearing military jackets and who had painted a single white line across their nose. It was happening.

The gig was a blast and the next day EMI offered Marco and me £22,000 for the rights to our song publishing. We accepted the offer and a couple of weeks later started demoing songs for the next Ants LP, *Kings of the Wild Frontier*, at a 16-track studio. We'd been signed by Brian Hopkins at EMI Publishing who then did a great deal of singing our praises to record companies. Brian became one of the unsung heroes of the Adam Ant story. He really knew his music. Because he was not really a corporate animal and we got on well with him, Brian would be the only person that Marco and I would play demos for over the next few years. There had also been major record labels at the gig, and they started making approaches to us, via Falcon Stuart.

Finally, on 25 July 1980, Adam and the Ants were signed to CBS, with two other companies also making offers. *Kings of the Wild Frontier* was cut, the sleeve manufactured, and after much work and talk and demoing of thirteen songs, the single hit the streets. I was incredibly nervous as all this happened, especially as the papers unanimously slagged it, and Malcolm McLaren's group of ex-Ants, Bow Wow Wow, became big, big stuff. Feeling like shit after being described as an old man by McLaren in an *NME* interview, I took a deep breath, had a haircut and went looking for Mandy. I felt low, despite the fact that Marco and I had grossed £70,000 in three months and the work was so much better than before.

I began to feel like a prick for having held Malcolm so high. Still, I told myself, I will win. It would not be easy, but we would be bigger than Bow Wow Wow.

We set about recording a new album in early August. For a month we worked at Rockfield Studios, which was actually a small cottage in Wales, recording eleven songs. I played bass on all but four tracks, with Kevin recording those. The single 'Kings Of The Wild Frontier' only made it to number 48 in the official charts, which didn't surprise me. We needed a TV appearance to get it any higher. *Sounds* had put me on the cover again, and I had a pop at Malcolm (who had claimed that he 'had to dump Adam'). I said that the difference between him and me was that I lived out my own fantasies rather than getting other people to live them for me. I could have added that he and Vivienne had no sense of humour, and that they were not from the gutter as I was, and that I would fight to keep the Ants at the top when Barbe, Ashman and Gorman had slipped into nothingness. I thought all of that, but kept it to myself. I didn't say it to the *NME*, *Melody Maker*, *The Face* or *Record Mirror* when they interviewed Marco and me. Clearly the music press was changing its opinion of Antmusic, as I knew it would. But just as I knew that television could help to break us big, I thought that the daily newspapers could be a great help to us, too.

In those days the newspapers didn't cover pop music in the way they have done since. There was no daily column in every tabloid reporting every fart and fall of minor 'celebrity' singers and 'pop idols' like there is today. They only took notice of a pop star when they were really big. They'd covered the Pistols in a shock-horror, 'must we fling this pop filth at our kids?' kind of way, and would occasionally run stories about Rod Stewart or Mick Jagger having affairs with models or some such nonsense, but the British newspapers hadn't really gone big on a pop act since T. Rex in the early 1970s had been proclaimed as 'the new Beatles'. Maybe they were too busy covering wars, politics and the collapsing economy at the time, who knows? But I thought that I could use them in a way that I couldn't use the music press, because the music press was useless, really. None of the weekly music papers sold more than 200,000 copies, whereas the *Sun* sold over five million a day. Not that I'd ignore the new bunch of teen mags being launched, like *Smash Hits*, or the older ones like *Record Mirror* or *Look-In*. It was just that the daily newspapers would give us a far wider exposure to people than they ever could.

A newspaper had given me the idea for 'Dog Eat Dog' when I'd read the line reportedly used by Britain's newly elected Prime Minister of the day, Margaret Thatcher. It was a powerful image and one that appealed to me in my then mood of anger at McLaren and determination to succeed. CBS liked the song enough to release it as a single on 3 October that year. It went into the charts at number 50 and then went up to 37. We had broken the Top 40 for the first time, which was a surprise, since CBS hadn't allowed us to make a video to promote it.

Although this was before MTV had launched, increasingly bands had begun to make short films to accompany single releases, mainly because it allowed them to 'appear' on TV shows like the all-important *Top of the Pops* in Britain while they were touring in another country. Since the recent introduction of video technology, the cost of making promotional films – which had previously only been affordable to major bands like the Beatles and Queen – had come down to the point where even new acts could afford to make them. We had made a low-budget video for 'Kings Of The Wild Frontier', which Steph had directed, and I was determined we'd use a still from it for the cover of both the single bag and the album sleeve. It hadn't helped sales, though, because it hadn't been shown anywhere. The cost of promo videos would always eventually be paid by the band, although their record companies, who footed the original bill, had to be sure that their act would sell enough records to be able to pay back the initial outlay before they'd do so. Maybe CBS were still unsure about our prospects, given the failure of 'Kings' to make the Top 40.

If they had been unsure about our chances of success, they changed their mind when the producer of *Top of the Pops* rang in the third week of October and asked if we'd be able to appear on that week's show to perform 'Dog Eat Dog'. The call came on a Wednesday morning. Could we be there that afternoon? Did bears shit in the woods?

•

'You fucking prick, call yourself a punk? Fucking stupid clothes and poofy make-up, you're shit.'

Four young guys wearing donkey jackets with '4 be 2' sprayed on the back, Dr Marten's boots and woolly beanie-hats were giving me and the Ants and Mandy a verbal lashing as we walked through the BBC foyer in Wood Green, W12.

'Oi, darling, want a real fuck?' one of the idiots shouted at Mandy. That was a mistake. She turned, flashed them a V-sign and said, 'You couldn't handle it. Adam's more of a man than you'll ever be, dickhead.'

'Fuck off, cow,' came the witty reply.

'Yeah, fuck you, go and pick on some kids who won't hurt you,' Mandy shouted back.

I steered her in front of me and down the staircase that Marco and the rest of the band had already descended. I didn't really want to get into a fight at our first ever *Top of the Pops* performance. They were the kind of scum who would take pleasure in such a thing, but I was determined to not lower myself to their level.

'You cunt. Get him . . .' shouted one of them.

I felt a kick in the small of my back and fell down the stairs. There was a rush of feet following me.

'Get him,' said a voice. 'Go on, get the bastard.'

I looked up as a beer-and-fags-stinking, spotty-faced moron leaned over me. I threw up an arm just as the monkey went flying backwards. Mandy had whacked him full on the nose and sent him flying. The tiny corridor in which I was sprawled suddenly filled with big men in uniforms and white peaked caps. The BBC security guards had arrived, at last. They grabbed the bovver boys and carted them off, tried to calm Mandy and asked if I was OK.

What a way to end our first major TV appearance. The guys in the donkey jackets were a skinhead band, named 4 be 2. The name was possibly because they were as thick as two short 4 by 2 planks. I was furious, not only because of the danger we'd been in – how the hell did those fuckwits get in to the BBC? – but also because I had become increasingly wary of attack since my run-in with the Glasgow punks at the gig in Edinburgh. I had not employed any security for the band, but now I would.

Mind you, it did prove me right about the daily newspapers helping to get us over to a bigger audience. The day after the attack, the *Daily Mirror* ran a headline which read, PUNK STARS IN TOP OF THE POPS RIOT and went on to mis-report the whole sorry affair. It took Peter Powell to go on air on Radio One the next day to tell the public this was not the case. That night, though, there was probably a slightly larger proportion of the TOTP audience waiting to see Adam and the Ants perform than there would have been if nothing had happened at the taping.

I had enjoyed the show enormously, despite having to mime during several run-throughs. I could never conserve energy when I was on stage and so put everything into each 'take'. The white stripe on my face had to be redone (by Mandy) a couple of times, and I sweated a hell of a lot in the David Hemmings cavalry jacket, but all of the hard work was worth it. We seemed to come across pretty well when the show was broadcast, because that appearance on the only major music show on British television resulted in a massive increase in sales of 'Dog Eat Dog' and awareness of Adam and the Ants. Overnight we became famous. The single shot up the charts and made number 4.

It was only a couple of weeks later that the album *Kings of the Wild Frontier* was released, and instead of spending any more time or money promoting 'Dog Eat Dog' – by making a promo video, for instance – CBS put all of their efforts into getting it into the shops. Which was fine, but as usual I felt that they could do more.

The success of 'Dog Eat Dog' had brought a lot of new fans to the band, which was great. In order to say thank you to all our old fans and to let the new ones know that we were not any new, flash-in-the-pan, overnight pop success, I insisted that the original pressing of the *Kings* album included the *Adam & the Ants Catalogue*. This was a black and white, twelve-page booklet that told the history of the band, included photographs and biographies of the band members, selected reviews from the past three years, a full discography and a complete listing of all the gigs that I had played since 1976. It took some persuading, but eventually CBS agreed.

They also agreed that there should be another single from the album before Christmas and that this time there should be a proper promo video to accompany it. I chose 'Antmusic'. For the video we hired my old haunt, the tiny Sombrero club in Kensington, and filmed us 'performing' the song to a crowd who are reluctant at first to dance to it, but eventually get completely into the song and surround us on the under-lit dance floor. The only part of the video not to be filmed at the Sombrero was shot at a tiny studio where we'd built an enormous plug and socket set to emphasise the 'Unplug the jukebox, and do us all a favour' line. That proved to be the most difficult part to film, of course, with the plug not fitting or constantly being dropped because it was too big to handle easily. It wasn't exactly *Lawrence of Arabia*, but the 'Antmusic' video did have a story line and wasn't just a film of us miming, which was important to me. I was determined that our future videos would have better production, a real story and even famous stars.

The video helped 'Antmusic' make the number 2 position on the charts in December 1980, only missing number 1 because 'Imagine' by John Lennon had been re-released (Lennon had just been murdered by Mark Chapman).

We were on tour through to the end of that year, so we were sitting in a hotel in Edinburgh in mid-November when we heard that the *Kings* album had gone into the chart at number 4. Marco and I literally danced around the room, chanting 'Number 4!' It was an incredible feeling to realise that after three years of hard work and slog, I had 'made it'; that not only did I have a single hit, but I had an album hit, too. I had always expected it to happen and there was a part of me that was relieved that the wait was now over, while another part felt apprehensive about what was to come next. I wanted to go straight back into the studio and make another album and set up another tour, to be as busy as I possibly could in order to keep the 'high' that I was feeling going. I knew that work would made me happy, that keeping myself busy meant keeping the depression at bay.

The tour was a mix of magic and mayhem. Because of the success of 'Dog' and now 'Kings' and 'Antmusic', at several venues hundreds of people turned up who couldn't get in. Having not expected to be big pop stars when we booked the venues around the UK, several were too small for the demand. We had to cancel shows in Shrewsbury and Lincoln, and rearranged one in Manchester from the Poly to the Apollo. Hundreds of fans who couldn't get into the venue in Sheffield staged a mini-riot outside and wrecked cars, while in Hull they tried to set fire to the doors that were closed to them. There were hundreds of fans screaming at me as I ran into the back doors of all the places we played. Our hotels were surrounded by fans, our van was followed by scores of cars to find out where we were staying. It all felt like I'd walked into the Beatles' film, A Hard Day's Night.

The final night of the UK tour was at the Lyceum, and was a cross between a victory rally and a party. Unknown to me, CBS had invited Les and Doreen to the show – the first time that they'd seen me perform live. Apparently, when we began and the crowd erupted with their usual pogo-ing frenzy, Les's jaw dropped and he sat, stunned, for the rest of the performance. I had a great time. There were more people wearing the white stripe on their faces, lots with feathers in their hair and nearly all of them sang along with all of the songs. The hairs on the back of my neck were at permanent attention.

For the first time, two British broadsheet newspapers reviewed the show. The Times reporter was very formal in his praise, writing that, 'There is an undeniable and oftproven excitement to be had from the sight and sound of two trap drummers resolutely performing synchronised or unison figures.' Unfortunately it was a bit too long to include on any future promotional material, but it would have been great if we could have. The Guardian's female reporter unfortunately wrote of me that, 'he isn't very sexy'. That made Mandy mad, but Marco laugh. A lot.

•

The Kings tour had been badly organised and we still did not have a contract with a manager. Falcon had appeared infrequently during it, and I had become close to Don Murfet, whom I'd hired as head of security.

After the fight at the BBC a call had been made to a security firm, Artists Services, which was run by Don. He was very powerfully built, suited and booted in a sixties style, and proved to be a great combination of business and muscle. The first thing he did was to track down 4 by 2 and give them twenty-four hours to get out of town, which, to my knowledge, they did – and never came back. On the tour Don was always a gentleman and never raised his voice, yet always got things done and made sure that I had whatever I wanted. He made me feel safe, which was a first for me on a tour. Back in London, Don invited me to his house for a weekend roast, with his lovely wife June and their three children. It was to be the first of many visits to come.

When Falcon came to me before the Lyceum gig asking for a contract, I said no. I had already decided to ask Don to manage the band.

Don went to see the legendary Peter Grant, manager of Led Zeppelin, for advice. I was then 'summoned' to see Peter when he expressed an interest in managing us instead; we went to visit him after he'd seen us at the Lyceum. It was an odd experience. Grant was a huge bear of a man, with a full beard, bald head and enormous stomach. He had been Led Zeppelin's manager from the beginning and stayed with them throughout their career, in the process making a reputation for himself as a kind of Mafia-style godfather. He got the biggest advance ever paid to a band when he signed Zeppelin to Atlantic Records in 1968, but had not worked with anyone else since. He was fierce in his support and work for Led Zep, and Don obviously picked that up from him. It was whispered that when promoters failed to pay Grant money for a gig – and he always asked for cash after the show, it was said – he would draw a gun and point it at their head until they gave him his dues. After a pleasant afternoon spent drinking tea and chatting, he waved goodbye to us and we never heard from him again. Which was just as well because I wasn't sure that I could handle him as our manager. But Don had said 'Yes'.

Early in 1981 the *Kings* album went to number 1 on the charts. I felt fantastically happy and proud, but knew that we needed another single out there to keep us in the public's mind, since Marco and I were about to start writing and recording songs for the third Ants LP. We were also planning an all-important first tour of America.

Since we had had a video made of 'Kings' and it was the album title track, it made sense to re-release that as a single, I thought. They took some persuading, but eventually CBS agreed to it. After all, they could use the existing video to help sell it. In it I am wearing the Hemmings military jacket, as in the video for 'Antmusic', and I had worn the same outfit on TOTP, so there was a continuity that could only help new fans to recognise it as being by Adam and the Ants. In February it made number 2 in the UK charts.

Another hit gave me another reason to promote, do interviews and appear on kids' TV shows, like Noel Edmonds' *Multi-Coloured Swap Shop*, on which I spoke with kids live on the telephone. It being my first such show, I struggled to be as straight and honest with the kids (and Noel) as possible when they asked me ever more inane questions. I treated the 'interview' as if it were *The Times* or something, and gave answers that were far too long and intense, but I soon learned that all I had to do on TV was smile a lot and be nice to people, keep the answers short and wink at the camera occasionally.

We also appeared on the BBC's *Old Grey Whistle Test*, playing live, which was at totally the opposite end of the television promotion scale to kids' TV, and a chance to show the hippies who watched that we were not just a teen band, but a gig-hardened and tight live outfit. We recorded *Whistle Test* the day after I returned from my first trip to New York, which had been a meet-and-greet with Epic, the US arm of CBS that we were signed to for America. I loved New York – it was just as I'd hoped and imagined. The massive buildings, constant noise and energy of the place were incredible. I played Stevie Wonder's 'Living For The City' non-stop during the cab ride into Manhattan, and gawped at the sights like a true tourist. In England, meanwhile, the *Sun* newspaper had declared that I was going to be the biggest pop star of 1981. And we had been invited to perform at the Royal Variety Show at London's Palladium Theatre, in front of Princess Margaret.

In the four weeks leading up to the Royal Variety Show I was interviewed twice for British TV, had day-trips to Holland, Paris and Germany to accept Gold Discs, and appeared on TV. I also began demoing songs for the forthcoming *Prince Charming* album with Marco, our second, and spent any 'spare' time writing new songs or being with Mandy.

The week before the appearance on the Palladium stage, the band recorded the music for the actual show. Only I would perform live – the band would mime. It has been said that the miming was what upset Kevin Mooney so much that he felt that he had to object in some way. It's also been suggested that he thought that we shouldn't play for royalty. But for me, appearing on the Royal Variety Show was a highpoint of my career to that point, as was meeting Princess Margaret afterwards, still in my make-up and still shaking with annoyance at Kevin's childish antics. (The photos of the Princess and me were all over the front pages of the tabloids the next day.) I said it was an honour for me, and the music press took the piss because I'd given her two children an autograph.)

I wasn't aware that Kevin was swinging his bass around behind me until we'd almost finished performing 'Antmusic' and he dropped it completely. I kept furiously signalling him to pick it up as we were taking our bows, but he ignored me. Marco later told me that Kevin's strap had broken and he was trying to hold on to the bass, but I was furious with him. I felt that what he did was completely unprofessional. It was the last straw.

He'd begun to annoy me while on the *Kings* tour, when he'd often shout at the audience and swing the bass around while playing, which was affecting his performances badly. I decided after the Royal Variety Show that he would have to go. He agreed to leave, and his contract was paid off. Luckily Gary Tibbs, who had been a member of the punk band the Vibrators before going on to play with Roxy Music, was available and jumped at the chance of joining the Ants when we asked him.

Gary went straight into rehearsal with us, helping with new material as well as catching up on old songs. We had several TV and awards shows to play in February and March. Among them were *Jim'll Fix It* (when we were joined by a kid who wanted to drum with us), the Nationwide/*Daily Mirror* Award Show, an Annie Nightingale Radio One session and appearances in Amsterdam and Sweden. Then, at the end of March 1981 we flew to America for the first Adam and the Ants US Tour.

•

In the week before leaving for America I had met the film director and now master of the music video, Mike Mansfield. We had a dinner together, arranged by Don Murfet. I had been explaining to Don how I saw the video for the next Ants single, which was to be called 'Stand And Deliver', should look. Don thought that if I could talk to Mike about it, he might be able to help me translate my ideas into a video.

I wanted to make something that had the feel and look of a Hammer Horror movie, something with costumes and a story. Mike, a calm guy with long white hair and a quiet voice, listened to what I was saying and responded positively. He'd love to make something like it. Why didn't I draw up the storyboards – each scene set down on paper in a series of squares, as if from a camera's point of view – and let him have them? I promised him I would.

Many videos at this time were not about anything except allowing directors to try this or that technique in order to make the band look exciting. The only other band doing anything remotely interesting in their videos were Madness, whose videos made me laugh, and I considered them the opposition at the time – especially Lee, the saxophone player, who was very funny.

Later that week I'd also met a new woman. Tessa Hewitt was a *Sun* Page 3 girl. Blonde and as curvy as a young Marilyn Monroe, she was not a typical dumb blonde at all. We had met at a club and danced for ages before heading back to my place, a new flat in Earl's Court that I'd barely had time to sleep in since moving at the end of 1980. I had also continued to rent Redcliffe Gardens for a couple of years, despite not living there, and had let an old friend, Dave Gibb, move in. When I had the time I was going to buy a place of my own.

Mandy and I had been seeing a lot of each other since success had hit me, but we had also started to argue a lot. When we did, we'd not see each other for weeks and I'd end up missing her like hell. Inevitably it would be either my jealousy that caused an argument – I was convinced that she was seeing someone else – or her jealousy over me. Of course, I was usually also seeing someone else and my hypocrisy also hurt me. If I wasn't in love with Mandy it was because I couldn't let myself be. I associated being in love with too many painful memories, not least the death of Stuart and my illness.

I met Tessa during one of our cool-it periods. She and I only had a few nights together before I flew to New York to begin the tour, but I hoped that we'd see more of each other when I got back.

Despite my best-laid plans and demands that Epic prepare everything properly for us, I found that we had to go through a lot of glad-handing and meeting and greeting with the press and record company people in New York before we could start performing.

MTV had been playing the 'Kings' and 'Antmusic' videos and so we already had a level of fame in New York (MTV wasn't nationwide at the time). It was enough to have attracted the attention of an American Indian organisation, and they had taken exception to my wearing a white stripe across my face because they said that it was warpaint. Epic had told me about their objection before we'd left England, and so I asked to meet with them when I got to America. I met with ten American Indian chiefs (led by a man named George Stonefish), and they put their case to me, claiming that I was exploiting their heritage without knowing anything about it. Because I had read so much about their people, I managed to convince them that I knew a lot about the customs and history of the North American Indian, and that I wore the stripe as a tribute to their spirit. I also promised that, if they insisted that I no longer wear the stripe after they'd seen me perform, then I wouldn't. In retrospect, I admit that this was a risky thing to have said. Luckily, they loved our American debut performance in Boston, and I kept my stripe.

We worked our way across America from the East to the West, occasionally returning to New York for a TV spot, such as one on Channel 7 News with Mick Jagger and Daryl Hall of Hall and Oates. (Jagger was extremely professional about the show and businesslike with me.) We landed in Los Angeles a couple of weeks after New York, playing the *American Bandstand* TV show after a couple of personal appearances to promote 'Kings' in San Francisco and Pasadena. We then played two nights at the LA Roxy in April 1981, at which Rod Stewart, Elton John, Britt Ekland, Warren Beatty, Neil Diamond and Frankie Valli sat in the audience watching me! It was hard to believe, and even harder to believe that the LA press were referring to an 'Ants Invasion' in the same terms as they had the British Invasion in the 1960s led by the Beatles and the Dave Clark Five. All the stars briefly came backstage after the show to say hello, and I felt like a kid again. I was simply a happy fan as I stood in front of Rod and Britt. I couldn't think of a thing to say except 'Hi' and 'Thanks'.

The shows were great, but I didn't particularly enjoy LA. I didn't get to see much, because we had to be in Chicago the day after the second gig. Then we worked our way back to New York via Canada. We had two days off in New York before appearing on the networked NBC Tom Snyder chat show, which was hard work, because he was a very conservative guy, and he had the film director John Huston (father of Anjelica) also on the show. There were these two old guys in suits, over seventy or looking it, and me in full make-up. They didn't know what to make of me. I sat there after we'd played a song, in costume, talking to Tom, who seemed surprised that I could even speak English.

'How can you possibly live up to all of the advanced billing that has preceded your arrival here, and measure up to the expectations so many people have for your success here?' Snyder asked, adding, 'It seems to me that you're under a lot of pressure.'

I looked at him for a half-beat and replied, 'I think you quite simply just stop talking, put your clothes on and get out and play for people, very simply.'

Which I was determined to do, in spades. During the tour I made several personal appearances, and we played TV shows when we weren't playing gigs. The pace was fast and furious. The only escape from the pressures of work and fame was sex. My seemingly tireless drive to succeed and the non-stop work to stay up there masked the symptoms of my illness. By keeping myself busy I was almost self-medicating. My permanent activity meant that my body was manufacturing enough serotonin to keep me stable.

Drinking, smoking or taking drugs would take its toll on anyone who was going through the kind of physical experience that I was, and I was having none of that. I kept fit by being on stage. The performance for me was more demanding than anything set up in the gym with a personal trainer could ever be. My way kept me lean and mean. I would sweat out a stone with each gig. At the end of a show I would go straight back to the hotel and slip into the bath, play *Apollo* by Brian Eno, then maybe go down into the lobby to meet some kids who had followed us back. Sex was available every few feet, and with the right vibes and a little chatter I'd have a lovely girl in my room and very soon in my bed. It felt great to have somebody sleeping next to me, and I doubt if any travelling musician would tell you different. Boredom is the worst part of touring – that and bad food. Sex is the escape. As far as I'm concerned, anyone who says otherwise is a liar.

Travelling across the USA in a tour bus was a real eye-opener, and a great experience for a boy brought up watching American movies. I loved getting to meet real Americans, especially at truck stops, where our English accents usually scored highly with the staff's sense of humour. Getting a bowl of rice pudding, my favourite dessert, always caused a bit of a drama, though, because it wasn't a common dish. In fact, food in general was a problem on US tours. Anything provided at the actual venue would invariably be inedible, and getting a steak and salad seemed an impossible task for the local catering company, wherever we were playing. I would prefer to eat about two hours before a concert, then let my food digest a bit, but that wasn't always possible – unless I'd settle for a pizza or burger, which I wouldn't.

As it came to a close, I realised that the whole US tour and round of personal appearances had been really hard work. It had been like starting over again in many ways. Just as I had done for the previous three years in the UK, I thought that Adam and the Ants should tour America almost constantly, keep releasing singles, keep working at it until we'd really 'cracked' it. My record company had other ideas, though. Still, we finished the tour playing the Palladium in New York and went home on a high.

Adam and the Ants had been in America for a month, working hard, playing hard and partying hardly at all. In the process I had discovered that Marco hated being on the road

and that I loved certain parts of America. Now we had to go
back to England and create the video for our next single, 'Stand
And Deliver'. We hadn't had a record in the charts for at least a
month.

8

STAND AND DELIVER

BRRRRING-BRRING!

The ringing of a telephone cut sharply through my sleep. I fumbled for the receiver.

'Hello?' A soft, high-pitched voice echoed down the line to me. 'Hello,' it repeated again, 'is that Adam Ant?'

The voice had an American accent, sounded vaguely familiar, almost as if . . . as if it was . . . My fuzzy brain reacted angrily.

'Terry,' I said sharply, 'stop pissing about. It's four a.m. and I'm trying to sleep.'

'No, it's not Terry', said the soft voice, 'It's Michael. Is that Adam Ant?'

'Very funny, Terry, now fuck off.'

I slammed the phone down and rolled over to try and get back to sleep, cursing my drummer.

A few minutes later the telephone rang again. I let it ring for a while, but it kept going, kept annoying me, stopping me from sleeping.

'*Hello,*' I barked into the receiver.

'Hi, no, really, it is me, Michael Jackson,' said the funny voice at the end of the line, 'and I just want to ask you . . .'

'Terry, if you don't stop this I'm going to come over there and fucking thump you. Now stop pissing about.'

Bang. Again the phone went down. Again I rolled over.

Again the telephone rang.

I grabbed the receiver and shouted into it, 'Terry! That's IT! Stop it.'

'Er, hi, is that Adam Ant?' This time the voice was deep, slow, sonorous, American and calm. It didn't sound anything like Terry Lee.

'Oh, oh,' I stammered. 'Yes, this is Adam. Who are you?'

'I'm Quincy Jones, calling from LA. Sorry, we probably woke you, but I'm here with Michael Jackson and he'd like to speak with you. Is that OK?'

Fuck me, I thought, it really is Michael Jackson. 'Yeah, sure,' I said. 'Put him on.'

A pause, and then that same soft voice. 'Hi, Adam, it's Michael. Sorry if we woke you.'

'Oh, no, sorry to have been so rude,' I apologised. 'I thought that it was one of my band playing tricks on me. I didn't realise it was you until Quincy told me. We were supposed to talk a couple of days back, right?'

'Yes, sorry, but I lost track of the days, I've been in the studio. I just saw your video on TV for "Kings Of The Wild Frontier", it's great. How did you get the tom-tom sound?'

'Oh, thanks. Well, we use two drum kits and then add loads of other percussion on top of them—'

'That's great, Adam,' Michael interrupted. 'I really like your jacket. That one with the gold on the front. Can you tell me where you got it?'

'Huh? My jacket?' I stumbled a bit, trying to think. 'Dave Whiteing got it for me. He works at Berman's and Nathan's in London's Covent Garden, they supply costumes for movies. In fact my jacket had been worn by the actor David Hemmings—'

'Oh, the guy from *Blow-Up*?'

'Yeah, but this was for *The Charge of the Light Brigade*. I rent it from them, for about £30 a month.'

'You rent it? Wow. That's great. OK, thanks for the information. How do you spell that again, Bowman's and who?'

'No, Berman's, B-E-R-M-A-N-apostrophe-S and N-A-T-H-A-N-apostrophe-S.'

'Great, thanks. Let's meet up next time you're in America, huh? Bye.'

The line went dead.

That was Michael Jackson, I thought, calling me. Am I dreaming? There was no one with me that I could wake and ask if I was awake, so I called Marco. He answered after two rings.

'Marco, it's Adam. Were you asleep?'

'No. Just running through a few of the songs. What's up?'

'Am I awake? Are you awake? I just had a telephone call from Michael Jackson and I can't believe it.'

'Wasn't he supposed to call a couple of days ago? What did he want?'

'He wanted to know where I got my jacket from. The military one.'

'Ha!' Marco snorted. 'Didn't want to guest on the new LP, then?'

'Oh, I didn't ask him. Maybe I could call him back . . .'

'Adam, no. Go back to sleep. I'll see you tomorrow. 'Night.'

'Yeah, 'night, Marco.'

There was no way I could sleep now, though, so I made a cup of tea and went out on to the flat roof that led off the landing window at Redcliffe Gardens where I was living once more. It was the last day of April 1981. I had been back in London for four days and was about to head off for a European tour, beginning with two days in Madrid in mid-week, when we were expecting 'Stand and Deliver' to enter the charts, hopefully in the Top 10.

I sat on the roof wearing Chinese slippers, a kimono and black silk trousers, drinking tea, watching the sun come up and London awake. There was a low hum in the background and only the slightest chill in the air. I reflected on the events of the past few days. We'd gone almost straight from the plane to the video shoot for 'Stand and Deliver'. I had sent Mike Mansfield my storyboard drawings from America, and he'd put everything in place. Mandy had rounded up a few mates to dress up and appear in the video, Dave Whiteing was also in it (he and Mandy are the couple that I 'rob') and had helped with the costumes. I wore a black tricolour hat, black cape, mask and big white shirt over breeches. Mike had hired a stagecoach and I had done my own stunts – the leaping through a sugar-glass window had been the riskiest and I'd cut my head a bit, but the two-day shoot had been great fun and the result, Mike had told me, was looking great.

It was important, I felt, that we had a memorable video to promote the single because CBS had arranged for us to tour Scandinavia, France, Italy, Switzerland, Germany, the Channel Isles and then Cornwall throughout May and early June. I wouldn't be around to promote the single too much. I'd argued with CBS that we needed to go back to America, but the best they had managed was for me to spend three days in New York in mid-June, just before we began recording the third Ants LP, which was to be called *Prince Charming*.

'Stand And Deliver' went straight into the charts at number 1. The video was played on every kids' TV show in the UK, it was played on *TOTP* and on rotation in New York on the MTV channel. The 'dandy highwayman' storyline gallows ending caused a bit of controversy when the BBC, having already shown it, then 'banned' it for some strange reason. I am helped to 'escape' the noose by my band, of course, but the sight of the rope apparently upset some people. The humour of the 'Stand and Deliver' video brought Adam and the Ants to more people in the UK and Europe than any tour could ever have. As MTV wasn't then networked across America, it only made the need to be there to promote ourselves more urgent to my mind.

In June Don and I made our three-day trip to New York to tie up merchandising deals and settle our US publishing deal. While there, I got to see Martin Scorsese and Robert De Niro at work as they filmed *The King of Comedy* movie. They were shooting scenes with Epic's other big UK act of the time, the Clash, on that day, so a record company PR took me to the set on Sixth Avenue. I watched the filming from the side for a while, enjoying observing how things were done. Movies seemed like fun to make when they were done like this rather than the way Derek Jarman had gone about it.

The headlines in the *Sun* newspaper that greeted my return to the UK were not happy news for me. I should have expected it, but hadn't. Tessa Hewitt, being a Page 3 girl, was considered the 'property' of the newspaper. That she was 'dating' me, a famous pop star, made her front-page news as well as Page 3 flesh. So they ran a story about 'Adam's New Love', which included an 'interview' with Tessa inside.

The attention that the daily tabloid newspapers were paying me was increasing in direct proportion to the number of records I sold. The Sunday tabloids were also starting to run stories about me, my family and my friends. Reporters were assigned to follow me and question anyone I spoke to, let alone slept with. As well as the newspapers, there were those insistent, persistent 'fans' who made it their mission in life to find me and make contact with me – any kind of contact that they could. I set about buying my first flat because too many people seemed to know where I lived.

When 'Stand And Deliver' became such a big hit, Don suggested that for my own safety and in order to get some peace and quiet, I take a room on permanent hire at a London hotel. I had decided that the Montcalm in Great Cumberland Street, just north of Hyde Park, would be my bolt hole, my home-from-home. Only my closest friends knew that I was there. Which meant, of course, that Mandy knew where I would be the morning that I arrived from New York to the *Sun* head-lines.

Her telephone call ran along the lines of, 'You bastard. Who is this tart? Do you know her? How long have you been fucking her? I've had bloody reporters trying to get me to talk to them about you for three days, now. What am I going to do?'

Mandy was about to start at drama school in September and wanted to leave home. In a week it would be her nineteenth birthday and we were still seeing each other off and on. With my recent touring commitments it had been more off than on, but she had every right to be pissed off by Tessa's public declaration. I was pissed off. We agreed to meet later in South Molton Street, where we had a coffee, a good cry and ended the relationship. Or rather, tried to end it again. We would continue to see each other for a while yet.

In the meantime I began another relationship with a beautiful red-haired former topless model-turned-dancer named Carole Caplin, who worked with a troupe called 'Shock'. We'd met through Tessa, and although I was, supposedly, 'with' Tessa, the attraction between us was too powerful to ignore. We met several times that summer of 1981, usually at the Montcalm. We enjoyed an illicit love affair, in private, with no one knowing that we were enjoying one another for several months. It was a gorgeous romance, tainted slightly by the guilt I fought. Carole was calm, relaxing to be around, sensuous and soft.

I distanced myself from Tessa, physically as well as emotionally, after the *Sun* story and spent most of July and August recording the *Prince Charming* album and dealing with the various attentions of the press.

Then the *Sunday People* newspaper ran a story about my illness and suicide attempt of 1976. I was furious about this, mostly because it seemed as if it might end my career when it was really only just taking off, but fortunately no one seemed to notice. They printed some photographs of early Adam Ant shows with me in leather and bondage gear, and the paper also used an illustration that I'd created in 1979 of Margaret Thatcher, dressed as a leather-clad dominatrix, sitting on a stool. Stupidly they hadn't cleared permission to print the drawing, so I sued them for it – and won.

I was much angrier with the bastard reporter who, a little later, wrote a story about my mum. POP STAR'S MUM WORKS IN A LAUNDERETTE, ran the headline, or something like it. A smart journalist had 'found' my mum at work. She ran a launderette in St John's Wood and loved the job. I'd offered to take care of her so that she didn't have to, but she genuinely wanted to carry on working. She loved the people that used the launderette, and since she'd always worked, she said, she wouldn't know what to do if she didn't. Because of the paper's story the launderette was not too hard to find, so she had to quit. Too many Antfans kept turning up, bothering her for my address or a photograph or whatever.

It was obvious that my life was going to have to be lived in public unless I did something about it. Meeting new people, especially women, became difficult because I had no idea if they were going to sell their 'story' about me to a newspaper as soon as I'd left them. I came to rely more and more on the small group of people that I'd known for a long time, among them Mandy, Marco, Danny Kleinman, Dave Gibb and Don Murfet.

Marco and I helped Danny to get a record deal that year, and we produced a single for him that scraped into the Top 40 ('Bike' c/w 'Spaghetti'). I spent many weekends in August at Don's house, recuperating from the recording of the album and preparing the next Adam Ant promo video, 'Prince Charming'.

The weekends spent at Don's house, and the problems of living in London, made me want to buy a house in the country. After searching for a few months I eventually found an old thatched cottage just up the road from Don. The Old Thatch had been built in 1632 and used by Cromwell to house his cavalry during the Civil War. Apparently the house had survived Cromwell's destruction of the surrounding area because his son was in love with a girl who lived in the cottage. It was on a lovely spot, high up and looking down on open Hertfordshire country-side. It had a separate building that I was going to use as a recording studio. However, because it was Grade I listed, all the work that I wanted done on it had to be meticulously monitored by English Heritage. It would take four years of hard work before I could move into the house, which I renamed Luxe.

Weekends at Don and Jane's became a base for me, from which I could oversee work on the house and escape from the city.

·

The video for 'Prince Charming' is the one that most people remember and seem to like. It was spoofed for an ad on British TV at Christmas in 2004, for instance. Shot on a sound stage at Shepperton Studios, it took longer than any of the others to complete and was the most expensive to make. I'd decided that I'd really like Diana Dors, the great British actress of the 1950s and 60s, to star in the video and she had eventually agreed, but not until I'd wooed her a bit with flattery and dinner at nice restaurants. She was a star and wanted to be treated like one, which was fine by me. She was very warm and funny and not at all precious. The shoot, directed by Mike Mansfield again, used sets that had to be created from scratch. I'd decided that we'd turn the Cinderella storyline around, with me as Cinders and Dave Whiteing as one of my ugly sisters. Diana played my fairy godmother. There was a cast of thousands, as usual, all doing a dance that Steph had invented and which she claimed meant something – each arm movement represented parts of my char-acter, she said. To prepare for the shoot, I'd researched the commedia dell'arte, from which British pantomime had grown. While people might just think that 'Prince Charming' was 'panto', they should know that there's a lot more to the tradition than men dressing up as women and fake cows. As with 'Stand And Deliver', I had drawn the storyboards for 'Prince Charming'. Because of the changing scenes, it had taken longer than 'Stand

And Deliver', but the result was as good, if not better. I really enjoyed dressing up as Valentino, Clint Eastwood and Alice Cooper.

I'd written the song with the idea of the video in mind, which is probably why both were successful.

With 'Prince Charming' I was moving closer to what I thought was my future. Ever since *Jubilee*, producers had been sending me film scripts to read and possibly make with them. Some I read, others I ignored, but the idea that acting would be a part of my future was firmly in my mind.

During my first American tour, various interviewers had asked me about what Antmusic was, and just as I'd explained to the music press in 1978, I told them that it was 'our' music, that it wasn't like anything else around. I didn't want to be regarded as 'punk' or 'New Romantic', the new term being used by the music press to lump a bunch of different bands together. I was an entertainer, a part of showbusiness. The music press never got it. They could understand pop stardom, but the videos they were dismissive of because they weren't anti-establishment in the way they wanted. On the US tour I had stated several times that I didn't drink, smoke or do drugs, and that that was an old-fashioned and pointless idea of rebellion. What I wanted to put across was that there was hope in the world, that people shouldn't be discouraged. Which is why 'Prince Charming' has the chorus, 'Ridicule is nothing to be scared of'. It meant, 'Go out and do what you want to do, believe and you'll succeed.' After all, I had – despite being rubbished by the music press.

Just before the shoot had taken place in July 1981, I had had another massive argument with Mandy. I had bought a flat in Primrose Hill and moved in only a few days earlier. Mandy had a key to the place and she had let herself in, where she found and read my private diary. Again. Again we screamed at each other, again she stormed out of my life. I didn't hear from her for a week, during which time I wondered if she'd read the diary

again in order to try and build up enough resentment against
me to end things for good. If she had, then, as I wrote in my
diary at the time, it was probably a good thing.

> She needs to be free of me 'cos I am bad for her. It breaks my
> heart to accept and record this because it is never easy to admit
> weakness, frustration and disappointment in yourself. I wrote
> her a note, which said that I was still her friend if not her lover
> and that I would always be there for her and that I didn't want
> to hurt her but I am what I am. Every time I go home I pray for
> just one message from her, just one line.

Three weeks later, Mandy accompanied me to the airport
from where we were to fly to New York and finish the last leg of
the *Kings* World Tour. We had made up a few days earlier and I
was glad to have her back in my life. I was so glad that, after
saying goodbye inside the car and getting out to face the barrage
of photographers alone, I leant back in and asked her to walk
with me to the departure gate. I knew that it would result in
another load of THE WOMAN IN ADAM'S LIFE headlines in the
tabloids, but I didn't care. I wanted the world to know that
Adam Ant and Amanda Donohoe were an item. It would certainly give Tessa the message that she'd been ignoring for the
last few weeks. Of course it would also let Carole know that she
and I were not destined to be, either.

Unfortunately Tessa got the message OK, but she took it
very badly. She made a silly attempt at 'ending it all' while I was
away (I have no idea how, or really even why), which resulted in
more newspaper headlines for her and me – ones that we could
both have done without. I called her when I heard about it and
she was apologetic and feeling foolish. She'd be OK, thankfully.
Carole seemed unconcerned about Mandy and me.

While I was in New York for a few days during August 1981
doing PR and promotion for the single release of 'Prince Charming', I suffered a bout of depression. I felt low and empty, verging
on tears, but at the same time felt like laughing. It had begun a

couple of days before, but hearing that 'Prince Charming' had only gone into the charts at number 2 made things worse.

My mood was lightened slightly by meeting Robert De Niro. He'd asked to see me to say thanks for having got his daughter Dreena, who was an Antfan, tickets for our Palladium gig back in April. We'd given her the best seats, of course, plus a bodyguard, too. She came backstage after and met the band, got some signed photos and was very happy. It was an awkward meeting, though. He's so shy that all he could do was mutter 'Hi'. I mumbled 'Hi' back and there we stood, two shy men, me in awe and him feeling awkward. He signed a photo for me, 'To Adam, best wishes Bob De Niro'. I told him that *Raging Bull* was a great film and that I hoped he would win an Oscar for it. A few days later he did, which was doubly good because I'd said to the band that if he didn't I'd never sing again. When they announced the winner, I jumped up and down on my hotel bed in celebration. It was the best I'd felt in days.

A few days later, in Los Angeles, I wrote in my diary that although some people might think that I'd made it, I certainly didn't, and that I would have to work even harder to *really* make it. Marco and I were discussing my making a solo LP, just as Bryan Ferry had while he was still part of Roxy Music. With the *Prince Charming* LP ready for release when we returned to the UK at the end of the year, my thoughts turned to the next look, the next set of songs. I had already decided that the white stripe would go from my face, along with the gold-braided military jacket. For the *Prince Charming* campaign I would wear a naval-style tail jacket, a white cravat, silver trousers (like Iggy's on the cover of *Raw Power*) and two red stripes on my right cheek. Although I knew that I would be Prince Charming for almost another year, I was already planning the look for after that.

While in LA I met with Monty Python member Graham Chapman to discuss both acting in and writing the music for his forthcoming non-Python movie, *Yellowbeard*. He seemed eager for Marco and me to create the soundtrack, what with our piratical look and the film being based on the life of Blackbeard. Although we met a couple of times after this to discuss the film, nothing came of it. The movie turned into a disaster, running well over budget, and suffered from the death of the leading man, the great wall-eyed British comedian Marty Feldman, during filming in Mexico. The film was panned on release and is not a great testament to either Chapman (whose last film it also was) or Feldman.

•

In mid-September we made our first trip to Australia. Despite having to do numerous TV and public appearances in the first week, I immediately took to the country. The weather was fantastic, and the people were very friendly and easy-going. Even the press seemed to be friendly. While there, 'Prince Charming' spent three weeks at number 1 on the UK chart.

It was in Australia that I first got to see Liza Minnelli on stage. Her performance wiped me out. She was fantastic. Afterwards I went back to her dressing room to meet her. It was so showbiz – there was a photograph of her mother Judy Garland and a note from Frank Sinatra next to it, and loads of flowers. Liza was as warm and sincere as her show had been, and when I left she hugged me and I felt sure that we'd meet again. The show had inspired me so much that I wanted to go straight out and perform an Antshow. It made me think differently about my live performances, and feel that I was an idiot for not enjoying my success so far. I was incapable of enjoying my success back then, because I could never take the time to be still, to not work, to lie back and simply enjoy things. My mind wouldn't let me. I had to be active, to keep pushing myself and everyone around me for . . . what? I wasn't sure. I just knew that I had to be constantly working.

Liza and I met once more in Australia, at a reception for her.

She asked me to walk the room with her, which I did, gladly. She looked gorgeous with her rough-cut, short black hair and enormous eyes. She was very fit – her tour keeping her as trim as she'd been in *Arthur* (with Dudley Moore) – and dressed immaculately in a shimmering gown that was slit up the side to show off her great dancer's legs. Liza was off to Japan the next day. I was going there soon after. We arranged to meet in Tokyo.

We met again in Japan on the night before she was to fly back to New York. We went with Marco and his girlfriend to a club, and after an hour or so of chat and laughs, I asked her to dance. I couldn't believe it as the words left my mouth, but she said 'Yes' and there I was, dancing with Liza Minnelli! We danced for ages, holding each other tight, her with her eyes closed, me wanting so much to be a part of her life somehow, knowing that it was impossible right then but hoping that maybe in the future . . .

When the DJ shut up shop at the Japanese club, we demanded one more song and finished the night dancing to Stevie Wonder's 'Lately'. It was a great night, and she was in tears as we parted – her for her hotel and me for mine. She'd asked me to visit her the next morning, though, so that she could give me some advice on what to wear when I met Queen Elizabeth, since a couple of days earlier we had heard that Adam and the Ants were to play for the Queen at another Royal Variety Performance in London in November.

The next morning, armed with two dozen red roses, I visited her in her suite.

'Adam, you must take your make-up off before you meet the Queen,' she stated as soon as I entered the room. 'You must wear a suit and look her directly in the eyes if she speaks to you, after kissing her hand. Now, I've made a list of what you have to wear and here it is.'

She handed me a piece of hotel stationery on which was written:

1. An Italian Tuxedo – slim satin black lapels.
2. A not-too-wide bowtie in silk.
3. A white, pleated-front shirt with an old-fashioned collar with no ruffles ('Or I'll kill ya,' she added as I read it).
4. Velvet pumps/slippers in black with a bow.
5. Silk socks – black with a fine weave.
6. White doeskin gloves (you're not supposed to touch the Queen).
7. Cartier cufflinks + 3 studs for the shirt – sapphire and diamond. Get them insured. Make sure they're square-shaped.
8. Slick that hair back and show that face.

As I wrote in my diary, 'Liza asked me to do this for her, and I will.' We kissed chastely, said goodbye and she promised to visit me some day, 'in your cottage'. I left feeling as if I could walk back to England.

•

Back in the UK in November, I had no time or use for resting. The *Prince Charming* album picked up between 500,000 and 750,000 advance orders, despite being slated by the music press (predictably). The size of the pre-release orders made me determined that the tour to promote it, which would begin just before Christmas, would be a truly original live experience, so I started work on preparing the Prince Charming Revue, which would involve a team of dancers, a horn section and a changing set – including a galleon ship that would be pushed on to the stage complete with rigging and sails and all. I worked fifteen minutes to change costume into the middle of the three-hour show, but that was the only time that I was offstage. The Revue was going to cost me a lot of money, but I thought it was worth it to give back to the fans who'd supported me by buying my records.

Before that, though, CBS wanted a Christmas single. I was doubtful, thinking that unless it went to number 1, it would be a waste of time and effort. The record company, however, were confident that it would be the Christmas number 1, and asked if they could release 'Scorpios', the first track on the album. I said no because I didn't have a vision for it, no ideas for a video. Instead I suggested that if anything was released it should be 'Ant Rap', which Marco and I had remixed and which was sounding like a good dance record. I also had an idea for a video script for it. Although I wasn't entirely sure about the song, it was easy to believe that anything I released would be a hit at the time.

The last nine months had seen an unstoppable, hardly controllable attack on the media and world audiences, and the launch of a new look as Prince Charming. It had all happened quickly because I'd wanted it to, but I was beginning to wonder if I hadn't become too cocky. This caused a lot of self-doubt, which meant that I had to have a video that boosted the power of the song. It took me a week of painful writing and rewriting and sweat. It really had to be the Christmas blockbuster of all blockbusters to compensate for the limitations (musically) of the 'Rap'. I was almost desperate that it get to the top of the charts. I now think that I shouldn't have adopted the Dandy Highwayman look so soon. The white stripe and cavalry jacket should have stayed for another album at least. I changed my look too fast and confused fans.

My reservations about Ant Rap were well founded. While the video was great fun to make – and I got to wear armour that had been made for John Boorman's recently released Arthurian movie Excalibur as well as to work with the lovely Lulu – it didn't help the single to get to number 1. It peaked at 3.

On 24 November Adam and the Ants were to appear in front of the Queen at the Royal Variety Performance. After performing 'Antmusic' (which I would sing live while the band mimed), I was to be presented to Her Majesty. The morning of the show I was summoned to a sit-down with Terry, Merrick and Gary.

They were pissed off that they were not going to meet the Queen. I said I was sorry, but it wasn't a decision that I could make. We had been told that only I would be allowed to meet her, standing in line (dressed just as Liza Minnelli had suggested) next to Tim Rice, Lulu, Henry Cooper, Lonnie Donegan and Marty Wilde. Their complaint made me angry as much for their insistence that it was my fault as for the fact that I couldn't do anything about it.

I also had many other things to worry about. Knowing that it was wrong, but unable to do anything about it, Mandy and I were still an item and I had even contemplated asking her to live with me, though I'd realised it would have been completely the wrong thing to do. Instead I had helped her to get a bedsit to live in. Added to that I had an album that was stuck at number 2 and a weak single out. Then there was the ever-growing and expensive Revue coming up. I really could have done without a near-mutiny from the Ants just before meeting the Queen.

Returning to my Primrose Hill flat after the sit-down, I drank tea, listened to Marvin Gaye and sewed up the split fly of my Sex leather trousers for the sake of having something to do. After regaining my temper I went back to the Theatre Royal and determined to go through with the performance as professionally as I could, while thinking about sacking the whole band and continuing with just Marco again. The performance went well, and afterwards I met the Queen in my rented Moss Bros tuxedo and wing-collared shirt, patent pumps and fifty thousand pounds' worth of diamonds and sapphires. She shook my hand and asked if I minded playing to old fuddy-duddies like her and said that she could hardly recognise me without my make-up. I mumbled something back and couldn't stop thinking, 'Christ! It's the Queen. I'm meeting the Queen!' After she'd moved on, both Lew Grade and Bernard Delfont, the first moguls of British TV entertainment, came up and were nice to me. Did I care that the NME thought I shouldn't have done the gig, and if I did, that I shouldn't have worn a tuxedo? Did I fuck.

The day wasn't over yet, though. There were a couple of bizarre events still to occur. The first came after packing away my gear, as Don and I were leaving the dressing room. We found two men on stage having a bloody fight. It was surreal. They weren't shouting at each other, just hitting and kicking the hell out of one another. There were splatters of blood on the white boards of the Drury Lane stage where I and others had just entertained the Queen. Don and a couple of other guys broke up the fight and we eventually left. Tired, bored and hungry we went to Stringfellows, a recently opened club around the corner. After a short while there, I got up to leave, having had enough of the arguing couple behind me and a guy across from me who was bad-mouthing the waiter. Then I spotted an angel in the DJ box – a gorgeous, small, blonde and finely featured woman in her mid-twenties. I went over to speak to her and discovered that her name was Mo. She had, she told me, a very jealous boyfriend. He has good reason to be, I told her, and left, thinking, 'I'll be back.'

Driving north at the end of the evening with Don to my place in Primrose Hill in his car, I chatted to his wife June for a while until two guys in another car started cutting us up, racing through red lights to tail us and flicking V-signs at us. On Camden High Street Don pulled over and so did they, blocking the front of our car. Two youngish guys got out and came over to Don's window. He rolled it down, an argument started and one of the guys punched Don. He threw a hand back, then reversed sharply and drove off quickly. We lost them and I got home somewhat shaken, my heart in my mouth and my pulse racing so fast that I couldn't sleep. It had been the strangest day I'd had in a long while. I wrote the events into my diary, recording that I wished that the phone would ring, even though it was four-thirty a.m. and I knew that it wouldn't.

I childishly hope for company. It seems strange that my life can be so empty when I'm supposed to be so attractive to the opposite sex. I feel it has definitely scared off some people like Carole who seems put off by my material gains + wealth. Who knows? Maybe it's just me.

•

Much of early December was spent in a huge sound studio in Borehamwood, rehearsing for the Prince Charming Revue. We kicked off the tour in Cornwall on the fifteenth. The album had slipped to number 3 and 'Ant Rap' entered the singles charts at number 9 (it would rise to number 3, 'higher than it deserves', I thought at the time). I felt responsible for everyone on the tour, responsible for telling them how to dress and where to stand on stage, as well as for my own performance. The pressure I was putting myself under, and would be under throughout the seven-week tour, was huge. By the first night I was dreaming of a holiday and then the next look, album and video, which would be needed in order to pay for the Revue, I soon realised.

I spent Christmas with Mandy. On the day itself we went to a kids' hospital to hand out gifts and hopefully cheer them up a bit. It was upsetting and beautiful at the same time. Afterwards we went to Don and June's for lunch. The rest of the time was spent having fun with Mandy, watching TV and drinking tea by the gallon. I also visited Marco in his new flat, a large, beautiful top-floor apartment in the West End, where he still lives.

Then it was back to work and the Revue. On 29 December we played in Brighton. It was one of the worst performances that I'd ever given. The reason was that I was furious with Mandy, who had turned up unannounced the previous day and then spent almost the whole of that night arguing with me and screaming at me about my 'affairs'. I barely slept and the arguing continued the next day. By the time I hit the stage I was still furious and I couldn't hide it. For the first two acts of the Revue I kicked things, butted the microphone stand, spat and scared everyone on stage and in the audience, I think, into grovelling submission to my ego. I was calmer for the last act, but I still can't forget how badly I treated that audience. I was still fuming when I left the stage.

Don drove Mandy and me back to London that night, and when we dropped her at her place, I told her that I didn't want to see her any more. She leaped out of Don's car, slamming the door. I told him to drive and I didn't look back at her once. I couldn't, in case I softened again.

And so I began 1982 without Mandy by my side. I was optimistic about the coming year, though. Marco and I had demos for a whole new album, while *Prince Charming* had gone up the LP charts again and the Revue was being enjoyed by fans, even if it was costing me money to keep it on the road. There was a lot to be thankful for.

•

On 18 January 1982 I was the cover star of the *New Musical Express*. Inside, over four pages, their star writer Paul Morley struggled to come to terms with the fact that he'd enjoyed the Prince Charming Revue, which he'd just seen in Manchester. Perhaps confused by what he'd seen in the show and the fact that he had enjoyed it, he questioned me as if I was a traitor to his cause. Morley and the *NME* at that time were the champions of Joy Division, New Order, the Fall, the Smiths and the rest of the serious, indie, post-punk bands that wore grey overcoats bought from Oxfam and dared not smile in public.

'Some see you reducing pop to a very clean essence,' he said to me at one point in the interview. As if that was wrong.

'I'm sick and tired of being told that because I don't drink and don't smoke that I'm a goody-two-shoes,' I replied, adding, 'OK, so I'm a goody-two-shoes. You know? So what? I don't like drugs and that is a threat to the rock 'n' roll establishment? Rock 'n' roll has become the establishment.'

'Don't you think you're merely an addition to a long line of glossy entertainers who don't actually stimulate young people to find out or look out – just a lolly to be licked?' he asked.

I replied, 'What can an entertainer do but provide hope through entertainment? All kids have been given over the past twelve months by a lot of people is a load of negativity. One big downer. I pick up the music papers and you might as well read the *Observer* colour supplement. It's not about a celebration of music, it's politics, politics, politics.'

'You talk of conviction, of being convinced, of quality, originality and diversity,' Morley continued, working away at his 'accusation' that I was too clean. 'But some of the things you do seem to undermine the fact you can have faith in such things. Perhaps you're often dismissed [by the music press] because people see more conceit than cunning. Revealing that a highlight of 1981 for Adam was meeting the Queen perhaps confirmed this "cleanness" I've mentioned.'

I took a deep breath before answering. 'I won't go along with anyone's preconceptions of what somebody involved in as decadent and as sordid a business as the music business should say and do. I basically think that the Royal Family are all right. I was asked and it was an honour to do the Royal Variety Show, it was a challenge and you don't run away from them.

'I'm not worried about credibility. Those things are illusions. It would have been exactly the negative, inward-looking rock thing to have turned it down. And of course it was good exposure, I'm glad I did it. Hey, were you pissed off when Robert De Niro wore a tuxedo to get his Oscar? No! It's the same thing.'

The interview was a stimulating encounter. I think that I got Morley to understand that I was a song-and-dance man at heart, that all I wanted to be was an entertainer. He did write that, 'The Revue . . . demolishes 20 years of standard pop star appearance. It is the work of someone who is at the very least 20 times better than anyone ever pretended.'

One of his last questions was to ask me what I thought was the point of living, to which I replied, 'To seek out happiness, to work hard and eventually get into a position where the work you do you don't consider to be a job.'

I wasn't there yet, but I was working hard to get there.

Morley's questioning had sparked my use of the phrase goody-two-shoes and it stuck in my head, inspiring what would become my first solo single in May that year.

The Revue, with all the dancing and costume changes, was good preparation for my next move into mainstream showbusiness: an appearance on the Cannon and Ball Show.

First though, I took a holiday.

At a record signing in Birmingham during the Revue tour I had found myself about to scribble over my own signature on a copy of the Kings LP. I looked up at the girl who handed me the record and she said, 'Remember me?'

I did, and the realisation hit me that it was two years since I'd been there and two years since I had had any kind of break from working. I had been and still was constantly worrying about my performance when I wasn't performing, thinking about new music and a new image. Earlier that day I had been considering the idea of 'stripping' and being considered a stripper for fans and women as I performed, an idea that I would take further in the future. As I autographed Kings for a second time for that Birmingham girl, I decided that I needed a break. That night I had asked Don to arrange it.

Four weeks later I lay on a golden beach in Barbados with nothing to do and only my old mate Danny Kleinman for company. The plan was to be there for ten days, soaking up the sun for the first time in six years (I'd last holidayed in Corsica with Eve, before Adam had been born), recovering from the Revue and everything else. I would have time to think about everything that had happened over the past four years and to plan for the future.

As it turned out, it was the worst thing I could have done. After only two days my mind was crowded with thoughts of Mandy back in Blighty sleeping with someone else, and with concerns that my record company was doing nothing but feeding off me, that I was never going to have another number 1 hit record.

With nothing to do and no woman to occupy my time, mind and body, I became depressed, unable to sleep and worried about everything. My deepest fear nagged at me, that of rejection. I obsessed about Mandy and missed her as much as I resented her. I decided that I couldn't live without her, but that we were no good for each other. Because I felt that she had rejected me, I had to have her back in my life. At one point I wrote in my diary that I might even 'LUV' her. And I never used the word and hadn't since Eve, Muswell Hill and the suicide attempt.

After four days in Barbados, I called Don in London and had him arrange to fly Carole Caplin out to be with me. She arrived the next day and we had three days together before I had Don book us on to flights back to London, damning Barbados as a tropical hell. I felt that if I didn't get off the island I'd really go nuts. I felt frustrated, that I was wasting time. The endless days of sun, sea and food left me twitching with boredom and having terrible thoughts about what Mandy might be up to – despite being with Carole, of course. She enjoyed the lazing around, as most people would.

On returning to London, I called Mandy and arranged to meet her that evening. She came to my Primrose Hill flat. Close to tears but clearly decided, she told me that she didn't want me any more and that I was going to play no part in her life at all. I collapsed, literally, and crawled at her feet, begging her not to go. She looked scared and tried to get me up on my feet, all the while telling me that it was too late. I felt broken inside.

As she turned to leave, I snapped and started ranting at her. 'You're scaring me!' she shouted. I stopped dead, stunned, desolate and disgraced by my behaviour. What I had wanted to be a reconciliation between us had become a trauma. She pushed me aside and half ran out of the door into a rain-sodden street. I don't know how long I stood there, but after a while I stumbled down the steps in the rain, trying to follow her. She'd gone and I didn't know where. I returned to my flat and lay on the bed, not able to sleep until five a.m., veering between despair and panic about what I'd done and not knowing how to make it better.

Sitting in the early morning light I decided that there was only one way to get over the previous night and that was to work. I booked myself into a studio for two days and spent the whole time alone with a bass and some tribal chants and drums that I'd recorded months before, making music.

On the third day, I left the studio and called Carole. She was away, working up North, so I called another woman and attempted to obliterate all thoughts of Mandy by having sex with her. It worked only as long as the sex lasted, of course.

Five days after our terrible meeting, I waited at the foot of the steps into the Central School of Speech and Drama until Mandy came out. Thankfully, when she saw me, she smiled. We had a coffee and talked for hours. I apologised profusely, she forgave me, we made it up. I was so happy that I told her I thought I loved her and that maybe, just maybe, we should think about living together. In the meantime, would she come to the Grammy Awards in LA with me? Of course she would.

Two weeks later, back in London again with a Grammy Award to add to my Ivor Novello Awards (for Best Single 1981, and Songwriter of the Year, with Marco), I reflected on the fact that I had a London flat (Primrose Hill), a house in the country, success and money. I had Mandy beside me. And I felt miserable. I had remembered how awful it had been living with Eve and what that had led to, and I really didn't think I could go through that again, live with anyone again, including Mandy. Eventually I told her all of this as honestly as I could. Amazingly, she said she understood. I said that I thought she'd come to LA with me because she was scared of what I might do to myself if she said no, and she said that was true.

In the end, we agreed that we really could be friends, that whatever bad ideas I had about her life without me were totally untrue and that we shouldn't live together. We should simply see each other when and as we wished.

It was the only way that we could part.

I wouldn't take another holiday for a long time.

•

Cannon and Ball were the last in a long line of great British comedy double acts. Just like Laurel and Hardy, Abbot and Costello, Martin and Lewis or Morecambe and Wise, there was a straight man (Cannon) and a funny man (Ball). There was an obvious physical difference between them in that Cannon was taller than Ball. He was also slightly better looking and exuded an air of control, however mistaken that was. Because they were on the UK's only major commercial channel, ITV, they were considered to be at the cheaper end of the entertainment scale than the BBC's Morecambe and Wise. I had been asked to appear on the Morecambe and Wise show but had declined, in favour of Cannon and Ball, because they had higher viewing ratings. (I thought about it for a short while before saying yes, though. What would the NME say?) From playing the Vortex to the Cannon and Ball show in less than five years, from playing to less than a hundred people in 1977 to being beamed into fifteen million living rooms. How could I say no?

For the show I had to wear a black Mexican outfit with tight trousers, a wide-brimmed black hat and a false moustache. I also had to pronounce a ridiculously long name – Juan Carlos Gonzales Miguel Pedro Rodriguez Dino Marco Francesco Pele Pirroni Hernandez Julio Orantez Domingo Diego Santana Vincente . . . Smith. After performing a flamenco dance comedy scene, I then sang 'Three Caballeros' with Cannon and Ball. I had a great time and got both men to sign a photo of themselves for me. I also got to sing my new single, 'Goody Two Shoes', for that massive audience, which was the main point of doing it.

A week after my appearance on the Cannon and Ball Show, on 20 May 1982, 'Goody Two Shoes' was released and entered the charts at number 5. I appeared on *Top of the Pops* without the Ants or Marco, dancing with the in-house dance troupe Legs and Co instead (I was apparently the first singer to do so). I designed three different sets, and outfits to go with them, for the show, and then rehearsed, with Flick Colby working me as hard as the girls to get everything right. I'd dressed them in very short skirts and styled them as Helen of Troy, a principal boy from panto and a French maid. All of which were obvious looks, but still great. I also had the dancers mouthing the chorus with me during the routine.

It was very, very important to me that 'Goody Two Shoes' be a hit. And not just a Top 5 hit; it had to go to number 1. Then I could forget about the failure of 'Ant Rap' to make the top spot (it had peaked at number 3) and feel strong enough to go out and work as hard as I could to establish Adam Ant as a solo singer and performer. Which was why I was appearing on as many TV and radio shows as I could before 'Goody Two Shoes' was released. We filmed the video for it two weeks after its release at a spooky old Victorian sanitarium in Virginia Waters. Mike Mansfield was the director once more, again perfectly interpreting my storyboards on film.

I had asked Faye Dunaway to be in the video, but she had declined, so instead I hired former Hammer Horror and Bond girl Caroline Munro. I also got the great Graham Stark (the sergeant in Peter Sellers' *Pink Panther* movies) to appear as my butler, and the long-suffering wife of TV's Alf Garnett, Dandy Nichols, to appear as my cleaner. The shoot was fun, despite the surroundings, mainly because I had my usual crew of extras working on it with me. But the video didn't exactly have the desired effect. On the Tuesday that the chart was announced, in which 'Goody Two Shoes' was to have risen to the top, I thumped the table in anger and yelled at no-one in particular, *'Number fucking two! Number fucking two!'* CBS were happy and even went as far as to call me and congratulate me on such a 'triumph'. But I couldn't bear it.

Later that day I sat bewildered in my fave place, the Troubadour café in Earl's Court, with a cup of coffee in front of me, wearing my boxing boots over black baggy karate trousers and a small black leather jacket. I felt that I'd worked my buns off, and that was the main cause of frustration. I had finished what I thought was my best, most accomplished video to date only for it *not* to get me to the top slot in the chart.

I was distraught at not going to number 1. I was working as hard as I could and didn't feel that my record company was helping me enough (or that anyone else was, either). I felt that the number 1 was essential so that I could establish myself as a solo artist and move on to other things, such as an acting career, safe in the knowledge that I could go back to music at any time. CBS were disappointed that the video for 'Goody Two Shoes' wasn't moodily lit and 'deep' and 'grown-up', but that wasn't me – I was a song-and-dance man, I told them. I wanted them to think of me as a kind of Frank Sinatra, not David Bowie. I had plans for the release of the first Adam Ant solo LP, *Friend Or Foe*, in July or August (Marco and I had already begun demoing songs for it), and a video *Greatest Hits* for Christmas.

In my desperation for the top spot in the singles chart, I blamed CBS for not doing enough to get it there. I'd telephone them every day, talking to different departments from the managing director through marketing to the press office, trying my hardest to get them to do anything that would get me there.

The next week it stayed at number 2 and I became resigned to it never reaching number 1. I decided that I had been boring too many people who had no reason to be interested with details of my business, and so I made a note in my diary to not talk about my professional problems with people who weren't in the business. I continued to appear on as many TV shows as I could get on, and did as many newspaper interviews as I could. Just before the third week's chart was announced I wrote that I was in three minds about what to do. I could work harder to conquer the shitty music business, I could throw it all away and leave the business, or I could go and work hard at getting acting parts and come back to music, like Bowie had done.

And then the single made number 1! As soon as it was announced I felt calmer, and confident that now I could move on to the next stage of my career.

That began with the recording of *Friend Or Foe*, the first Adam Ant solo album. Marco and I recorded it with a new band, the Ants – Merrick, Terry Lee and Gary Tibbs – having come to the end of their contracts, and almost their health, with the schedule that we'd undergone in the past twelve months. The sound was to be Motown-ish, with soul-sounding horns and rockabilly guitar, the beat being big as usual, though not Burundi-like. And all produced by Marco and me (for the first time). The song lyrics reflect what I was thinking and feeling at the time, as most of my lyrics do. So the newspapers got a bit of a kicking in 'Goody Two Shoes' and 'Desperate But Not Serious' (which BBC children's television would later ban because of the line, 'Mr Pressman with your penknife always asking about my sex life.' Well, that and a vampire kiss in the video).

'History And The Right To Lie' covers my feelings about fame and how in Britain people love to knock you down when you're on top. 'Made Of Money' was a message to Eve, who'd made a silly demand for a divorce settlement earlier in the year. 'Here Comes The Grump' is all about me, of course – I wasn't feeling sorry for myself when I wrote it, just ready for the fight that I thought I was in with everyone, from the press and my record company to the people who worked for me. In 'So You Shall' I told the Adam Ant story again, with lots of nods to the music press and their accusations of my being a 'panto dame'. But it's the title song, 'Friend Or Foe', that best sums up my attitude at the time. I didn't care for half measures. If you got to know me you either became an admirer or an enemy, and I didn't care which. I couldn't take *indifference* about what I did and who I was.

The bill for making the album, combined with the bill for making the 'Goody Two Shoes' video, had troubled me and made me assess exactly what my financial situation was. I had paid out £250,000 to put on the Prince Charming Revue, and the album had made £2.7 million for CBS, of which I only got 10 per cent. After I had paid for these recording sessions, I would not own the tapes, but CBS would. It didn't make sense. Falcon Stuart had told me to accept a new publishing deal from EMI of £100,000 while I was touring, but I had not agreed, simply because I didn't have time. I was glad about that when, after hiring a new business manager, Tony Russell, he told me that he thought he'd get ten times that. That was something to look forward to.

Meanwhile I had to deal with the fact that I had paid almost £40,000 to a lawyer who was advising me on the legality of my original deals with Decca and Do It, only for him to tell me that I couldn't do anything about either.

It all made me determined to get another publishing deal and a new recording deal decided as soon as possible, and that both of them should be as good for Marco and me as they could be.

•

In the middle of recording *Friend Or Foe* and designing the graphics for the sleeve, I took an afternoon out to meet one of my idols, Terence Stamp. We met in the tea room at Fortnum and Mason, me wearing an anarchy shirt, camel overcoat, Sex leather trousers and suede boots, he resplendent in an immacu-late two-piece grey suit, white shirt and blue tie with a white pattern. We talked for almost two hours about movies, not just ones that he'd made, but our favourites. He told me great stories about Fellini, his speech full of cockney-tinged, 'Fucking hell, cunts and pricks'. He also gave me some great one-liners, such as Anthony Newley's 'When in doubt, do nothing'.

I told him that I wanted to get into movies but didn't want to take the kind of parts that I was being offered, most of which were parts as a pop star. Terence said that at least I knew what I didn't want to do, which was a start. He also said that I shouldn't be afraid to do something and make a mistake, because that showed I was human. Across from us at another table sat Colin Welland, the Oscar-winning scriptwriter of *Chariots of Fire*. Terence nodded at him and told me that I should go and introduce myself, give him £1,000 and ask to get together for a couple of afternoons because I had some ideas. He'd listen to me, said Terence, because I was Adam Ant and hot property at the moment, and it gave him the chance to go home and tell his family, 'Guess who came up to me today?'

My conversation with Terence Stamp was one of the most memorable I'd had in a long while. His advice stayed with me, even if I didn't go up to Colin Welland and give him a grand. Later in my life, when I was acting in movies and on TV, things that Terence had told me came back to me and helped me.

I had also met Bryan Ferry for the first time that year, while promoting 'Goody Two Shoes' in Italy on a TV show in May. He was dressed in a tuxedo, having his photograph taken, with Andy Mackay and Phil Manzanera of Roxy Music in the casino hotel that I was staying in. We said hello and spent fifteen minutes chatting, and he was friendly. He offered some advice about keeping out of trouble (which I can't remember) and as we parted I thought he was just like I'd expected him to be.

In the middle of July I moved into a new flat in North London (I kept the Primrose Hill flat, too). It was to be my escape, the place that only a few people knew about. I began a new relationship with a dancer named Karen at the same time – the first and only woman to know about the flat, because when, in September, I awoke one morning, opened the curtains and found a row of schoolgirls in blue uniforms trooping past on their way to class, I knew that I'd have to move out. It was sold before the end of October.

I still had periods of missing Mandy and the occasional dream about leaving everything behind and going somewhere that no one knew me so that we could be together, one on one. It was too late, though. We both knew that. I knew that she had a new boyfriend, and I could accept it, but only because I didn't really believe it. It didn't make me sad, because I wouldn't let myself feel anything.

Early in September, Doreen, my father's second wife and the woman that I had called Adamum, died. She hadn't been the woman that I had known and loved for some time because of her illness, and I was heartbroken at the news of her passing. She had been going through hell in a secure mental hospital and her death was something of a release, in truth. I hadn't visited her while she was there because Les told me that she didn't recognise him so wouldn't know me and because I was simply too busy. And so I said goodbye and told her that I loved her at a funeral which I arranged and organised. I had the most beautiful marble headstone that I could find put in place and stood at the grave with Les, feeling strangely protective toward him. He took it very badly. He was clearly heartbroken. Despite the troubles that he and Doreen had endured, he loved her and would miss her enormously. He had taken to the bottle in the week leading up to the funeral, but was sober for the ceremony. After the funeral I took him shopping and bought him two new suits and transformed the pathetic empty man who was my father into an almost handsome bastard. I also bought him a motorbike and told him to go and get a job and a new life, that this was the chance for a new beginning. Would he take it?

At the time of Doreen's death, 'Friend Or Foe', the single, had been released and entered the charts at 22. As the summer drew to a close, I had begun rehearsing with a new band, getting ready for a tour to support the new album release. For the first time, I was beginning to suffer stage fright. I talked it over with Karen and Mo, even Don's wife June, looking for some help in understanding why I had become genuinely scared of going on stage. I didn't know why. Maybe it was because I wouldn't have Marco with me on stage for the first time in two years (he simply refused to tour any longer). Maybe it was because it was Adam Ant and His Men and not Adam and the Ants who were going to be up there. Either way, the Friend Or Foe Tour was a gamble and one that I had to win. As I had done throughout my career I was putting everything on the line. Less than two years after becoming successful I was changing everything again. Would the fans understand and still support me?

I couldn't afford as big and expensive a show as the Prince Charming Revue had been, and so I'd have to give my all on stage. I had to swallow my fear and press on.

The touring band took shape quite quickly, with three Q-Tips horn players and drummer Bogdan joining guitarist Cha Burns and bassist Chris Constantino (whom I rechristened Chris DeNiro) along with a second drummer, Barry Watts, in August. The rehearsals were good, hard work with no complaining. I told them that we had to 'spit fire and crap thunder' and they seemed to be up for it. Marco didn't come to rehearsals, of course, so I had to teach them the guitar chords for all the songs, which was fine because it really made me feel like the band leader.

The band would be working with me on a big tour of America in the autumn. I knew that I had to make it there with this album, or it might not happen at all. I'd decided on a different singles release schedule for the US, and would put out a remixed version of the Doors' 'Hello, I Love You' (which would only appear on the Friend Or Foe LP in the UK) instead of 'Desperate But Not Serious'.

In England, meanwhile, I directed the video for 'Friend Or Foe'. It was the first that I'd made without Mike Mansfield and he was a bit upset about it. It wasn't because I thought Mike had done a bad job, it was simply that I wanted to direct it myself. After all, I was writing the thing (as I had all the previous videos) and storyboarding it, so why not? If only to see how difficult it actually was, I told myself. The storyline for the video was loosely based on the Adam Ant story, with some surreal touches, such as my tap-dancing with a panto cow. I took serious tap-dancing lessons in preparation for the shoot (and so that I really could claim to be a song-and-dance man, of course). My new girlfriend, Karen, directed the choreography for the video (rather than Steph who had done that for all of the previous shoots).

Mike wrote me a letter after he'd seen it, saying how I needed someone who cared behind the camera, someone who cared in charge of the lighting and so on. We met for dinner and talked it over and agreed that he would be back in the director's chair for the next video, 'Desperate But Not Serious'.

After the stress of the 'Goody Two Shoes' release in May, I was determined that I wouldn't live my life from chart day to chart day with 'Friend Or Foe'. Which was just as well, because there were plenty of other problems to occupy me in the first few weeks of its release, not least those concerning what would be an almost disastrous UK tour. (The single got only as high as number 9.)

The night before we were to make our live debut at London's Astoria on 30 September, the wardrobe mistress told me that I had only three pairs of trousers and one jacket ready for the whole band and we had to make do. Despite that, the Astoria gig was a triumph, I felt, and I was very happy that Marco got up on stage for the encore. Unfortunately all of the reviewers thought differently. Among the insults they threw at us, the worst was that we were copying Dexy's Midnight Runners, who had recently swapped their little black hats and tight suits for braces and flat caps. It wasn't just the look, though, it was also because I had included a horn section on the album and the stage. As if Dexy's had thought of it first! Thoroughly pissed off,

I had the outfits redesigned and new ones made before the main part of the tour began. I then set out to promote the album as heavily as I could, signing one thousand LPs in one sitting at CBS, appearing on TV and agreeing to the *Sun* newspaper accompanying us on the tour which began on 4 November – and which had not sold out yet.

I started a promo tour of personal appearances in Manchester, and the next day *Friend Or Foe* the LP made number 5 in the charts, which was a good beginning, I thought. Unfortunately, that was the best it would do. Interviewers were asking me if I thought that it was all over for me, if my bubble had burst, and shouldn't I have kept the Ants?

Fuck you all, I thought. I will succeed.

The night the tour began, in Brighton, guitarist Cha Burns broke his wrist. Things didn't get much better after that. The band felt sloppy, and they argued over the set list, suggesting that I drop songs such as 'Grump' and 'Made Of Money'. I refused, convinced that if everyone worked harder then we'd get better and better. We did. In Ipswich we were evacuated from our hotel in the middle of the night because the building next to it caught fire. The next morning the BBC told us that they would not play the video for 'Desperate' that Mike had finished editing the week before (it was inspired by the *Rocky* movies). The LP slipped to 20 in the charts. The *NME* described our Glasgow appearance as being a 'cockroach on a dunghill'.

By the end of the UK tour, though, I thought the band was tight enough for the US, and had been heartened by the great response that we'd had from the paying public at all of our appearances. I had to be optimistic. Even if it felt like starting all over again there. It was now or never, I thought, as we touched down in November at JFK airport.

9

STRIP

THE PAIN WAS TERRIBLE. Three songs into the set and my knee had exploded. It felt as if someone was sticking a red-hot poker into it. I had to stop singing and slumped backwards on to a drum riser. Bogdan's bass drum thumped into the back of my head as I sat, my face scrunched up in pain, leaning back on his kit. He didn't know what was happening and so kept on playing. Cha was looking over his shoulder at me with a quizzical expression. If I'd been a football player I could have signalled the trainer on. Instead I looked towards the wings where Stan Tippins, our vastly experienced road manager, was standing and waved him on with my right hand, while the other kept a tight grip on the source of my agony.

He ran out and knelt by me. 'What's up, Adam?' he shouted.

I couldn't talk, just pointed at my left knee and leaned into his shoulder.

Stan helped me up and half carried me off stage. The band ended the number we were in the middle of and followed me off stage. The Cleveland crowd were booing and clapping at the same time. What a place to collapse, I thought – the home of rock 'n' roll.

'What happened, Adam, what's going on?' Stan was trying to get a hand on my knee, but I kept pushing him away and swearing.

'Fuck, fuck, shit, fuck . . . my knee!'

Someone ran up with a plastic bag full of ice and handed it to Stan, who put it on my knee. That helped. A bit.

'Get someone out there to let the crowd know that we'll be back,' I ordered anyone who'd listen.

Finally a doctor arrived, eased my hands from the knee and gently felt around the joint. 'Can you bend it?' he asked, trying to raise my leg.

'Fuck off . . .'

'OK.' He gave up trying to move it. 'I think you've bust a cartilage.'

'OK, but can I get back on stage?'

'You want to?' The doctor couldn't believe it.

'Yeah. Give me something to ease the pain and strap the knee. I'll get it looked at tomorrow.'

He shook his head, got a couple of Tylenol from his bag and passed them to me as he also pulled out a bandage.

Twenty minutes after I'd collapsed, I went back on stage and finished the gig on one leg, hopping about and trying not to 'dance' as I did. The crowd seemed to appreciate it, which was good, because I'd not just torn a cartilage, but wrecked my knee.

It was 21 February 1983 and we were nine dates into a 48-date tour of America that was supposed to seal the conquering of the USA by Adam Ant.

•

The American tour of November and December 1982 had been depressing at first. Booked into the kind of clubs that I'd last played in England before 1980, we had been ordered about by the US record company and promoters, been given rudimentary care and didn't get on stage until ridiculous hours – usually between eleven p.m. and one a.m.

When we'd arrived there had been only one car to meet us at JFK airport, and when we got to the hotel our rooms had been double-booked. I was suffering from conjunctivitis and my knee was beginning to trouble me – it had been bashed so often on monitors and speakers that God knows how it lasted as long as it did.

Sitting in a tiny grey room in the hotel in New York on that first trip, I reflected that three years of hard work had led to this – dates at clubs the size of the Marquee. I knew I should have been back sooner, but CBS in London and my desire to be number 1 in the UK had postponed the trip. Well, I'd done it before, so I had to do it again. I was as determined as ever to succeed. If I were an unknown again, then I'd work as hard as it took to become known.

After dates in New York, Washington and Cleveland and several TV and radio appearances, things started to turn around in Chicago. The hotel was decent for the first time and the show was at a decent-sized venue. I was grumpy, though, and not just because my knee was playing up and I had to wear an eye patch because of the conjunctivitis. It was because in England the single release of 'Desperate' had entered the charts outside the Top 10 (at 33) and the album had slipped out of the Top 30. Yet the gigs in America were going really well, and the fans seemed to enjoy it, especially when Marco got up on stage to play the last couple of numbers. He was enjoying the tour for a change because he didn't have to play all night, every night. And the really good news was that 'Goody Two Shoes' was shooting up the US singles chart while *Friend Or Foe* was doing the same in the album chart.

So it made it all the more annoying to be travelling across America – from New York, through Minneapolis and Chicago to New Orleans, Houston, Dallas and Los Angeles – in a bus. It was such a throwback to the early days that I almost started to think that I had never been a hit anywhere, and that news of the single and album working their way up the charts was all untrue. As I wrote in my diary, 'What a mind-destroying pastime touring can be.'

I was also beginning to think that Don Murfet was out of his depth as my manager. We should never have been booked into such small venues, I thought. He should have been constantly harassing CBS UK to make sure that their American office took notice of us and believed that we were bigger than the toilets we were playing. Maybe we needed an American manager to handle Stateside affairs. Marco and I discussed it as we slowly crawled across the country, heading toward Christmas and Los Angeles. He was the only person I felt able to confide in and talk to about a future for Adam Ant.

Our publishing deal with EMI would run out in June 1983, and they had made us a new offer, already, of £1 million each to buy out the rights to all of our songs, for ever. It was tempting, but we decided not to make a decision until the deal ran out, or at least until it had almost run out.

And then, with the increasing success of the single and album in America, tickets to the gigs started selling out rapidly and we were asked to add two dates to the tour, in Seattle and Portland (Oregon), before finishing in LA on 14 December. Plus, girls had begun chasing us wherever we were spotted. It was just like being back in England.

In LA at the Palladium, the Doors' guitarist Robbie Kreiger joined us on stage for 'Hello, I Love You', to a great reception. From such low beginnings, the 1982 American tour ended on a very high note. The UK tabloids had changed their mind about me, too. In early November they were asking if it was all over for Adam Ant, but by the time I flew back into Heathrow in mid-December the *Daily Mirror* centre spread was bearing the headline ANT WORSHIP. It also ran a review of the last gig in LA that was almost ecstatic. I may have had my first failure in the UK for three years (in 'Desperate But Not Serious'), but I was definitely not ready to retire.

•

Bang-bang-bang-bang-bang.
  'Manuella!'

Uh. Where am I? What's that noise? Who . . .?

'Adam, wake up. Is my boyfriend.'

A gorgeous Swiss woman, Manuella, was shaking me awake. It was light out, so obviously a new day had begun. After a muddled few seconds I recalled that we were in her flat, in her bed in which we'd had a lot of fun the night before.

This awakening was not anywhere near as much fun, though.

Bang-bang-bang-bang-bang-bang!

'Manuella! Open the fucking door!'

It looked as if I was caught, although I was determined that I wouldn't be caught with my pants down.

I half fell out of bed and scrabbled around the floor for my clothes. With my white shirt on but undone, I pulled my black leather trousers on and grabbed everything else, making for the kitchen.

At the front door the boyfriend was trying to kick his way in and sounding like a castrated bull. He was Spanish and screaming abuse in his native tongue. I was terrified, trying to hold on to socks, pants, rings, watch and boots as I darted for the back door. My eyes were blurred, having slept all night with my contact lenses in. I was shaking so much that I hadn't fastened my trousers properly and they were half falling down.

In Manuella's tiny kitchen I struggled with the six ridiculously complex buckles of my light tan suede World's End boots. Christ, fucking boots! They could cost me my life, or at the very least my face. My throat was dry, my head banging and my ears full of rushing blood as my heart pumped furiously. If El Toro busted through that door I had no excuses, no reason to be there that early.

Finally, the buckles fastened (or most of them, anyway) and I pulled open the back door and ran out.

Shit.

It was a basement flat and there was no way out of the garden except through the flat. I hesitated, thought about trying to climb the drainpipe to the flat above and going out through their front door, but decided that I'd never make it. I stepped back into the kitchen and listened. The screaming and banging had stopped.

Christ, it sounded as if the crazy man had left. Relief flooded over me. Right, I thought to myself – move!

I unbolted the front door, ran up the steps into the road and, amazingly, there was a black cab passing – with its light on. I stopped him and jumped in the back. Still panting from the adrenalin that was rushing through my body, I slumped back in the seat and told the driver to go to the flat in Redcliffe Gardens. God, I was glad to see Dave when I got there. I took him to breakfast at the Troubadour and told him all about my ridiculous Great Escape.

I had been stupid, I knew. If that guy had got hold of me, the triumphant tour of America that was to begin next week would have been off.

Of course, it wasn't the only time the tour was put in jeopardy.

The massive second tour of America during the first three months of 1983 made my accountant happy. Well, happier. Marco and I had to spend at least nine months of the year away from the UK for tax purposes and so we planned to travel on to Sweden afterwards. There we'd meet with Phil Collins at ABBA's recording studio and he would produce a new single or two for us. That should take another couple of months, we figured, and then after that we'd see what opportunities arose.

I had taken on an LA agent named Michael Black who was working on getting me parts in movies. I had read the script for Martin Scorsese's *Last Temptation of Christ*, and although I knew that it would be a great movie, I also knew that there was no way that I was ready for a part in something like that. I had met with the casting agent for the film and had an interesting chat with her. Unhappily, she was as unimaginative as everyone else I'd spoken to had been about my acting up to that point. She suggested that maybe I should find a part that cast me as a rock star. Groan. So far only Terence Stamp had given me any decent advice or encouragement about being in movies. Don had suggested that I 'try a guest slot in a TV series'. I was amazed that he'd even think that I'd consider such a thing, although I shouldn't have been.

Don had been very tired by our US tour in the autumn of 1982, and so both Marco and I insisted that he stay in the UK in 1983. Instead we hired a big, funny American named Michael Kleffner to manage the tour. A former head of A&M in Los Angeles, he was brash and pushy, which was exactly what we wanted.

It wasn't a totally new team for the tour, though. It was the same band and the same road manager, Stan Tippins. A very great responsibility for the success or failure of any tour falls to your road manager. Luckily, we had the best in Stan. I could almost pity any promoter who tried to cut us short, or who failed to provide us with the basics in our dressing room or on stage – I wouldn't have liked to face the wrath of Stan. An experienced road manager of some years practice, he also had a great voice and had once sung backing vocals for Mott the Hoople on tour, although he claimed that he was always hidden from view behind a curtain.

Stan originally came from Hereford, and supported Hereford Football Club, who were always at the bottom of the league. This had taught him to handle disappointment, so he was unfazed by the small things that occurred every day that would have tested other people. He used to keep a list of all the ways his surname had been mistaken over the years, for instance. It included Tiplets, Teepees, Triplets, Criplins, Treblets and so on and on. A big Johnny Kid and the Pirates fan in his youth, Stan claimed to have once thrown a fire extinguisher at Cliff Richard during a gig.

As a father only to daughters until that tour of America, he and his wife were waiting for a son – and she was pregnant. His wife gave birth just as we came to the end, and it was a boy. We held a celebratory party in one of the rooms for Stan, who never drank while on tour, but that night he made up for what he'd been missing all those years. Normally he was the straightest, most together guy on the road. He had researched the local laws for every state that we were to visit, for instance, and had sheets of information on the kinds of laws that bands on tour might break and issued them to every band member when we arrived in a new state. At some point during the celebratory party for Stan's new son, someone called the cops. When they arrived Stan jumped out of the window, luckily landing in a huge trash cart that was parked directly below.

The next morning, thankfully unscathed, Stan was put at the back of the bus, the curtains were pulled across, a wet flannel was put on his brow and he was left to rest. That night at the gig he was fully restored to fighting form.

Stan was tough and always calm. One night at an open-air show in Milan on a European tour, a huge riot broke out and tanks were sent into the audience, blasting everyone with water cannons. Stan studied the situation for a while before snarling to us, 'All right, lads, on you go.' As we were trooping out on to the stage, though, Stan (who was leading us up the steps) saw a guy with a gun in his hands backstage. He stopped dead, turned to us and very calmly shouted, 'All right, lads, off you come now.' And did we get off that stage as quickly as possible. A while later, when Stan said it was all clear, we played a very speedy set. Talking to us about it after the show, Stan typically played the whole thing down. 'A diabolical liberty,' he said, huffily.

Because we were playing big gigs and staying at decent hotels on the February 1983 American trip, Stan decided that the band could and should have a party after every gig, either in someone's room or, more often, in the bar or a specially reserved room elsewhere in the hotel. He'd make sure that there were women, booze and food present at every party, and it mostly made for a happy band and crew. Although I would go to many of these parties, I couldn't stay for long. Being around drunk people made me very uneasy, and I was never attracted to women who were drunk and sycophantic (as they invariably were at such parties). I would leave after a short while, alone, and return to my room or go to meet people I'd arranged to see earlier in the day.

Before the 1983 tour had begun in America I had recorded a session as the first guest Video Jockey for MTV, which had just gone national. Later the same day I presented the Top Female Singer prize at the first Contemporary Music Awards show. It was an incredible honour for me to be there, handing out awards alongside Luther Vandross, Randy Crawford and David Bowie (who, I had just heard, had requested that every one of my videos be sent to him). Standing backstage as the seemingly endless show went on, I was approached by first Quincy Jones, who gave me the greatest compliment I'd ever had by saying that he really liked my work, and then by Lionel Ritchie and Nile Rodgers (of Chic). I was also introduced to Al Green and the founder of the Tamla Motown record label, Berry Gordy. He asked me if I would appear at a special birthday concert for Motown. Of course I said yes, and left the awards show feeling like a happy schoolkid.

My mood was helped by the fact that accompanying me was an African-American model-turned-singer I'd got to know on my last trip to New York. Then she was called Denise, but now she was known as Vanity. As we were making for the door, Rick James approached her and said, dumbly, 'Why you leavin' with that white boy when I got something thick between my legs for you, baby?'

'Uh-huh, sure,' said my girl, and pulled me through the doors and into a waiting car.

Denise had become Vanity when she had joined a Paisley Park group named Vanity 6, one of Prince's many offshoot bands who were about to release their first single. I was very happy for her and we would see a lot of each other on tour. Unhappily, though, Prince didn't like her seeing me. In San Francisco, later in the 1983 tour, we bumped into him in the lobby of our hotel and he went apeshit at her for being with me. I think it was professional jealousy, although it was just as likely to have been romantic jealousy, too. I had met Prince on my last trip to America and he'd seemed a little arrogant, but I couldn't help but like him, maybe because I really liked his music and his videos.

Vanity and I had been photographed leaving the awards show and soon, according to the British press, we were 'insep-arable' and about to marry. I was almost as amazed about that story as I was about another one in the *Sun*, in which a woman claimed that she and I had been married at a register office in New York. She had also appeared on various TV news pro-grammes on the US East Coast as 'Mrs Adam Ant'. Had anyone even thought of contacting me to find out if either of these stories was true? Of course not. At least I'm being written about, I thought, and any day that I'm in the newspaper means that neither Boy George nor Duran Duran are. Both acts were 'chal-lenging' my position as the number 1 pop star in the UK at the time, and I was acutely aware of it.

I was also becoming annoyed that Sting was being offered, and accepting, acting work on TV and in movies when I hadn't been approached properly about making a film since *Yellowbeard* in 1981. It seemed that, just as it had been with my music career, so it would have to be with acting – I'd have to push for it all by myself.

As the tour entered Cleveland, then, I was feeling deter-mined that the rest of the year would be spent playing great gigs, making a great album and getting myself into a position of strength to get acting work. And then my knee exploded.

•

The X-ray showed that my kneecap was floating – it had come away from the knee completely. The doctors were talking about surgery and at least three weeks' rest. I was thinking of continuing the tour in a kind of Gene Vincent way, with my left leg straight, leaning in to the microphone stand. I could even get an all-black, all-leather suit made . . . *Friend Or Foe* was at number 16 in the US album chart and had gone Gold. I couldn't cancel now, I kept telling anyone who'd listen.

But the reality was that I couldn't hobble, let alone walk. I couldn't even put my own socks on. I was given a set of crutches, but after a couple of hours they were hurting my armpits almost as much as the knee was hurting. The Cleveland knee expert recommended that I return to the UK and get expert surgery. I asked Michael Kleffner, in between his dealings with insurance companies and promoters, to find me an American knee specialist. Much as I would have loved to be back in my lovely, sky-blue Primrose Hill flat so that I could be treated by the doctor who fixes knees for the Royal Ballet, I couldn't go back to the UK. If I did then the taxman would get a big chunk of the little I'd earned in the last year.

So the band flew back to London, while Marco and I flew to New York and settled into a quaint old hotel in uptown Manhattan. Marco hired some acoustic guitars and, with my leg in a brace, we spent a week writing songs. In that time Don and his wife flew out to New York and arranged for me to see a doctor in Los Angeles. Three days after arriving, and the day after I had talked with my mum on the telephone and wished her Happy Birthday, I was wheeled down to the operating theatre feeling apprehensive and unsure. The orderly taking me down crashed and banged the bed into walls and other tables, stopped for a chat with another Hispanic orderly, and then, pushing my bed against the wall outside the theatre, proceeded to shave my leg with an open razor and no foam. He was surprisingly gentle and quick, which almost made up for the dreadful drilling noise that was coming out of the theatre. As he finished, the orderly looked up at me, gave me a gold-toothed smile and nodded towards the door behind which a pneumatic drill was pounding away.

'You next,' he said.

I gulped. It was my first operation. A hundred different thoughts flooded my brain at once. 'I haven't had sex for ten days,' was one. And I really needed the tour to resume as soon as possible.

Then the drilling ended and a bed was pushed out of the theatre past me. I tried not to look. The anaesthetist came over and asked if I was allergic to sodium pentathol. I didn't think so. My bed was rolled into the theatre and I lay under enormous, bright white lights. My left arm was straightened out on an adjoining table and a needle smoothly inserted. 'Count backwards from fifteen, please,' asked a friendly voice. I didn't get past thirteen.

•

I was woken by a chubby, cheerful nurse. 'Hello,' she smiled.

The operation had gone perfectly. They had removed all of the torn cartilage from my knee. Don was waiting for me when I came round, and we chatted about everything and nothing for a couple of hours. After a couple of days in the hospital I was driven by Don via the sea to the Sunset Marquis Hotel, where I stayed for a couple of weeks.

Throughout my stay in LA I spent the mornings having physical therapy on my knee, and worked on songs with Marco for the rest of the day. In that time we wrote and recorded a demo for the next and only single of the year, 'Puss In Boots'.

Two weeks after the operation, I had a read-through of a script with Walter Hill, the director of Warriors and 48 Hours, which Michael Black, my film agent, had arranged. From there I went to the Hitsville recording studio to lay down the backing track for my version of 'Where Did Our Love Go', which I was to perform at the Motown 25th Birthday Concert.

A couple of days after that, limping stiffly, I made my way to the show itself. It was the strangest thing, to appear on a show with my musical heroes. I spent the whole time backstage staring at stars like Stevie Wonder, my jaw hanging down. But I needn't have worried, the whole thing was just like a big party.

Having rehearsed for two days before, I knew that my version of the Supremes' hit 'Where Did Our Love Go' would go well. I made my entrance on a revolving mechanical 'M' inside the huge Motown logo on the stage. I was set in front of a huge heart, nose to nose with a very pretty dancer. On the seventh bar she gave me a gentle prod, pushing me away, just as I sang 'Baby, baby, baby, don't leave me . . .' The dress rehearsal the day before had impressed all, especially Berry Gordy, who later assured everyone that I was 'sensual'.

Backstage I met so many legends it's as much as I can do to list them. First, there were the Four Tops and the Temptations, and then a very sparkly Mary Wilson. After a while the tent outside where everyone was waiting became too cold for me, so I went into the theatre and waited on the second floor. After watching a few acts, I went down and waited backstage. As I stood alone, quietly and respectfully enjoying watching the show on an engineer's monitor, I felt a tap on my shoulder. I turned around and there, beaming at me, standing together holding out their hands, were Marvin Gaye and Smokey Robinson! I told them it was my honour to meet them and that I carried their music with me everywhere on tour. They thanked me and we chatted. Next, a very trim, slim and serious Richard Pryor came up and said, 'Thanks for doing the show.' I also met the other two Supremes and a deceptively young-looking Martha Reeves.

Then Stevie Wonder arrived, wearing a soft leather suit and an African beaded hairdo with a long ponytail. He stood, looking helpless and lost, clinging to the people with him. He'd whisper into people's ears as they approached him to speak. He played a remarkable medley of hits on stage and gave a touching and sincere speech about how precious the communication of music is. I thought, watching him, that somehow Stevie Wonder had become 'holy', like a priest, almost. Bullshit, I knew, but his music means so much to me, still.

Next up was Michael Jackson, performing 'Billie Jean' and debuting the Moonwalk, while wearing diamond socks and one matching glove. He brought the place to a standing ovation. Guess who was up after him?

It was my 'moment of truth'. I was introduced by Jose Feliciano, who said to a clearly stunned-by-Jacko audience, 'And now, from London, England – Adam Ant!' On I went for my first ever solo outing in front of the Hollywood elite. It was my intention to introduce them to a little English, cheeky sexuality, so I wanted to be almost over-the-top and melodramatic. It was the first show on my damaged knee, so I took care to use my hips and arms more than the knees as I moved. It went pretty well, I thought, and I 'danced' through the instrumental middle eight, moving over to the left-hand stairway as I'd rehearsed. Suddenly the crowd went crazy, clapping and cheering.

'Christ! I've cracked it!' I thought. 'I'm killing them.' So I got up off the stair to sing the last two verses and looked towards the centre of the stage, and there, in a tight, glittering pencil-dress, pulling her hair up over her head like a black Marilyn Monroe, was Diana Ross! My jaw hit the floor and I thought, 'Please, leg, don't give up on me.' The crowd was going nuts and so was I. Somehow my shock turned to confidence, and I slinked over to the beautiful superstar, singing 'I've got this burning, burning, yearning inside of me' into her big, brown eyes. She was really enjoying it. As I circled her, she said, 'Oh yes,' and I felt like her slave. The song ended, and before I had a chance to say anything, she scooted off! I left the stage to much applause, though.

As I came off I was congratulated by Marvin Gaye and Smokey Robinson. Then a guy came up and said he was from the Jacksons and they'd like to meet me 'now', so I followed the guy and passed through four cordons of security guards, up a steep set of stairs, my knee killing me all the way. At the top of the building I saw the Jackson brothers in a narrow corridor and shook hands and chatted with Michael, who loved my outfit. He looked thin but confident, and it was as if we already knew each other (he remembered our telephone chat, of course). I told the brothers how much I loved their music and left. During the finale, with everyone on stage, I managed to get close enough to Diana Ross to kiss her and say thanks.

I was on an incredible high when it was all over. During the last year of touring and staying in bleak hotel rooms and riding dingy buses I'd forgotten how special showbusiness could make me feel. Perhaps the Prince Charming days were over, but this surpassed it all because it was true and pure. Everyone there made me feel good and welcome.

I only just managed to sleep that night. It seemed that every time I closed my eyes I'd be back on the stage with Diana Ross and I'd mumble 'Oh fuck' and 'She-it!'

Four days later I was back on stage with my band. The tour had begun again, after only four weeks' rest. It was great to be performing once more. We played two 'warm-up' gigs at a college outside LA, and my knee was swollen afterwards, but it didn't seem so bad. An ice pack and sex with a gorgeous masseuse soon made it feel better.

Adam Ant was back on the road again.

•

By the beginning of May 1983, I had worked out that over 250,000 Americans would have seen our show by the time we finished on 18 May in Dallas, Texas. For almost six months I had worked hard at persuading the American public that Adam Ant was worth seeing and hearing. Mostly the tour had gone well. There had been a couple of upsetting incidents, though. A female fan had approached me at lunch one day and asked for my autograph. As usual I obliged, as I had done ever since Marc Bolan had given me his autograph in 1974 and I'd realised how upsetting it would have been to me as a fan if he'd refused. The girl took the piece of paper back from me and ripped it into shreds before throwing it in my face and calling me a jerk. 'I used to like you,' she spat, 'but now I hate you.'

In Indiana I had a visit backstage after a show from two former Vietnam veterans who were now cops and had been upset by my treatment of their flag. Someone had thrown a Stars and Stripes on stage, and I had picked it up and draped it over my shoulders for a while before putting it over the drum riser. According to the cops, that was against some law or other and they were clearly upset about it. Don gave them the flag, which they then ceremoniously folded into a triangle, and they left holding it (and a few dollars from Don) as if it were the Crown jewels. I later learned that they did the same thing to another couple of British bands who passed through their town. They'd hit on a successful way of adding to their cop wages.

If you didn't know differently, the idea of a six-month tour of America might seem romantic, but the reality is far from that. Apart from the ninety minutes spent on stage each night, the days are an endless round of travelling, sleeping and trying to find ways of passing the time. For some musicians the bottle and/or drugs are an obvious form of escape from the boredom of touring. For me, of course, it was sex. But even that could become another routine unless it was spontaneous, exciting and sensual. For that I had to be in the right frame of mind, and touring would often make me angry, bored and desperate for home. After every performance I had to sit for a while and alternate hot towels with ice packs on my knee until the swelling went down, which meant that I couldn't – and wouldn't – party with the band after the show.

Yet through it all, the performance was a reason to exist. Which is why in Oklahoma, with a night off, we played an impromptu gig at a punk club and then bought some studio time in a local recording studio. Not that we recorded any music. Instead, Marco, Chris and I made our own version of Peter Cook and Dudley Moore's *Derek and Clive* tapes, with lots of laughing, swearing and very disgusting discussion about band members and each other. It was very funny.

By the time we played our last date in Dallas in May, I felt as if my leg was about to go again and was relieved that it was all over. Phil Collins had received a demo tape of 'Puss 'n Boots' and let me know that he was ready to start work on it. Marco and I planned to fly to Paris in order to finish writing the rest of my next album, after I'd popped back to London for a couple of days in order to catch up on things.

One of those things was Carole Caplin. I took her and my old friend Steph out for dinner on my overnight stay in London. After a pleasant meal, with jet lag starting to hit me, I took them back to Carole's for a cup of tea and a chat. There Carole ambushed me. She had become an Exegesist since we'd last met, and so she sat, being 'enlightened' and telling me how fucked-up I was. Exegesis involves the detailed reading of religious texts, or at least that's its literal meaning. In the early 1980s it came to be a catch-all name for the reading of anything and then reading too much into what you'd just 'studied'. Instead of leaving, as I should have, I stayed and argued with her until we were both exhausted and in total disagreement. Then I went home to my Primrose Hill flat and slept like a baby.

The next day I joined Marco in Paris where we'd booked a 16-track studio in Montmartre to write new songs. We wrote almost all of the seven songs needed to complete the new album, including 'Strip', which could, I thought, be the title track. All of the songs are about women, sexual encounters, love and romance, and all of them are more mature than previous Adam Ant songs. I planned a new look to go with them that would also be more 'mature', with less make-up but keeping a Romantic element to the clothes.

Despite Karen joining me for four days, my stay in Paris passed slowly and I felt like a tourist in a snotty city and didn't enjoy being there. But then, Marco and I were both exhausted.

Being away from England for so long was beginning to affect me, too. I had suffered physically from the massive tour of America, yet didn't realise it. As usual, I expected to be able to go straight from one thing – the tour – to another, the new album. I should have had a holiday in between, but after the horrible experience of Barbados I couldn't face it.

So I was glad to finally get to Stockholm and work with Phil Collins. He was a delight throughout the three weeks that we worked together. He and Hugh Padgham, who worked with him, were professional and adventurous, willing to try a number of different things in the studio and taking care of what I called 'drudge' work, making things sound exactly as they should. The drum sound was perfect, of course, as were the horns. One day they persuaded Frida of ABBA to come into the studio and record a spoken-word section for the song 'Strip'. Later both Benny and Bjorn would visit us at work in their studio, which was also a thrill. At the time they were writing a musical with Tim Rice (*Chess*), and the following year they asked me to record one of the songs for the soundtrack, which was an honour, even though it didn't make it on to the album.

By the third week of June, enough work had been done on my album (which was to be called *Strip*) to allow me to take off for a long-needed rest. After another stop-over in London, I flew to Los Angeles, determined to rest while at the same time working on getting into movies. My agent, Michael, had lined up a few things for me, and I was determined to push him to get more – mostly they were dinners with directors, an occasional read-through of a script, getting to meet producers.

Before things got under way, I went to visit Michael Jackson at home. Motown president Suzanne de Passe took me to Neverland (but before he'd named it that). Dressed in a red V-neck pullover, white shirt with bow tie, black turned-up jeans, white socks and sneakers, he still looked like the Michael Jackson who had first become famous with his brothers. I met his mother and sisters – and instantly fell in love with Latoyah as she handed me a 7UP. Michael took me into his private cinema and we watched James Cagney in *White Heat* ('Look Ma, top of the world!'), preceded by the video for Michael's 'Beat It', which was kind of strange. He didn't seem to want a response to the video, but of course I told him how good it was.

Throughout that afternoon I mostly sat quietly, trying to be English, reserved and polite. After the movie we went to see his pets – a llama, a ram and two deer (there was no chimpanzee at the time). As we walked around he told me that he was talking to Steven Spielberg about making a movie, and I said something about working with people of that calibre would guarantee it was a hit. He stopped walking and turned to me, his big brown eyes stared straight at me for possibly the first time that afternoon, and he said, 'If you work with the best people you can't go wrong.'

On the way back to my Sunset Strip apartment in a limousine, I felt incredibly privileged to have been a guest at Michael Jackson's home. I'd come a long way for a man with a silly name, I thought. It was a thought that would come back to me several times in the next few weeks.

•

At the beginning of July I fell head-over-heels in love with an actress named Jamie Lee Curtis, daughter of Tony Curtis and Janet Leigh (star of *Psycho*). At the time, Jamie was proving to be very impressive in the role of a hooker in Eddie Murphy's film *Trading Places*. She had the most beautiful body I had seen in years. I met her at a dinner party given by a photographer friend of Michael Black's. She was also one of Michael's clients, and had told him how excited she was about meeting me. It was electric when we met, and I felt very, very attracted to her. It was like a first date where you're both ultra-polite and giving sneaky touches as you pass by, starting conversations just so you can look into each other's eyes. And because she was so ambitious I felt intrigued by her as well as being slightly envious.

All night I tried to get close and grab a moment with her. Yet I got the impression that she knew that in order to be really successful you have to be ruthless and, above all, independent.

When she left the dinner party, we stared at each other briefly before kissing on the lips quickly, but with as much tenderness as company around us would allow. In the hallway at one point she touched my hand and I held hers. I felt as if we were made for each other.

A couple of days later we had lunch, but neither of us ate very much because we were talking so much. Afterwards, we went to a photo shoot for my agency photos at the same house where we'd first met. As I sat waiting for the make-up woman to arrive, Jamie leaned over and gave me a quick kiss on the lips. I went red and pecked her in return. 'Sorry,' she said shyly, 'I had to do that.' The make-up woman appeared and I had to go to work. Jamie left, but sent a card to my apartment just as I was leaving for Sweden again. It read, 'Adam, I'm sorry I had to leave . . . I would have loved to stay with you . . . I hope I get to see you again somewhere . . . You are very special. With much affection, Jamie.'

Back in Sweden I had decided that the album needed more work, and wanted to re-record at least three of the songs. Unfortunately Phil Collins was no longer available to produce them, and so Marco and I had begun asking around to find another producer. We tried former Bowie producer Tony Visconti, but he couldn't do it, so Marco and I began producing it ourselves. After a week or so we employed Richard Burgess, who had most recently worked with Spandau Ballet. He proved to be very efficient and very hard-working, as I'd hoped he would be. July turned into August, and the album took shape. I worked on storyboards for 'the Puss 'n Boots' video at the same time as planning the next American tour.

After finishing the 'Puss' storyboards, I began writing a script for the video to the second single, which would be 'Strip'. It wasn't proving to be easy, probably because the album work was beginning to bore me. I had also begun to worry about releasing a single at the most competitive time of the year in the UK (Christmas), especially after almost a year away from England. And I had just been forced to rewrite a track for the album titled 'Dirty Harry'. I had requested permission from Clint Eastwood to use some excerpts from his movie of the same name, and Clint had called Michael Black in LA himself to say that he'd rather I didn't, as he had a new *Dirty Harry* movie in production. But he also said that he'd seen my videos and was a fan. Indeed, his kids wanted him to let me do it. In the end the track didn't make it on to the finished album anyway.

It was decided that *Strip*, the album, would be released in the middle of October with the 'Puss 'n Boots' single coming out a month later. I employed Susan Blane to make me costumes for both the *Strip* cover shoot and the 'Puss' video (she had designed the clothes for Peter Greenaway's *Draughtman's Contract*, which I loved). Despite the movies not coming to me, I was determined to go to them. I had brief second thoughts about 'Puss' being commercial enough to succeed as a single, and decided that in America, 'Strip' would be the first single from the album, both being supported by another big tour. In the meantime I could spend a whole week in London making the video for 'Puss'.

My return to England was greeted with a delightful contingent of teenage girls and the four major Sunday tabloids, all of whom wanted to know what I was going to do next.

Come to that, so did I.

The 'Puss' video had an enormous budget but no leading lady. I had asked for Suzanne Danielle, a small, sexy French actress, or Finola Hughes, John Travolta's co-star in Sylvester Stallone's *Staying Alive*, neither of whom could do it.

I had employed Christopher Tucker to make me a rat face-mask (he had designed John Hurt's make-up in *Elephant Man*), but he couldn't deliver it in time for the shoot. The CBS MD,

Maurice Oberstein, then refused to foot the £50,000 bill for the shoot, so, with only three days left before the filming was due to begin, I cancelled the original script and spent a weekend rewriting it, shaving the budget to £35,000.

Because of the tax situation, I had to get out of the UK while the shoot was rearranged, and so I spent a week in New York. While there I worried about making my 'comeback' after a year out of the UK pop charts. Because Jamie was filming in LA we couldn't get together, so I returned to London and the video shoot feeling anxious and unable to sleep. On 4 October, I wrote in my diary:

> Tonight the ground opens up and swallows me with fear and loathing. The fear is of failure in the next few months with Puss 'n Boots and the follow-up Strip, the album and then Playboy the next single. The plan is made.
>
> The left side of my head aches since banging it on the soap rack of a New York hotel. I loathe the people around me who seem totally incapable of seeing the effort required to adequately serve this piece of work. I understand that Duran Duran (who, a year ago, wouldn't have caused a pause in a sentence) release simultaneously with me. They are very strong and I'm apparently to prove how good I was/am.

The next day, at seven-thirty a.m., I began filming 'Puss 'n Boots' with my dancer girlfriend Karen as the leading lady. It turned out that my worries were unfounded. She was great, the video looked fantastic, and when the single was released with the video getting heavy airplay on kids' TV shows, it did the trick. It sold 100,000 copies in its first week, entering the charts at number 21 and eventually climbing to number 5, one place ahead of Duran Duran's 'Union Of The Snake'. It was helped by a live performance of 'Puss' on Jonathan Ross's *Late Late Breakfast Show* and a choreographed *Top of the Pops* appearance. There were also rushed appearances on other kids' and music TV shows, magazine interviews and radio promo before

I had to leave England once again, this time for at least three months.

Back in Los Angeles at the end of October, at least I found that I could sleep again. I didn't care about journalists asking if I thought I could come back from the dead any more, because I knew that I had. Instead I just looked forward to seeing the woman who had been in my mind for the past four months. Jamie.

•

I had to wait three days before Jamie and I could meet, but when we did, it was as if we'd never been apart. She was waiting on my doorstep as I returned sweaty and grimy from a work-out at the gym. I pecked her, invited her in and rushed to the shower. A couple of minutes later, dressed and refreshed, we started again, with her going out of the front door and knocking, me letting her in. Then we both just grinned at each other and started touching and hugging with a great deal of kissing, too. We spent a week together making love, laughing, eating break-fast in public, talking about out lives. We snogged in the back row of a movie theatre 'watching' *Danton*, and ate dinner in intimate restaurants. I felt relaxed and at ease for the first time in so long it was almost unreal. Jamie was one of the most positive and 'up' people I had ever met. She was always happy to see me, very tactile and generous with her affections. When she wasn't working on a movie, she would spend time every day at the gym, working out and keeping her body as strong as her happy mood.

During that week, though, unfortunately Marco had a major split with his long-time girlfriend, who admitted to him that she'd met someone else. I spent several hours on the telephone with him before he finally agreed to come out to LA. I then also invited his mother and father out, to help look after him. He was truly heartbroken, and I wanted to do as much as I could for him.

In the middle of November I was asked to crown Miss World and the seven runners-up. I had to think seriously about whether to do it before my Hollywood agent Michael Black pointed out to me that seven hundred million people would be watching. So of course I agreed. The night before, I went to the movies with Jamie and her mother, the beautiful Janet Leigh, and then had dinner with her father, Tony Curtis. Despite a small squall of press in the UK when the *Daily Mirror* published a photo of Jamie and me, it seemed as if I was living in a dream.

On a one-night stopover in London to pick up an Antony Price suit for the Miss World pageant, I took my mum and Tony for supper with Don and his wife June at a swanky restaurant. After a while, as waiters sucked up to me, the pop star, I looked across at my mum, and there she sat, pale and lovely, small and almost shivering with fear. Suddenly I realised that while we all sat there confident and assured, my mum, who had probably only ever been out to supper at most a dozen times in her whole life, was scared and unsure of how to act. I felt ashamed of myself and how big and full of shit I had become.

The next morning, as I was leaving, my mum came to say goodbye. I pulled her to my chest and she exploded into tears. She was genuinely sad to see me leave again, and I could only coolly explain that I had to, without any tears on my part. I realised then what a hardened person I had become in the last five years.

Back in Los Angeles I saw Jamie as much as her schedule and mine would allow. She'd come over between auditions and I'd take time between interviews to promote 'Strip', the single and album, to see her. In the UK, Don called to let me know about the LP's performance in the UK while Jamie and I were celebrating her birthday – the album had only made number 20 before dropping to 32 (although it had sold 100,000 copies). By the time I got off the phone she was asleep, and I was feeling angry and disappointed.

After almost a month in LA, Jamie and I went to New York so that I could promote the album. Before leaving, I'd had dinner with producer Giorgio Moroder, who asked me to contribute a track to the soundtrack of his remake of the Fritz Lang classic, *Metropolis* (I recorded 'What's Going On', with Moroder producing for it). But that had been the only positive meeting about movies that I'd had since arriving. I was beginning to get the feeling that Hollywood didn't want me. I knew that I could play on my relationship with Jamie to get in to see important people to get parts, but I really didn't want to do that.

In New York I once again became unable to sleep because of worry about 'Strip'. The video for the single release of the title track had caused a national scandal, apparently, and been banned by children's television. It never made it past number 41 in the charts.

Jamie and I had agreed to spend Christmas in England, at my new house in the country (Luxe), and with Don and June. Jamie had to go ahead without me – not only because I had to spend a couple more days promoting the album in New York, but also because the UK tabloids had decided that she and I were ready to get hitched. One paper sent a female reporter to interview me with the express mission to get me to reveal that Jamie was the love of my life. In England the press chased Jamie everywhere from the moment that she arrived with the same questions. As I wrote in my diary at the time, this was not a bad thing for either of us, press or careerwise, but, 'I am not in any shape to get too serious about anybody'. Jamie was very special to me and I cared about her, but I still could not even think about getting totally involved with any one person. Then there was the fact that I didn't want to be known simply as the boyfriend of a famous Hollywood actress, which she was rapidly becoming.

After making early preparations for a tour of America early in 1984, I travelled to the UK for Christmas. While there, I took Jamie up to visit my mum and Tony in their council flat. She was such a joy to be with and treated my parents with such respect that within a couple of hours they were all hugging and kissing.

Since my house in the country turned out not to be in any shape to stay in, we spent eight days in my Primrose Hill flat, with trips out to see Don. Those eight days proved to be almost the end of the relationship. It felt too much like being married, to me. Jamie was always so positive and bubbly, and I was such a misery that, as I wrote in my diary, I would be surprised if she ever spoke to me again. A real relationship with someone of quality like Jamie was blocked to me. It always ended in apologies from me and my feeling ashamed, as if I was involved in a withering marriage. Even though I tried to, I never kissed her enough, not like she would have liked.

Yet Jamie was an optimist and did not give up on me. It wouldn't be until several months later that she would summon up the courage to end our relationship.

•

I spent New Year's Day 1984 in Copenhagen with Marco and Don, planning another assault on America and coming to terms with the failure of 'Strip' to put me back on top of the charts. I decided that work was what was needed (as ever) and that I had to get in shape properly for the forthcoming US tour. I booked time at Compass Point Studios in Nassau for myself, Marco, Don and the band to prepare the live set. For almost three weeks I would begin work at nine a.m. with a fifteen-minute pedal on an exercise bike. That was followed by twenty push-ups, leg stretches and other stretches and bends, and after strapping five-pound weights to my ankles, I'd take a five-mile hike with Antmusic old and new blasting through my Walkman. The walk, along the fabulous coastline of Nassau, was wonderful and reinvigorating, building the muscles around my damaged knee to help withstand what would be another gruelling US tour.

While there, I employed Michael Kleffner, who had been tour manager on our last US outing, as our US manager. Strip had sold almost 300,000 copies in America but had begun to drop down the charts. I needed someone in charge there who would help me to fight for sales and success, and I knew Michael would do that. Suzanne de Passe of Motown had agreed with me (via telephone) that Michael was the best man for the job, and so we settled on a deal that gave him a nice bonus if the album (or its follow-up) made the Top 20 in the US.

By the time the sixty-date American tour began in Alabama on 28 January 1984, I felt confident, fit and positive that this would be the one to finally break me in America.

After an opening consecutive five dates, I celebrated six weeks of total celibacy with an ice pack on my knee and a cup of tea. The show ended with me immersed in a perspex tank of water that stood at the back of the stage, rising from the water wearing nothing but shorts as the band played 'Strip'. Getting in and out of the tank played havoc with my knee, but exercise had replaced sex in my life at the time, which helped strengthen my leg. The album had stopped its slide down the US charts, while the single had entered the charts at number 80 and rose each week as we toured. The gigs were going well, with each venue sold out and our performance always good, sometimes excellent. Which is probably why I began to become obsessed with making it as an actor again. My tour diaries are full of my thoughts on and hopes for an acting career. Having decided that Hollywood was not going to come calling for me, I had spoken with my English theatrical agent, Simon Astaire, about finding me a stage part in the UK.

On 9 February I saw Jamie for the first time since Christmas, in New York. To prepare myself, I'd been to see her in her new movie, Love Letters. It was an odd experience watching her having sex with another (older) man. It was strange because the sex scenes were almost real, and yet I felt only protective towards her after seeing it. I didn't feel jealous.

We spent the next four days making love as much as possible, with breaks for me to record *Saturday Night Live* (performing 'Strip' and 'Goody Two Shoes') and an MTV special interview, before Jamie flew back to Los Angeles and I went on with the tour. And worrying about why no acting offers had come in, missing England and my family and friends there, reading the occasional film script (three came in during those four months on the road) and talking to Jamie on the telephone when I could.

After four weeks I began to get road fever. On tour, time, like everything else in a touring musician's life, is not fixed. As long as I made the stage at the right time and got on the bus or aeroplane in time to make the next gig, then anything else could happen at any time. One hotel room is much the same as any other, one steak much like any other, one hotel gym the same as the next.

After a while, the exercise routine I had set myself proved to be not enough to keep my spirits up, and I wrote in my diary that I had to have sex. As with previous tours, it was a different woman in every town or city. All of them were unique and interesting. All of them were necessary for me to keep my sense of self intact and my inner self calm.

By the end of March I was sleeping as much as I could between gigs, watching terrible TV, and popping into the awful after-show parties only to be assaulted by kids asking what my real name was. And then a brief respite came up in the form of a two-day shoot for a commercial selling Honda motorbikes (which was ironic, since I couldn't drive) with Grace Jones, to be filmed in Hollywood. The fee was nice, too ($75,000). After two-thirds of the tour, a third wave was needed to help propel me through to the end, and maybe this would be it. Filming would take place in mid-April.

Meanwhile, I spent three days with Jamie staying at her penthouse in LA. The first day was great and it was almost dreamlike seeing her, touching her and sleeping in her bed. She rose at six-thirty a.m. to get to the gym, and I slept until one p.m. In the kitchen, eating 'breakfast', I felt human for the first time in so long that it was like coming out of an anaesthetic. By the end of the second day I began to feel like a wallflower, though. She was busy, and I tried desperately to be chirpy, with little success. I read a script of a movie that she was making with John Travolta (*Perfect*), and told her that I didn't think it was very good. I added that I was fed up being treated (I felt) as if I were another pet in the house and let go at her about the script. After dinner we ended in tears, most of them mine. On our last day Jamie was moody, obviously because of my comments about the script. After a walk with the dog late that night, Jamie came back to her penthouse and blurted out her feelings to me. She was confused that our relationship wasn't total. That she didn't put it about and that I was 'the one', and she usually moved in with a guy when she felt that way. I was flattered and thankful that she felt that way, but I was as confused as she was, I told her. I didn't and couldn't live with a woman. It had gone so badly wrong the first time I'd tried it that I didn't want it to happen again. We went to bed that night with the air between us cleared of resentment, at least, if not confusion. The next day, when Jamie dropped me at LAX airport, she was in a sensible mood, if a little sulky for her.

Three weeks later I was back in LA making the Honda commercial. Grace Jones was lovely, and we listened to King Sunny Ade in her trailer as we waited for our call to the set. It was nice to be dressed well for a change, in my gun-grey, two-tone Antony Price suit, and to be made up. Getting away from the band and the road helped me feel more positive about finishing the tour. (The ad would cause something of a stir when it was released, because Grace decided that she'd bite my ear-lobe in the final shot and the director kept it in. America didn't like the sight of a beautiful black woman biting a nice young white man, it seemed.)

While in LA for the filming, I met up with Jamie, of course. She was very serious and told me that she had to be in control of everything in her life, including her relationships, in order to get through her work. While I understood, there was still no way that I could take her in my arms and say that I would be her man at home, the one that she could come back to and trust with her life. Our goodnight kiss was chaste, and, as it turned out, final.

•

At the end of April the tour ended. Jamie and I were going our separate ways, which was for the best for both of us. I was excited and very happy to be going back to Los Angeles because I had a part in a movie at last. I was to play the lead villain in a supernatural thriller called *Nomads*, written and directed by John McTiernan (he would go on to make *Die Hard*, *The Hunt for Red October* and *Last Action Hero*, among others). As I wrote in my diary,

> People may have forgotten me but that's not too bad. I wasn't too proud of the person they last saw, anyway. It's over. I'm standing.
>
> Now a new, fresh start.
>
> Don't look back.

Unfortunately, after only a couple of days on the set with Pierce Brosnan and my 'gang' (I was the leader of the Nomads), I realised that this was going to be far from my big Hollywood break. It began when the director and his wardrobe woman rejected my personally chosen outfit – I'd found a fantastic, ankle-length cattleman's duster coat in the Paramount Studios wardrobe department which, the man in charge told me, had been worn by Steve McQueen in *Tom Horn*. I'd teamed the coat with all-combat gear because my character was an ex-Vietnam

veteran. Instead McTiernan decided that I should wear a ridiculous, camp punk outfit with tails and a leopard-print waistcoat.
It seemed that he'd recently discovered punk and thought it was
the coolest thing around.

I refused to wear their clothes and stuck with my first choice
of garb, which is possibly one of the reasons why my scenes in
the movie are reduced to just one, in which I am whacked over
the head by Brosnan with a rubber tyre iron, all seen in long-
shot. Pierce was a very serious actor and really got 'into' his role.
In fact, he got so into it that despite the tyre iron being rubber,
I ended up with a gashed head – he hit me so hard that the
thin metal centre of the bar broke through the rubber. He was
apologetic afterwards, but during the filming of that scene, he
'became' his character, and I could see the fury and determination to 'kill' me in his eyes.

None of my close-ups made it into the finished film. But
then, feeling distinctly conned, I had insisted after those first
two days that the credits read 'Special Guest Appearance by
Adam Ant' as opposed to the 'Introducing Adam Ant' that had
originally been agreed by my acting agent, Michael Black.

The experience showed me how hard it was going to be for
me to 'break' Hollywood.

At the end of the shoot I flew to Montreux and met up with
Marco and the boys to perform live at a pop festival and be
filmed by the BBC. It was a great weekend and I really enjoyed
playing live, but was really looking forward to getting back to
England. I had been away for too long and missed everything
about my home.

Or rather, nearly everything.

10

ROOM AT THE TOP

'HELLO, NAN. WHAT'S UP? Are you OK? Has something happened?'

'I'm all right, dear, don't worry about me. It's your dad.' Nan's voice sounded small and frail through the telephone.

Of course it is, I thought to myself. 'What's he done now?' I asked with a big sigh.

'Well, don't get yourself too worked up, Stuart . . .'

'OK, Nan, I won't. Has he been drinking and bothering you again? I'll bloody . . .'

'No, no, not me. It's the police. He's been arrested.'

'Drunk and disorderly? Drunk driving? He hasn't hurt anyone, has he?'

'Well, no. It's awful, though.' Nan sniffed, she'd obviously been crying. This was not the first time that Les had caused his mum heartache, of course. But it wasn't like her to not come right out and tell me what was wrong. I gave Sonya, my office manager, a questioning look before I continued.

'Nan, don't worry, just tell me what he's done and where he is so I can go and bail him out.'

'Oh, you don't need to, love, he's home. I just thought that you should be told about it before anyone else tells you. He's been arrested because a thirteen-year-old boy says he made improper suggestions to him.'

The world stopped. I stopped breathing. What the fuck? my mind kept asking, spinning, unbelieving. 'Are you sure, Nan? Have they got the right guy?'

'Oh yes, dear. He called me and told me himself.' She sniffed again. I had to do something to help her, protect her, make her feel better.

'Don't worry, Nan, I'll sort it out. Is Les at home now? I'll call him and call you back later.'

The date was Monday, 17 June 1985. I had dropped into my office in London on my way back up to Manchester where I was well into a six-week stint starring in Joe Orton's *Entertaining Mr Sloane* at the Royal Exchange Theatre, the irony of which escaped me for a good while to come.

•

A year before Les was arrested, in July 1984, I'd had another very difficult conversation with someone close to me. Over a long and at times emotional lunch at Rags in London, Don and I parted company professionally. I had gone into the meeting in an angry mood, determined to let Don have it as bluntly as possible. I left the meeting, however, knowing that I liked, respected and felt close to him. He agreed that our split was for the best and let me know a few things from his point of view, too. His comments were spot-on. Even if I could only accept part of his criticism then, I now see how right he was (and why).

I would often not listen to advice from other people because I was determined that I knew best, Don told me. At best I tolerated people working for me because there wasn't enough time for me to do it all myself. He was right, of course – I did want to do everything myself, to do it 'now', and I couldn't understand why things ever went wrong. My mania drove me on constantly. Because it was all I knew, I thought that everyone should be as driven as me, that they should do as I asked when I asked. I would often vent my frustrations with the record company, tour promoters, the band and even Hollywood pro-

ducers on Don and the people close to me. No wonder he was
kind of relieved that he would no longer be managing me.

I didn't have anyone else lined up to take over, and I didn't
have time to go looking for a new manager, either. Marco and I
were busy recording songs that would become the album *Vive
Le Rock*. After my chat with Don I was determined – for a brief
while at least – that I should enjoy my life as a pop star. I had to
separate the character of Adam Ant from the me who was
writing and recording 'Strip', 'Vive Le Rock' and the other songs
in order to get a clear idea of how to develop my pop persona.
We had decided that Tony Visconti, the record producer most
famous for his work with Bolan and Bowie in the early 1970s,
would be the perfect man for the album, and he agreed to do it,
saying 'It's a very important record for me.' He needed a hit as
much as we did, and I always believed in working with people
who were hungry for success.

The recording process was not as smooth as it perhaps could
have been, with Visconti justifiably walking off at one point,
unhappy about the way the recording process was going, but by
September 1984 we had the first single, 'Apollo 9', out. I promoted the hell out of it with a video directed by Danny Kleinman, appearances on *Top of the Pops* and other kids' TV shows
and plenty of press interviews. With all of that it made number
13 on the singles charts in the UK and sales of around 100,000.
It felt like I was back, and I looked forward to finishing the
album in the spring of 1985.

While promoting 'Apollo 9' in London, I had a telephone call
from Jamie, who was in Los Angeles. She was getting married. It
was the first time we'd talked in a few months and the call came
out of nowhere, but I was genuinely pleased for her. It was what
she wanted and I wished her the best of luck.

It was in September that I also landed my first proper acting
job in the production of Joe Orton's *Entertaining Mr Sloane* at
Manchester's Royal Exchange. Mandy Donahoe had suggested
the idea, and my theatrical agent Simon Astaire and I made a

trip to see her play Estella in a production of *Great Expectations* at the Manchester theatre in November 1984. After her performance we met her director (Mandy had broached the idea to him, and he liked it), and it was agreed that the announcement about my role would be made at the end of the month. There needn't even be an audition. I returned to London and began voice classes with a private tutor, which were slotted into a schedule that included recording demos for the album, trying to arrange a UK tour for February 1985 and overseeing the enormous rebuilding job on my house in Hertfordshire.

As Christmas 1984 approached my life was full of promise. The only real disappointment came when I wasn't asked to sing on the Band Aid single. I had no idea why I wasn't asked. My mind was soon taken off that, though, when I was approached by Miles Copeland with a view to his managing my pop career. The brother of Stewart Copeland, drummer with the Police, Miles managed the Police and Sting, and also ran his own record label, IRS (who first signed REM, among other bands). He was seen as being a bit of a maverick in the business, but was respected and certainly got things done.

In March 1985 Miles and I flew to Hawaii for a working holiday. He arranged meetings with the CBS America bosses in order to impress me with his managerial skills and impress the CBS bosses with my determination. Both seemed to work. Miles, with his redneck American accent and wild eyes, had a very direct approach to business, always getting to the point of any discussion (which was usually the money) as soon as the handshakes were over.

After a few days in Hawaii we flew to LA, where Miles introduced me to his US business partners in the wittily named CCCP (Copeland, Copeland, Copeland & Powers – at the time the USSR used the same letters, CCCP on their athletes' tracksuits). He then had numerous movie studio executives come to meet me at his offices with a view to getting my Hollywood career going. We dined with Mickey Rourke and a couple of budding

Hollywood starlets while there. How could I fail to be impressed? Despite being wary (as I always was) of anyone else running my career, we struck a deal.

Back in England to prepare for the release of *Vive Le Rock*, I asked Jordan to style the cover shoot, with photographer Nick Knight. It felt great to be working with her again – I trusted her opinion above anyone else's. (We had re-recorded 'Apollo 9' completely after playing Jordan the original for instance, because she didn't like it.) She did a great job with me on the cover, and despite protests from CBS about the final image, we stuck with the photo of me stuffing bank notes into my pocket with a guitar slung over my shoulder in a kind of James Dean in *Giant* pose. I felt good about the album. Visconti had made it sound epic and very rock 'n' roll. It could almost have been a Bowie album, *circa* 1973. Unfortunately, the public didn't seem to want Bowie *circa* 1973. On release in July, a week before my appearance on Live Aid, the title track was released as a single and entered the charts at number 64. I thought it was a disaster.

But as usual there was no time to ponder for too long on one thing. At the time of the release I was preparing to play Live Aid, my love life was as complicated as ever, of course, although I was still seeing Karen regularly, and whenever away from London for more than a week missed her like hell in the same way that I'd missed Mandy a couple of years earlier, and I was in the middle of my run in *Mr Sloane* in Manchester.

'Adam Ant is a guileless Sloane without enough vicious menace,' said the *Daily Telegraph* of my stage debut. However much you say that it doesn't, it hurts. Still does. After weeks of rehearsal and self-questioning, the reviews of my first night as Mr Sloane in Orton's play were not good. They were not totally bad either, but that one remark was enough to make me think again about exactly why I was taking such a risk. It wasn't the money, by any means. I guess it was because I could do it, and because I thought that appearing in a play would teach me about acting. Which it did. But it was not any help, despite my naively thinking it might be, in getting roles in movies. However, I did really enjoy the experience, and having the chance to act with the delightful Sylvia Simms and John Southworth was not something that anyone should turn down. Director Greg Hersov did his best, and after a couple of weeks of playing it in front of an audience I think we got to be bloody good. Pity the reviewers didn't come back.

And then, during a Sunday off and a trip to London, I made that telephone call to Nan and found out about Les being arrested.

After I'd put the phone down to her, I called Les and he told me his side of the story quite calmly. Anger built slowly and surely within me as he did. I could already see the tabloid headlines – ADAM ANT'S FATHER IN CHILD SEX SCANDAL or some such nonsense. I controlled my temper and told him that I'd get him the best lawyer I could find and that he wasn't to do anything until he heard from me. He'd already spent two days in the cells being questioned by police. Hopefully he'd told the same story to them as he had me (that the boy was making it up, basically). The thing was, I didn't know if I believed him – so would a complete stranger whose business it was not to believe such a story accept his version of events?

My next call was to my lawyers, Russells. They put me on to a criminal lawyer and I made that call, too. It was the first of countless calls to lawyers, Les, Nan, Mum and other people that I'd make about this matter over the next two years – which was how long it would take to be settled.

This all happened in the middle of *Entertaining Mr Sloane*'s run, which opened on 18 May 1985 and went on for six weeks. During the run I also shot the video for 'Vive Le Rock' (again styled by Jordan) and spent Sundays, which was the only day off, in London sorting through my music business affairs. Miles Copeland went quiet on me for the duration of the play's run, as he was in Europe looking after Sting. That meant that I felt frustrated because no one (i.e. me) was in London during the week to kick ass at CBS over promotion of the *Vive le Rock* album and single. Two days before Live Aid I turned down a request from my LA theatrical agent to appear as a 'special guest' in *Miami Vice* – a cameo with a few lines – because I thought the show was too trashy. Miles, Marco and Simon Astaire all thought that I should do it, which only made me question their judgement about what was best for me.

On Saturday 13 July I played Live Aid at Wembley. It was a crazy schedule the day before. I attended three TV interviews before midday, then a film interview and a sound check at Wembley before travelling to Karen's for pasta and a sleep on the sofa. I'd had three hours sleep in two days.

I met Princess Diana and Prince Charles in the pre-gig line-up, which went well. Di looked slender-faced and dinky but skinny. She said I'd melt in my leathers. I said I had to go on early so it was OK. I found that the preparation that I'd done for the play helped me get myself together under pressure – I remembered to fold my arms when I didn't know what to do with them, and talked clearly and concisely, gazing deep into the other person's eyes.

What happened at Live Aid numbed and thrilled me far beyond my wildest dreams. Right through the whole event there was a spirit of camaraderie, total dedication and determination from everyone involved. I can't remember my performance in any detail. As we went to perform 'Vive Le Rock' I saw a sea of faces, and the air was cooler and calmer than anywhere else I'd been that day. As the boys got ready I said, 'The world is watching, let's feed it,' and then went into a crazy, dynamic whirl that left me winded by the guitar solo – but on we pressed.

And then it was over. So quickly. The crowd wanted more and so did I, but orders were orders and we sprinted off.

As I watched Sting, Bowie and Queen play their numbers it all clicked. I've only just begun, I realised. There's no point moaning, just get on with it, I told myself. Write great songs. As Bowie played 'TVC15', 'Rebel Rebel' and 'Heroes', I gaped in awe. Here was a lesson in how to be a star. How far I had yet to go.

The appearance on Live Aid was a great honour. Now we had to tour to sell the single of 'Vive Le Rock', which had only crept up to number 60 in the charts. A forthcoming live tour wasn't selling out, either. With Bogdan on drums, Chris DeNiro on bass and Marco on guitar we played two warm-up dates in Malaga, Spain, in late August, before heading to New York to promote the release of the album. I did over thirty interviews in NY and LA, including a four-hour stint on the influential KROQ radio station as DJ with Richard Blade, whom I'd got to know quite well. There was also an HBO Special being filmed at the Hard Rock Café where I got to watch James Brown perform from a distance of about five feet, which was fantastic. That night a young stand-up comedian named Billy Crystal was compère and did a great impersonation of me, which was kind of flattering and embarrassing at the same time. It was a good impression, though.

During the trip to LA I met more studio executives with Miles Copeland, and came to realise that if I wanted to make it in movies then I'd have to move to Los Angeles and live there. I knew that my pop career in England was over. I would miss it, but there was no longer any point in staying in the UK. Back in London, to play a gig in Brixton, I almost cancelled the date because of flu – the doctor who saw me told me I had a temperature of 100 degrees and should rest. I laughed at him and we played the gig. The reviews of Vive Le Rock in mid-September 1985 were terrible and depressing. They hurt, and I felt like punching one reviewer in the face (but I decided to buy a Picasso etching instead. Why not?)

At the end of that month I flew back to America and went straight to the set of The Equalizer, a hugely successful American television series starring the English actor Edward Woodward. I played the bad guy. Edward was an old friend of Sylvia Simms and so we chatted about her when we were introduced. I realised then that doing *Sloane* had been useful, not only because it gave me bona fides in the eyes of legitimate actors, but because I found myself using techniques I'd learned on stage as I played my part. Making *The Equalizer* was a great experience for me. Woodward was the consummate actor, a true professional and great to watch. The writer of the show, Joel Surnow, became a friend (he went on to write some of the TV series 24 among others), and we would eventually write a film screenplay together, titled *London Bridge*. By the end of the shoot I felt that I could no longer say, hand on heart, that music was my sole love any more. Now there was something else.

I flew back to England on Concorde ('Its elegant design is marred by the economy-style cramped seats,' I wrote in my diary. 'It's a tourist trap in the sky') full of the joys of acting. Unfortunately I had to go straight into rehearsals for an upcoming European tour with the band.

We had dancing girls, extravagant lighting and a creeper-covered metal bridge across the stage that I could run along and over for the Vive Le Rock tour. The band was hot, and for a while it looked as if things might start improving on the music front in Britain. However, the opening night at the Hammersmith Odeon was almost wrecked when the lighting rig refused to work. Once we got to the US I told myself that I'd never play live in the UK again. In less than three weeks *Vive Le Rock* sold over 100,000 albums, whereas in the UK it entered the charts at number 42 and then dropped.

However, as the tour moved across America in November (promoted by another Miles Copeland company, the FBI Agency), the album promotion dried up and I felt that CBS were not helping us as much as I'd hoped. Miles kept telling me that they were cutting back on everything (and they were; it wouldn't be long before Sony bought them), but I thought that they were just cutting back on Adam Ant. We were playing and filling stadiums from Chicago to San Diego, Houston to Albany, yet other dates were being cancelled as the album failed to make the Top 40 charts.

In mid-December Miles Copeland informed me that CBS would 'let me go' if I wanted. All I had to do was chat with their head of A&R, Muff Winwood, and if we couldn't agree on how to work together then I could leave the label. I knew before Miles put the phone down how such a meeting would go.

I was leaving CBS.

I knew that I was stone cold as a commercial prospect at that moment, but I was determined that in 1986 I would rise again and CBS would regret letting me go.

•

I spent most of Christmas and New Year in London, worrying about Les, my future and what was going to happen next. I couldn't bring myself to visit my father, but was kept up to date on what he was doing by members of the family, whom he saw occasionally.

I believed that Miles would work wonders soon, but still felt lost, with no creative thoughts or direction to take. I'd now released two failed albums in a row. A third would surely take me out of the game altogether. Leaving the music career to Miles to handle, I moved to Los Angeles at the end of January 1986 and learned to drive, passing my test in two weeks – the cars are all automatic, and the test wasn't too difficult.

In February Les was finally charged with conspiracy to commit gross indecency against a minor and was put in Brixton prison to await trial. It could take another twelve months to come to court and bail wasn't immediately set, yet I wasn't too bothered by that and genuinely didn't know whether he might not be better off in prison anyway. At least there he couldn't drink and he was constantly watched and couldn't do anything too stupid. Of course he was kept out of the general prison population because of the nature of his crime. It gave him time to think about his life. However, that was not necessarily a good thing. He told me that on his arrival on the prison wing a bunch of inmates sang 'Stand And Deliver' as he passed. They all knew who he was.

Danny Kleinman had also recently moved to LA and so I had a friend there, along with all of the 'friends' that I'd previously made. There had been a change at ICM, my acting agency, in LA and Michael Black had left. I moved to a company called Leading Artists and was represented by Anne Dollard. A lovely woman, she was smart and powerful – in fact there were a lot of powerful women in Hollywood, many of whom had more power than men in the same companies. I liked that, and I liked Anne a lot.

I started to get myself 'seen' in Hollywood, attending parties. At one of the first after I arrived I met Cher, George Michael, Harry Dean Stanton, Eric Roberts, Prince and my old mate Steve Jones, the ex-Pistol, all in the space of twenty minutes.

It was good to be away from London, making a fresh start. I was going to readings for movies, being sent scripts and even being offered parts (including the role that Bob Dylan eventually took in *Hearts of Fire*) – although none that either I or Anne thought worth taking. I felt positive and fit, was eating lots of healthy food and even started working out. All I needed was something to happen to put me back in the public eye. Then, one early morning in March 1986 I found myself back in the newspapers. Unfortunately it wasn't particularly good news or particularly helpful to my career. It was around two a.m. and I was driving home in my rented Nissan Maxima having finished writing and recording demos of new songs at a small studio on Melrose. I came around a blind corner and noticed a helicopter hovering overhead with a searchlight almost on me. As I glanced up at it a small white Honda came flying around the corner in the opposite direction and swerved to miss me, but slammed into the side of my car anyway. Since the Honda was being hotly pursued by eight police cars I didn't have to wait too long to report what had happened. I skidded to a halt and held my breath as the police cars emptied and the officers all stood in the road with their guns out in the 'fire' position, legs apart, arms outstretched. They then pulled the driver of the other car out and beat the hell out of him with their truncheons. My car was totalled and there was glass all over the place – my side window had smashed, the whole near-side was wrecked. I wasn't bleeding, but a paramedic took my blood pressure anyway. I answered every question put to me politely with lots of 'Sirs' just as Don had taught me, before packing my tapes into a squad car and being driven home. The next day, apparently, the *Sun* reported that I had been dragged lifeless from the burning wreck of my Ford Mustang, close to death. As accurate as ever.

Two weeks later I took Raquel Welch out for a very nice meal and a movie (*Out of Africa*). She had called me a couple of times and I, like most heterosexual men of my age, was in awe of her. As we walked from her hotel to my car, Raquel sighed and said, 'The last person to pick me up at this hotel was Steve McQueen. On his motorbike.' I gulped as quietly as I could and helped her into my new Honda. That remark made me feel uneasy, of course, but what can you say about a date with a legend, an icon? She was great fun, gorgeous, funny and fucking smart. We had a 'pals' night out, no more. I knew that if anything more had happened, I'd feel like a toy boy. She let me kiss her on the cheek before walking off to her hotel.

Meanwhile I found myself missing Karen a lot, but also knowing that if I flew her out to be with me I'd be trying to get rid of her after three or four days, and that wasn't fair. I saw a few women, of course, and sex was nearly always available with a number of them, but there wasn't a special one.

Not long after the date with Raquel I was back in London for a couple of weeks and saw a lot of Karen. While there, I received a letter from Les. In it he wrote about suicide. 'If I had the strength of character or will I would finish it all knowing what is yet to come.' The letter continued, 'Well I brought it on myself. God what I've done to you, Mum and the family. I have not the right to ask your forgiveness, not even the right to ask you to regard me as your father. And yet I do so write. Try in time to forgive me my dear son.'

It was a hard thing to do at the time. I'm not sure that I did forgive him. I knew that I had to make a choice between Les and my family because if I publicly announced support for my father the media would put great pressure on my relatives. I chose the family and set about protecting them as best I could. My lawyers issued a warning to all newspapers not to include my name in any reporting of Les's trial.

The best I could do for Les was to try to understand, and help as much as I was able. I understood that the beatings he took from his father must have caused some damage to his mind and body. I also knew how naive he was and how lost he felt most of the time without Doreen or someone like her to look after him. Since Doreen's death, he'd spent his days at home making model aeroplanes, and the local kids had taken to hanging around his place because they used to enjoy making models with him and he liked the company. He was vulnerable and easy to exploit.

But then, I also couldn't help but think about the drunken beatings he'd given my mother and the filthy, booze-soaked swearing, and all those times I'd stood outside pubs eating crisps while he pissed away our 'day together'. It was hard to forgive him.

At the same time I became depressed by the lack of action on the music front from Miles. CBS hadn't simply handed over my contract, of course. They were talking about releasing a *Greatest Hits* compilation album and a *Video Hits* compilation for Christmas, which was positive, but I had written five new songs (including 'Manners and Physique' and 'USSA') which I thought were strong enough to get me a new recording contract. Of course, I had to be free of the present one before I could do anything. Eventually CBS agreed that the *Greatest Hits* would see my contract fulfilled, and I flew back to America to perform with a pick-up band featuring Steve Jones on guitar and my old mate Terry Lee Miall on drums for a Disney TV special concert. It went so well that Jones suggested that we write songs together. I was flattered but still believed that Marco and I had something to offer the world as a songwriting partnership and so declined.

At the end of May, Miles Copeland called me and said that MCA had offered an advance of £250,000 for my next album. The same day Brooke Shields called and asked if we could meet (unfortunately, we never did), and I hosted the 'Rodney Biggenheimer Show' on the KROQ station as two hundred or so teenage girls turned up and rioted outside. I always got on well with the DJs and producers at KROQ and had often appeared with their DJ Richard Blade. Not long after my stint on Biggenheimer's show (he is often credited with 'inventing' disco and had put Iggy Pop and the Stooges on at his LA club in their early days), Richard asked if I wanted to make a movie with him. I agreed and spent two weeks of June in Rome making a low-budget horror film called *Spellcaster*.

That month, Les's bail was set at £5,000, so I paid it and he was released. Unfortunately he immediately started drinking. Because I was in Rome, there was little I could do except talk to my nan on the phone and call Les to try to warn him off the bottle.

One early evening, sitting in the heat of the Italian capital, I reflected that at least *Spellcaster* meant that I was acting. And I got to see a lot of Rome. The only thing needed to make my life complete at that time was a decent film role, I thought.

It would take a couple more months, but in August I got one – I was to play opposite Tom Hulce (the Best Actor Oscar winner

• A heroic pose for a CBS publicity photo.
Left to right: Terry Lee Miall,
Chris Hughes, me, Marco
and Kevin Mooney.
(CBS)

• On the 'Ants Invasion' tour, 1980,
my Walkman was probably playing
Iggy Pop.
(Allan Ballard / Scope Featues)

• Mandy
(Amanda Donahoe)
and me in a photo
booth, 1978.
(Author's collection)

• At dinner with
Jamie Lee Curtis,
1981.
(Author's collection)

Me and the delightful Diana Dors on the set of the video for 'Prince Charming'.

(Mirrorpix)

- On tour Down Under,
  we were awarded
  several Australian
  gold discs. Left to right:
  Chris Hughes, Marco,
  me and Terry Lee Miall.
  (Author's collection)

- The Ants, after Kevin,
  posing to promote
  'Prince Charming'.
  Left to right:
  Chris Hughes,
  Terry Lee Miall, me,
  Gary Tibbs and Marco.
  (Alan Ballard / CBS)

• I first met Robert De Niro on the streets of New York while he was filming *King of Comedy* in 1981. He later signed this photo for me.

(Lorey Sebastian)

• The Queen shaking my hand, while Lulu looks on. My clothes had been chosen by Liza Minnelli. It was my second Royal Variety Performance.

(Richard Young / Rex Features)

• On stage in reach of the
audience during the 'Friend
or Foe' tour in 1982.
(Mirrorpix)

• I chose to appear on the
Cannon and Ball Show because
it had 17 million viewers, 1983.
(Mirrorpix)

• A photo-call with
co-star Sylvia Simms
for *Entertaining
Mr Sloane*, 1984.
(Mirrorpix)

• Heather Graham and
me on my parents'
sofa, in their flat, 1993.
(Author's collection)

Marco and me outside the Abbey Road Studios, when we recorded *Wonderful*, 1994.

(Tom Sheehan / EMI)

A promotional shot from 2000.

(Author's collection)

for *Amadeus* in 1984), Mary Elizabeth Mastrantonio and Harry Dean Stanton in *Slamdance*.

•

The first run-through of the script for *Slamdance* took place at a small theatre named The Zephyr on Melrose. We all introduced ourselves and then read our lines. My first impression of Harry Dean Stanton was that he would be very entertaining to work with (he was). Tom Hulce was very friendly. He had the most expressive face I'd ever seen and could do incredible impressions of other people. The two female leads, though, Mary Elizabeth and Virginia Madsen, were very quiet and cool, almost whispering their lines. I got through the read-through by using my usual uptown cockney accent but felt very much in awe of everyone there. I had to play Jim, Tom Hulce's best mate. Hulce played a cartoonist whose girlfriend (Madsen) is found murdered and the police suspect Hulce of doing it. Written by the guy who had written *Android*, it's an attempt at modern film noir that almost works. I was still learning how to act when I made it, really, but was given some great advice about acting by the director, Wayne Wang (who went on to make *The Joy Luck Club* among other films), and Tom Hulce. That advice came in useful as I picked up more film and TV roles over the next three years.

Barely two weeks after wrapping *Slamdance*, I was on the Universal Studios set for a role in Steven Spielberg's *Amazing Stories* television series (I played Ted Hellenbeck, 'man of the future'). It was a kind of television version of the sci-fi-horror comic books that became hugely popular in the 1950s. I met Spielberg, who asked me what I had been doing in a professional way, and was pleasant enough. I later heard that he liked my acting in the show (he was producer), which made him one of the very few, as it turned out.

A month later I started work on an independently financed movie called *Honour Betrayed*, which was later retitled *Cold Steel*.

Written and directed by Dorothy Puzo, daughter of Mario, the author of *The Godfather*, the film is gory and wasn't a success. At one point Dorothy admitted to me that she felt helpless as the producers took over the final edit of the movie. I played a speedfreak hustler who's not exactly a bad guy, just confused. The stars were Brad Davis, who had been the lead in *Midnight Express* but whose career was sliding, and Sharon Stone, who was not a big star back then. We got along fairly well. She was cool most of the time and quite businesslike. After a few days of the shoot we both realised that this was a B-movie and wasn't going to set the world alight, so we relaxed a bit and sometimes had coffee in each other's trailer. That stopped on the morning that her boyfriend (I don't recall who he was, I'm afraid) came in to Sharon's trailer unexpectedly. We were simply sitting, drinking coffee and joking with each other, but he was clearly jealous and I left before things could become difficult.

Throughout 1986 I was in demand as an actor. While making *Slamdance* I had turned down the chance to play the lead in a David Hare play, *Knuckle*, in London because I thought that it was a backward step in my acting career. It would also have conflicted with my next movie role, which was as the bad guy in a futuristic thriller titled *World Gone Wild*, opposite the great Bruce Dern. Shot in Tucson in February 1987, the film is kind of *Mad Max* meets *Waterworld*. Set in 2087, water is the most precious commodity in the world, which has been devastated by a nuclear war. Dern plays a kind of world-weary 'good' guy who rescues an outpost of civilisation from marauding bad guys, led by me. Tucson was the perfect place to make the film. I remember huge, endless blue skies, dust-swept plains and a small, arty centre downtown with the only espresso café in the whole city. Bruce Dern was smart and opinionated, offering suggestions as to how his character should be played from the first read-through, which encouraged me to do the same. The long days in the sun while making the film turned my face a bright red, while the cold, cold nights chilled me to the bone.

The production was well financed and the sets looked great. Bruce Dern was fantastic, too. The film wasn't a box office smash, but it earned fair enough reviews and has since become a bit of a cult movie.

Back in London briefly for Christmas of 1986, I managed to get Les to agree to see a psychiatrist, who prescribed anti-drinking pills which made him sick if he drank alcohol. The Director for Public Prosecutions then refused my lawyer's request that the name Adam Ant be struck from proceedings in Les's case. It was a blow since I had been hoping to keep my name, and therefore the family, out of the papers. I wanted to protect my mum and Tony (many people thought he was my real dad and had been giving him a hard time) from the inevitable tabloid shit-storm that would erupt when Les came to court. I had to go back to the USA to make my next movie, but as the case drew nearer (it was set for 27 April 1987) I gave instructions for my lawyers to act if any newspaper attempted to implicate me in the sordid affair in any way. A couple of days after I left, Les collapsed. He had stopped taking the anti-drinking pills and started drinking. He was hospitalised for a few weeks before being released and allowed to go back to his flat.

Two weeks before the case was due to go to court, Les's psychiatric report came through and it was not good reading. There was real doubt that he'd turn up for the trial and he was seriously suicidal. He was having a breakdown, and I knew it. A week later, he was in the hospital wing of the prison. He'd had a fit of some kind and bitten almost through his tongue. Nan then told me that he'd had a couple of similar fits in the past year but no one had told me.

For the first time in thirty years I sat and cried for my father. Not because of him, but for him. I kept feeling the loneliness and desperation he must have gone through, and thought how, finding no solution, he must have cracked and withdrawn into a terrible hell of insanity.

When I pulled myself together, I called Les's barrister and all agreed that he must, if possible, make the trial, otherwise all the others accused in his conspiracy trial would blame him and make him the scapegoat for all the charges.

In the event, Les pleaded guilty but still had to attend court. By the time it came around, I was in London on a brief break from film work in LA, although I stayed away from court to avoid the publicity. It was Tuesday, 4 June 1987 and the day before I'd attended the funeral of my old friend Danny Kleinman's father. I heard the news on the radio in a black cab. 'Pop star Adam Ant's father was sentenced to two years at the Old Bailey this morning.'

I felt relieved, both because it was over and because Les was in prison and could get help there. For almost two years Les had been gnawing away at me as I tried to resurrect my singing career and further my acting one. Now it was over. At least for a while.

•

My next film role got OK reviews. Shot in July and August 1987 (a month after Les had been sentenced), it was titled *Trust Me*, and in it I play an art gallery owner whose business is not doing as well as the competition. The reason, my character James Callendar figures, is because the other galleries host only dead artists. So I find an unknown, talented artist (played by Nick Conti) and set about getting his work on my walls and then murdering him. The film was fun to make – except that the production was so strapped for cash that they kept trying to get me to wear my own clothes. The role involved doing my own 'stunts' too, in a fight scene, which went OK. The only injury I sustained was a headache.

Next up I appeared in an episode of a comedy cop show in the US called *Sledge Hammer!*, which was fun, if brief.

In early 1988 I got a lead role in a TV film called *Out of Time*.

Intended as a pilot for a possible series for stand-up comedian Bill Maher, it also included Bruce Abbott, who'd starred in *Re-Animator*. Abbott plays a cop from the future who goes back in time to help his grandfather (Maher) fight crime in present-day Los Angeles. I again played the bad guy. I was beginning to worry that I was being typecast. It was a good experience once more, but it wasn't to be repeated for some time. I kept being offered horror movie parts to play, all of which I refused. There were also offers of cameo roles in *Miami Vice* (again) and other TV series that didn't seem to be worth taking. There was also, at one point, a chance to play the Joel Grey part of compère in a stage version of *Cabaret* in London, with Toyah Willcox as Sally Bowles. I politely made my excuses and declined. By the end of 1987 I had begun to concentrate on music again.

•

When Miles Copeland had told me back in May 1986 that MCA had offered £250,000 for my next album, I thought this represented a good starting point with which to approach other labels. However, Miles knew the people at MCA very well and thought we should go with them, but also wanted to push them for more money up front. While I made movies, dealt with Les's court case and continued to write new songs on my own in LA, I found myself increasingly frustrated with Miles.

Three months later I met with him at his LA house and we agreed that we should part ways. He had a lot of other artists to deal with and I, as usual, was being overdemanding of his time and attention.

I then spent over a year trying to get new management in place. The success of the video compilation in the UK (it went to number 7 in the video charts in the autumn of 1986) was countered by CBS's refusal to release a *Greatest Hits* album after all.

I had spent that Christmas painting walls again, this time at Karen's new flat in Battersea, South London. It was the first time since 1980 that I hadn't had a single in or around the seasonal charts. Early in 1987, while back in LA, I went on the hunt for new music management. At one point I thought Ron Weisman and Bennett Freed were going to take me on, but they eventually declined, which was a shame because I thought that Bennett particularly would have been very good for me.

Strangely, feeling as if I was rock bottom but sky-high, with no ties whatsoever, I saw Peter Asher (once Peter and Gordon of 1960s pop fame), Shep Gordon (Alice Cooper's manager) and Freddy DeMann (who managed Michael Jackson and later started the Maverick label with Madonna) about managing me. None of them seemed the perfect fit, though, and the feeling was mutual. Still, EMI Publishing funded a set of demos and I continued to write songs, sporadically at least.

Then, in May 1987, Bennett Freed took me to dinner and told me that he was starting his own management company, away from Ron Weisman, and he was calling it Loot. Did I still want a manager? He'd go straight into talks to MCA if I did, so negotiations with them on a deal for me could be resurrected. In the UK, only London Records had shown enough interest in my new album to be of any concern, so I said yes on both counts.

Bennett put me to work in a studio with André Cymone, a former protégé of Prince and Paisley Park from Minneapolis, now also managed by Loot. André had made a great start to his career as a producer by producing his girlfriend Jody Watley's solo debut single 'Looking For A New Love' and debut album *Jody Watley*. Both were a big hit in 1987. André and I spent weeks at the end of that year rewriting and recording demos of songs for Bennett to play to record companies. The songs were far more dance-oriented than anything I'd tried before, but I really enjoyed creating them – in my diary I wrote that the songs sounded like 'Parliament Funkadelic meets Dean Martin'. At one point Bennett suggested that we record a cover version of the Dazz Band's 'Let It Whip' (the head of MCA in LA had suggested it to him). I really didn't like the song, but we recorded it anyway. As time wore on with no contract presented for me to sign – we began talking seriously to MCA in January 1988 about the deal, but it wasn't finally signed until February 1989 – I began exploring the idea of working with other songwriting partners.

On a hot sunny day in LA in mid-1988, while visiting Brian Setzer (formerly of Stray Cats), he suggested we go to his home studio and write a song. We did. It was OK, but never saw the light of day. Back in London in September, I lunched with Kevin Rowland (of Dexy's Midnight Runners). We both moaned about the state of pop music and agreed to write together. The resulting song, 'If You Keep On', did make it on to my next album.

At the time, Marco was producing and playing with a band that had been formed by Kevin Mooney, named Max. Marco also worked with Sinead O'Connor, and it wouldn't be until 1989 that he and I got together as a songwriting team again.

In 1988 I found myself in the odd position of auditioning for British record companies. Bennett made appointments with half a dozen London-based record companies so that I could meet them and play the new songs. It was a depressing few days. One of the companies rescheduled and then cancelled the appointment. Two others passed within twenty-four hours of the meeting. Eventually the English division of MCA picked up the UK deal, but not before I'd been rejected too many times by companies that I vowed would regret it.

In the summer I was back in my hometown feeling as if the previous eight years hadn't happened. In order to keep myself busy I painted more of Karen's flat in Battersea, painted my Primrose Hill flat and contemplated doing over my godmother's council flat. Marco joked that I'd become 'Andy Mann' again when I turned up at his place to paint his back bedroom. I wasn't doing it for money, I was thrashing around desperately trying to keep busy, keep working at anything.

Thankfully, in the spring and early summer of 1989, Marco, André and I finally got to record and mix my fourth solo album, *Manners and Physique*. André played or programmed everything except the guitars, which Marco played. André also produced the album. Apart from backing vocals by Melanie Andrews, it was a three-man job and all of us were more than happy with the finished product. We just had to hope that the public felt the same. It was a very different sound for Adam Ant, so it seemed fitting that it would be released at the beginning of a new decade.

•

The years 1987 to 1989 were not particularly good for me. The movies that were released (*Trust Me* and *Slamdance*, notably) were not bad, but by 1988, and after the sad death of my acting agent Anne Dollard in a riding accident, I was not being offered any decent film or stage roles. I recall rejecting one offer to star in a stage version of *Around the World in Eighty Days* in London in the spring of 1988, and another to play Charles Manson in a biopic a year later. I had no record deal, and for two years no manager, either.

So for the three and a half years I filled my time trying to 'work', despite not having any. I read countless books, many of them biographies, and saw hundreds of movies. I told myself that it was all 'research' for the numerous screenplays that I was either writing or about to begin.

I wrote and then rewrote one screenplay, *London Bridge*, three times with Joel Surnow and three times it was almost made. In the end, despite being optioned by such legendary directors and producers as Hal Ashby and Hemdale, it was abandoned by both of us. I also researched and made lots of notes on a possible screenplay about the life and times of a Regency-era boxer from London named Daniel Mendoza, and had another idea about London-based gangsters in a screenplay that I titled *Piccadilly*, neither of which was finished.

After moving to Los Angeles in 1987 I had become interested in motorbikes, and in my typical manic fashion bought three before I could ride properly – a Harley-Davidson Heritage Soft-tail, a 1965 Triumph Bonneville and a 1959 BMW R50. I was inspired to buy them after taking a test ride along the Pacific Coast highway one beautiful spring day in early 1988 on a Harley. I only ever rode the BMW properly (it had the smallest engine at 500 cc), but spent hours cleaning and mucking about with the other two, which I also spent ridiculous amounts of money on having rebuilt. After eighteen months of oil spills in my garage and a slight accident when trying to start the BMW one day (which saw me dragged along the road for a hundred yards or so on my face), I sold the lot.

Before the move to LA I had hired a new accountant in London, Richard Cohen. Over the next three years I gave Richard a lot of work and spent a lot of time on the telephone to him, badgering him to sort out my many and various money situations. I had 'investments' all over the place, and I had bills coming in constantly from the work still being done on my Hertfordshire house, Luxe, which I also asked Richard to put up for sale. Once it was sold, I bought my nan a house in Cookham to be near her sister. I also made sure that Les wasn't told anything about it. I didn't want him troubling her when he was released, which was to be in the summer of 1989. Then I bought myself a house in Los Angeles. This was despite the fact that every three months I would decide that London was where I belonged, and not LA.

Slowly and surely I slipped into a period of depression during those years that was dull and numbing. I knew that my not working was making me ill. At Christmas 1988 I wrote in my diary:

Would it feel different if I were signed and working? Probably yes. Should I go back to London and watch TV to realise how much I've let slip? How much of a distant memory I've become? The continued effort (through the fan club, fanzines etc.) daily to assure people that I am 'recording my new album', out next year, is a charade and I know it. But some mechanism forces me to do it. I can't give up, it's all that I have that doesn't answer me back. I don't have to worry about it, just do it. It's a long-shot as I do nothing, but once things start happening, and the music is on tape, then the faith in myself will begin to come back.

Throughout that time I suffered from several physical ill-nesses, from eczema and the common cold to strange cramps in my neck and severe headaches. I continued to eat as well as I ever had, but because my days held no routine or actual work, I would sometimes sleep away whole days and then suffer from insomnia at night. Whenever illness or boredom got too bad in LA, I'd fly to London and stay in my Primrose Hill flat. For the first few days of peace, quiet and herbal tea in London I'd be happy and question myself on why I had moved to the West Coast of America, over six thousand miles away. I'd catch up with friends and family, eat at favourite restaurants and see old girlfriends. Invariably, though, by the fifth day in London I'd be eager to get back to LA where I was sure that work was waiting for me. Only it usually wasn't.

When working and at the height of my fame, I always had people around me. There would be other musicians, people from management, a road crew while on tour, lots of girlfriends when not making music. I would occasionally rant at people who worked for me – or girlfriends – when in one of my manic phases, but the objects of my anger were many and different. Unfortunately, during the late 1980s, Karen was the only person that I spent a lot of time with, and so she bore the brunt of my anger. Our relationship became a cycle of emotional show-downs, recriminations and making up.

By 1988 Karen and I had been seeing each other on and off for five years. After a particularly awful and tear-filled split and make-up in early 1988, Karen began suggesting, first that we get married, and then that we live together in Los Angeles. I was as resistant to the idea as I'd ever been. Karen didn't raise the marriage question more than once, but occasionally she'd stop me in my tracks by asking, 'Why can't we live together?' Why indeed, I thought. Because Adam doesn't want to, my love, I answered myself. It was not her fault, but I knew that it would end in tears if so serious a decision were to be made during such an indecisive era.

And yet, when I began looking for a house to buy at the end of 1988, I asked Karen to come to LA and help me to find one. I found myself thinking about having kids with her one minute, but then remembering what had happened when I was married to Eve, and then getting angry at Karen for putting me in that position. Still, I began to write 'we' in my diary during the search for a new house. In December, Karen arrived at a house I'd bought in Meadow Valley Terrace, Los Angeles, with a box full of Airedale puppy (christened Elvis) and a plan to become an actor herself. Over the next twelve months our relationship changed enormously. In January 1989, barely three weeks after she'd arrived, I wrote, 'Karen and I live together but I don't feel any desire to kiss or cuddle her whatsoever. She's a housemate helping me to settle in.'

When Marco travelled to LA to work on *Manners and Physique* with me, he stayed at the house. He and Karen didn't get on, and there was an air of hostility between them. They wouldn't talk to each other unless I was in the room. I was rapidly falling out of love with her, and that was a shame. I began to pretend that everything was fine between us as much as I could, and poured all of my frustration about our affair and the mess that she and Elvis were making in the house in my diary. I'd be perfectly nice to her in person when I could manage it. There were still times when I couldn't control myself, and I'd become cold, distant and brutally honest about her and us. Naturally it was upsetting for Karen, to say the least, and soon after an argument I'd apologise and we'd go back to a kind of bliss for a couple of days before my resentment about her 'cramping' my life would begin to build up again. How or why she stuck it out with me for so long I don't know, but by the summer of 1989, after the addition to our 'family' of another Airedale (a female, named Alfie), I'd begun to notice that Karen was spending a lot of time out of the house, despite not having any work to go to. She would occasionally get a choreography job that took her to other cities or states, but for the most part she was taking acting classes in Hollywood and remained in our house when I travelled to London. I began to suspect, and even hope, that she was seeing another man.

Then, on a visit to London during that summer to make the video for 'Room At The Top', with Danny Kleinman directing and Jordan styling, I rediscovered my libido with another woman, ironically also named Karen. One night, having entertained the new Karen in London, the telephone rang at three a.m. and Karen in LA's voice filled my fuzzy head. I was cool and off-hand with her, and after the shortest possible conversation said goodnight.

The next day, over lunch with my old friend Steph, she told me that I had to call Karen in LA and ask her to leave the house before I got back. I could then make a new start and get on with promoting the album, which had been set for a January 1990 release in America. I couldn't do it, though. I was focusing intently on getting back to the top of the charts. My desire for success was all. A painfully honest entry in my diary of summer 1989 shows how much I wanted the new album to succeed where *Vive Le Rock* had failed.

I'm disgusted at my chronic jealousy of others less talented than myself on MTV or in films. So like some bitchy brat I cry +

kick + scream for attention. 'Love me – I'm great,' is my demand from everyone. It's terrible, disgusting. But it drives me on. I know these three years have been a test, and although right now my stamina seems low, it's all in the mind. Reality is something else, of course, and I can't accept defeat the way I suspect many feel that I should after the decline of *Vive Le Rock*. I'm not an actor or a rock 'n' roll star, I'm Adam Ant. Whatever that might be.

Karen became the only person that I could vent my anger and fears on. When I wasn't preparing myself for the new battle with the press, record company and public to make *Manners* and 'Room At The Top' a hit, I was trying to drive her away. After almost exactly six months of living together, Karen came home one night to Meadow Valley Terrace from I didn't know where, late and clearly unhappy. She asked me if I loved her, and I said no. After a couple of hours arguing she packed her bags, kissed the dogs and left the house. I could feel the same sense of desperation coming over me as she packed that I'd felt when Mandy had declared our relationship over, but I fought it back. I didn't try to stop her leaving. The next day I cleaned the house from top to bottom and then invited another woman over for dinner. I was in strict training for the coming musical fight, and part of that training was regaining my powers of seduction.

Over the last days of summer that year I began to feel like my old self again. I worked out three times a week, started seeing different women and tried not to think about Karen at all. But, just as it had been in the past, as soon as I didn't see her, I began to want her again.

In the autumn she came back to live with me, and two weeks later we were right back where we'd been before she'd left, the only difference being that I had turned thirty-five, I was working, and 'Trust Me' had been released to good reviews in

America and the UK. I'd also got myself a new acting agent, Steve Lovett of Harris and Goldberg, all of which meant that I was feeling more optimistic and less depressed than I had in years. When I spent the end of that year in London giving interviews to promote the release of the new album, they went well and I found myself in demand for the first time in ages. My photo appeared in the national newspapers – without critical stories accompanying them. The new decade couldn't start soon enough for me.

•

In January 1990 I could feel that my confidence was returning as 'Room At The Top' went into heavy rotation on various American radio stations and the video was finished. At home, Karen and I were friendly enough with each other even if we no longer made love regularly or with any real emotion. My confidence turned out to be well founded. Amazingly, 'Room At The Top' went into the Top 30 in England, eventually peaking at number 13. Despite initial resistance from MTV over the video, as the dance mix began climbing the dance charts in America they put it into light and then medium and finally heavy rotation and I had a hit there, too. The video also made the Top 20 MTV chart.

I went to London in late February and was in demand from the newspapers and magazines for interviews. It seemed to me that the journalists who came to interview me were a bit younger than I remembered, and they were all very courteous and positive about the record. It struck me that they might well have been fans five years ago, and in general the pieces that appeared were positive.

So the first half of 1990 was spent in a whirl of work activity. MCA America decided that they should follow up on the success of 'Room' by rushing out the next single, 'Can't Set Rules About Love'. In between making personal appearances across the country on what were called 'track dates' (I would mime to a backing tape in odd places like school gyms, a practice that had made Tiffany a huge star in America), I worked on the ideas and then made the video. I flew around America, from St Louis to Chicago, Texas to Los Angeles and New York to Minneapolis, making appearances, meeting new people and working the single and album hard. Michael Cox, who worked for Bennett, travelled with me and we became firm friends – which was something that Bennett would eventually come to resent. Because I was busy and having sex again I felt strong and positive. Being a hit helped a lot.

The album went on to sell 400,000 copies in America and made the Top 30, while 'Room At The Top' made the Top 20 (and Top 10 on the dance charts).

Almost as if they had been surprised by the success of 'Room At The Top', MCA fluffed the release of 'Rules'. It peaked at 47 in the charts and then dropped after a couple of weeks. 'Room' was still being played across the country and it seemed as if no one noticed that 'Rules' had come out, so MCA agreed to a $130,000 budget to make a new video for another single, 'Rough Stuff'. That was a whole $130,000 more than they'd paid for the videos to either 'Room' or 'Rules'. It meant they believed in me, which was fantastic. They also admitted that they had been wrong to release 'Rules' so quickly. Danny Kleinman and I worked on ideas for the 'Rough Stuff' video in May and arranged to make it in London during June.

Meanwhile, after almost three months of constant promotion, I returned for a two-week stay at my house in LA with Karen. It was not a happy reunion. The phone rang almost constantly and hardly ever for me. That annoyed me, but at the same time I realised that she had to make a life for herself without me being there. We rowed almost constantly for the whole time before I flew to New York on my way to London.

In New York in early June, I made an appearance at the first

International Music Awards and met 'Downtown' Julie Brown, a
gorgeous MTV presenter who was just beginning a film and
music career. The daughter of a Welsh mother and American
airman father, she had grown up all over the world at various
US airforce bases. She was smart, very funny and beautiful. We
shared a limo to the after-show party and got on well enough to
make a later date for when I returned from England.

While in London to make the 'Rough Stuff' video, my life
began to go wrong again, however. I felt shattered and completely listless. The shoot was slow and hard work, involving
days of rehearsal in a small dance studio in Docklands before
getting to the sound stage. After the wrap, and on return to Los
Angeles, I reflected on the thirty or more track dates that I'd
made in the past three months, plus the press and radio interviews and the video-making. I was thirty-five years old with a
dodgy knee (which had begun to swell up again) and should
know better than to try and push myself the way I had when I
was twenty-one.

However, being back in the charts meant that I was back in
demand – from all directions. Harris and Goldberg, my theatrical
agents, were getting requests for me to read scripts and read for
film parts for the first time in almost two years. MCA decided
that I should have a new album ready for release in January
1991 (it was almost August 1990 at the time), and so I
approached a bunch of different producers to work with and
received positive feedback from Cameo's Larry Blackmon and
Chic's Bernard Edwards. Marco was finishing up a tour with
Sinead O'Connor but would be able to come into the studio
towards the end of the year.

Earlier in the summer I had been approached by a video
production company called Propaganda about becoming a pop
video director for them. Why not? I asked myself, and signed
on. (In the event I made just one for them (for Information
Society). It would take three months of my time, from January

to March 1991, and sink without trace, having caused me no end of sleepless nights and annoying meetings with MTV who rejected it after seeing a silent thirty-second rough cut!)

In September I began writing new songs with Bernard Edwards in New York. (They sounded like Bad Company meets Chic, I noted at the time.) And after a false start, when I spent two frustrating days in Miami waiting for Larry Blackmon to call me (his manager was fighting for a better deal for his client from MCA at the time), the Cameo man and I also wrote two songs later that year. In October I turned down a part in a television series that would have meant a five-year contract, and agreed not to renew my contract with Harris and Goldberg soon after. The only parts that they'd ever been offered for me were for low-budget, horror and sci-fi C-movies. Instead I signed with CNA on the understanding that I would be represented by Ellen Drantch. She was a fabulously tall, elegant woman, very beautiful and only in her late twenties, but she got things done. She commanded respect from studios and directors. Maybe it was because she looked like a six-foot-tall Jessica Rabbit, but whatever she had, it worked for her clients and I wanted to be one.

Around that time Bennett agreed to give Michael Cox a more senior position in the company, which was good news for me. Bennett had just lost his first star act, Jody Watley, and had some rebuilding of his reputation to do. I was his major act now, and expected to be treated in the right way – which as far as I was concerned meant getting a better deal out of MCA for the next album in terms of an advance. Unfortunately, despite a great video, 'Rough Stuff' had only been a hit on the Billboard dance charts and not made it into the main Top 20. So it was still all to do again. Yet I had scored another hit, which at times over the last few years I had seriously doubted would ever happen again. I pressed ahead with new songs, and by the end of 1990 had exhausted all the lyric ideas that I had scribbled down over the previous three months. But I still had six almost finished songs that I could commit to tape, with Bernard producing, in the spring of 1991.

•

During all the time I was working properly again in the second half of 1990, my relationship with Karen had deteriorated. If it hadn't been for the dogs, we would not have had anything to talk about. Finally, at the end of November, she had packed her bags and returned to London for good. We hadn't agreed that it was over, but I knew it was. Or thought it was. Julie Brown and I had begun a very enjoyable and passionate relationship in which we met whenever she could get to the West Coast or I could get to New York. It wasn't all lovey-dovey between us, though and as 1990 turned into 1991 and winter faded, so did contact between Julie and me. Once again I'd become involved with a woman who wanted a faithful boyfriend, and I couldn't be that. My libido had awakened with my renewed success, and I found myself enjoying affairs with new women and revisiting old flames, especially once Karen had left.

And then, once again, life slowed up. Bernard Edwards proved to be a painstaking producer and took weeks over each track before handing over the tapes. I landed a role in a Dennis Hopper movie titled Midnight Heat in May of 1991, but filming didn't begin until late July or August. To prepare myself I began attending acting classes in LA with Harry Mastrogeorge. It was an eye-opening experience from the start – not least because Ray Liotta was also in the class. Harry was an original, and didn't follow any 'method' except his own. He gave us all manner of things to read (including Samuel Beckett and Dylan Thomas). We would take turns to learn a part and then read to the class. It was clear that Liotta was streets ahead of everyone else. He believed totally in his role, no matter what it was. In my heart, I knew that I wasn't a great actor (although I would reveal that only to my diary at the time), but I hoped to learn enough from Harry's class to get better at it.

Harry's classes became the closest thing I had to work during the summer months of 1991. He became a kind of father figure to me, and he seemed to appreciate the fact that I liked to work hard on the scenes that he set me, so would often spend time outside class going over things with me. 'Treat the text as if it were your Bible,' he always told his class. 'Forget all that method business and learn the lines that were written.' I appreciated that enormously, because I didn't 'get' method acting, but enjoyed really getting to understand what the writer had created.

With the album on hold while Marco and I waited for Bernard to get everything ready to finish, all I had to do was garden and clean up the house. My lawn became an obsession to me. I would rise as early as possible and clip, reseed and care for it, trying to resuscitate it after two years of Elvis's and Alfie's antics. After breakfast I would spend time writing what would become the first few chapters of this book on my Apple Mac, or tidying the house and working out. I'd call London to arrange my business affairs as soon as I could, and then meet lovers or friends.

My mood was lightened briefly that summer by meeting one of my true heroes, Muhammad Ali. After a two-hour wait in line at a bookshop to get my book signed, I finally met him. There he sat, relaxed and calm, with a great sense of serenity and joy about him. I shook that huge hand, which was now soft, and looked into his brown eyes, and they seemed to look straight through me. Clearly his mind is alive, and he knows that his nerves don't react to his brainwaves. I gabbled happily, telling him how I'd seen all of his fights as a kid on TV in London, to which he replied, 'And now you're all grown-up.' Then he pulled me slightly toward him and put his cheek against mine. I felt elated, almost fit to drop. He's a great man, undoubtedly the greatest I've ever met. I remember thinking, 'That was a day to tell my grandchildren about.'

Inspired by meeting Ali, and after a night out with the actor Tim Roth, I set about developing my role in *Midnight Heat*. I played a biker named Danny, who I decided had to be on the edge, half mad and half ecstatic, as if he was making a film and none of it was actually happening to him. I could almost have been assessing myself. I saw nobody for two weeks before filming began and learned the part and my lines. As ever, being alone made me uncertain and panicky. As I wrote at the time, 'This time has left me vulnerable emotionally. Feelings come and go quicker than usual, mood swings and self-doubt for a second or two. It shakes me and I have to snap out of it. Sleeping is just a symptom of this.' Finally, in July, I began my five days' filming with the bit that worried me most – riding a Harley-Davidson on dark, wet roads. It went well. All of my work on the film had to be done at night, which meant that I'd sleep during the day, but it was a routine I'd become used to anyway. Poor Lori Depp (actor Johnny's ex-wife), a great friend who agreed to be my PA and help out with my hair and make-up, took a little longer to get used to it, though.

The work 'cured' my depression. To be working felt soothing to me, and I loved arriving home as dawn broke, being greeted by Elvis and Alfie, drinking coffee as the neighbourhood awoke, and slipping into sleep happy, knowing that I had things to do when I awoke.

Soon after finishing my work on the film I met with Bennett and Michael Cox and sketched out my work for the rest of 1991. I flew to London in late August and wrote new songs with Marco, demoing them at a small studio with Leigh Gorman, ex-Bow Wow Wow bassist, both playing and 'producing'. While there I couldn't resist seeing Karen again, and, horribly and inevitably, we declared our love for each other and I dreamed about us having kids together. Of course, back in Los Angeles two weeks later I regretted it and buried myself in work. I was offered the lead in a Vampire movie titled *The Reluctant Vampire* (eventually retitled *Love Bites*), which would mean returning to London briefly straight away to record all of my vocals for the album with Marco and Lee so that I could begin shooting in October in LA.

Realising that taking the role would mean an extremely heavy schedule for the end of the year, I took it.

While in London I finally told Karen that we could not be with each other, that we weren't right together, that I loved her when she wasn't there and resented her when she was. She agreed to give it a break but to 'see what happened'.

As the shoot for *Love Bites* began, LA suffered a heatwave that meant it was 110 degrees in the shade. I wilted. I felt sluggish, unable to do anything and almost slurring my speech. Thoughts of Karen flooded my brain with regrets and guilt. The thought of having children and owning a Georgian house in London and enjoying a family life haunted my dreams. Yet I knew that it was over and that we could never have that. I'm not sure how I got through the shoot, but it was almost over when I got news that MCA had refused to pay for a final mix on the album. They wanted to hear all the tracks before agreeing to finish it, they said. I demanded that Bennett pay for the mix and fuck MCA. Bennett tried to sort it out, and after a week told me it was OK and we could finish. It had to be done soon or we'd miss the chance to release it in the first quarter of 1992, which was the plan.

Three weeks later I began a new love affair with my leading lady in *Love Bites*, the delightful Kimberley Foster, formerly a star of the *Dallas* TV series. She was a typical California girl – petite, blonde, blue-eyed and in love with the LA life of dog-walking in the surf and power-breakfasting with producers, brunching with pals and dining with lovers. We flirted at the wrap party, which happened to be on the day before my thirty-seventh birthday.

Kimberley was the best present I'd had in a long while, and embarking on a relationship with her took my mind off Karen and the problems with MCA. We were like teenagers together, always kissing, holding hands and smiling at each other. For three weeks we had fun, in New York for a weekend, in LA at the beach where she lived, and at my house. Then, while Kimberley was in Texas working, I got another real shock. MCA announced that they were dropping me from the label and the album wouldn't be released. In truth I had kind of expected it. The company had new Japanese owners who seemed to be releasing any non-Gold-status artists from their contracts, and my first album hadn't quite made it. I was gutted by their decision, but equally determined that we'd take the tapes and find another label for it. Bennett assured me that he thought it was the best album I'd made and that he'd be able to sell it to someone else, so I set him on doing that.

In the meantime, I agreed to act in a small-time production of Steven Berkoff's West at an arts theatre in LA. I hadn't been on a stage for six years and was dying to do it. The rehearsals were only a couple of weeks and the play would only have a few performances, but it kept me busy during the day, while Kimberley's visits kept me busy at night.

Unfortunately, rehearsing the play caused my leg to swell up again. I sought professional help and my doctor put me on a rigorous new treatment, which involved floating in a pool of water with my legs anchored to the bottom and small electrical currents being fed to the knee through small pads. It seemed to work, but slowly, which meant I never made it on to the stage to perform in West.

As Bennett fought over the terms for my release from MCA, which included their paying for the recording I'd done but me keeping the album, I planned what to do when I went to London in January 1992. Over Christmas I turned things over in my mind. I had plenty to sort out there, including legal problems and the fact that large amounts of money had started to disappear from my English bank account for no apparent reason. I also knew that I had the best album I'd made in a long time ready to go. I was determined to get back out there and be a hit again, and decided that I'd go to London and act as if nothing had happened.

But of course it was never going to be that simple.

11

WONDERFUL

THE GUN, A SMITH & WESSON .38 SPECIAL, sat at the back of my bedside drawer. Next to it lay a box of shells. Made of blue steel with a hard black grip handle, the gun had been loaned to me by a friend after a stalker, Ruth Marie Torres, had begun to show up at my Los Angeles house screaming, ranting and raving, in late October 1992.

Now it was nine months later, and I lay in my bed sweating, terrified and hearing the gun call to me, 'Go on, load me. Squeeze the trigger and it'll all be over.'

If I wasn't such a coward, I told myself, I would get it out, load it and blow my brains out. But I couldn't. Instead, I left the house when the call of the gun became too loud and too insistent. Some mornings I'd drive, shaking, anywhere – to a coffee shop or a parking lot by the ocean. Once there I'd just sit and cry my eyes out for I didn't know how long.

What the fuck was wrong with me?

Despite my pressing problems in London in January 1992 – the mysteriously dwindling bank account with almost £60,000 missing from it, plus the loss of my record deal – I had not gone there. Instead I had remained in Los Angeles so that I could have another knee operation to remove another piece of cartilage.

During the recovery time in February, I had brooded on my

musical career and had numerous conversations with my manager Bennett Freed about what to do next. These discussions culminated in his resigning. The next week I discovered that my former lover Karen and actor Michael Praed had become a couple and were planning marriage. I couldn't help feeling upset that Karen was moving on with her life. Not long after, I suffered a different kind of shock that had nothing to do with Karen, when my accountant told me that my English bank account was missing several thousand pounds. Things were going to Hell around me. There was no way of getting my money back from someone that I had regarded as a good and trustworthy friend. If it hadn't been for the joy of sex with two beautiful women and the various acting roles that I was being offered, I feel certain that depression would have hit me sooner than it did.

Throughout March and April I was occupied with a TV show, *Tales from the Crypt*, directed by John Frankenheimer, the man who had directed the original *Manchurian Candidate* starring Frank Sinatra, and a play, *Be Bop A Lula*, about Eddie Cochran and Gene Vincent, which I produced but did not act in. Then there was Kimberley, my actress girlfriend, and Cheri, a gorgeous masseuse who had become a friend and lover, although in late March Kim and I had the inevitable Big Talk, with her wanting more commitment from me and me being unable and unwilling to give it.

When he heard that I no longer had a manager, Miles Copeland called me. We met and talked, and I agreed we could work together again as long as he hired Michael Cox, who had worked for Bennett and accompanied me on the US promo tour for *Manners and Physique*, to be my personal manager. He said OK and began shopping for a new deal for me.

With Miles taking care of the music, and armed with the songs that Marco, André Cymone, and Bernard Edwards and I had recorded for what would have been the second MCA album (tentatively titled *Persuasion*), I concentrated on other things. Determined that *Be Bop A Lula* would be a hit, I threw all my energies into it. It was not easy, and I probably made mistakes along the way, but the play ran for over a month on the LA fringe and was adjudged a hit. When it ended in late April I went back to brooding over Karen, and thinking that I'd missed a chance to be a husband and father – both things that, at times, I wanted, or thought I wanted, very much. I didn't know why, though.

In mid-May I went to London and started to write songs with Marco that would eventually appear on another new album (the first song we wrote was titled 'Wonderful'). While there I met with Karen, which helped me to fully accept that the relationship was over. Within a year she would have a child with Michael, and they eventually had another together.

Back in LA in early June, I worked out a lot, building my leg muscles, getting into shape. I resumed my affairs with Kim and Cheri, finding solace in sex. Things were going well until Kim and I visited Vegas (my first time) in July and had a major falling out. Gambling didn't seem as much fun to me as it did to her. I minded losing hundreds of dollars on the turn of a card or wheel, yet she – like everyone else there – found it great fun, so I retired to our hotel room and watched TV as she and the friends that we had travelled with enjoyed the casino. On our return to LA, Kim refused to make another date and we parted. I knew that it was over, but without truly knowing why.

My mind was taken off her when I landed a part in the TV series *Northern Exposure*, which took me to Seattle for three days later that month. Just before I left, Miles Copeland informed me that he had an offer for my next album from EMI. He also suggested that I record 'Wonderful' as a duet with Kim Wilde or Vanessa Paradis, which I didn't agree with. However, I arranged to fly to London after finishing *Northern Exposure* in order to get more songs written with Marco.

In London Marco introduced me to Boz Boorer, guitarist and musician, best known as a former member of rockabilly band

the Polecats and as a guitarist for Morrissey. Marco and Boz –
a great musician with a photographic memory for old singles, a
great quiff and lots of rockabilly clothes, even today – had been
working on songs together, and I was soon working with them,
too. We seemed to hit it off, and along with drummer Dave
Ruffey started playing old and new songs with a view to touring
to promote a new album release in 1993. Miles was still insisting
on my recording a duet, though, so I suggested that Morrissey
and a I duet on Johnny Thunders' 'You Can't Put Your Arms
Around A Memory'. Sadly it never went further than the suggestion.

While in London I discovered that Miles was talking to EMI
about a deal for me that included my being released through
IRS in America, which I was not happy about because IRS
was Miles's own record label. I wanted him to get a deal with a
big American label. It would prove to be a bone of contention
between us for some while. Meanwhile, Marco and I decided
that the next album should be completely new songs, and that
Persuasion (the never-released MCA album) was best forgotten
altogether. My month in London passed pleasantly enough, but
by the end of September I was ready to return to LA, and did so
with high hopes for both acting and music.

Which is when Ruth Marie Torres came knocking.

•

The first time Ruth Torres turned up at my house she rang the
doorbell and asked if I liked the flowers she'd sent. There had
been a lot of them; sometimes she sent them two or three times
a day. Didn't I remember her, she asked? I told her I'd never
seen her before in my life. Then she told me that she was a
virgin and was waiting for me, waiting to become my wife. She
stood there, her big brown eyes staring out of her gaunt face.
She was twenty-four, painfully thin, with hair that hung straight
down to her waist, and wearing a tiny miniskirt. Even that first

time I felt spooked by her, but asked her calmly to go away and closed the door on her unblinking eyes.

After that things were never civil between us. She'd turn up at my house at all times of the day and night, stand on the front lawn and shout or scream at me when I refused to answer her. She left cakes that she'd made for me on the doorstep, unless I was out, and then she'd crawl into the kitchen through the dog flap and leave the cake on the table with a note which read, in a big scrawl, 'Get the whores out of the house.'

I went to the police and they suggested that I keep a log of things she did and get back to them if she ever did anything dangerous. Apparently, breaking in and leaving a cake was not considered dangerous enough.

Torres came over more than forty times in a three-day period in late November 1992, leaving a garbled written note each time. After she smashed a glass birdfeeder outside both the front and back door (the glass of which could have cut the dogs badly had they run over it) and wrote a big 'Fuck off' in chocolate sauce on my neighbours' car, I decided to act. According to a lawyer friend, I needed visual evidence of her behaviour to get the police to do something, so, with Danny Kleinman and my friend Lori Depp as witnesses, I videotaped a Torres visit.

Seeing the camera, she came to the front door and talked directly into the lens, telling it her sad life story. As she spoke – of her poor upbringing and the murder of her best friend from high school – her mood changed from calm to angry to raging. All the time, as she spoke, she took off different items of clothing until she was down to a miniskirt and bra. There I ended the recording. She seemed happy that I'd filmed her, and left, waving and smiling as she did.

Armed with the tape, I finally managed to get the authorities to act and she was arrested with bail of $100,000 set. But after a couple of weeks in custody she was out, though charged not to come anywhere near me. Certain that she would break that restriction on her, I moved into a friend's house for a couple of weeks and sent the dogs away, too. It was just as well I did, because, sure enough, Torres returned, as the neighbours reported to the police a few days after her release.

She was arrested again and this time kept in jail until a trial could be held in January 1993. I didn't attend the trial – there was no need to, since the log of her visits that I'd kept and handed over to the police, along with the video footage of her shot by Danny, meant that there was a strong enough case to convict her. My presence at court would only attract media attention, and she'd had enough of that as it was.

So finally I went back to my Meadow Valley house in mid-December, and had a big, strong metal fence erected around the perimeter of the grounds and shutters put on the windows. Yet, despite knowing that Torres had been imprisoned and banned from coming within ten miles of me, or my property, for four years at least – and that California had changed their anti-stalking laws because of my experience with her – I could never feel completely happy there again. Which is why I kept the gun in the drawer by my bed, and why, on those hot summer mornings of 1993, as I lay in bed scared of everything and nothing, those shutters seemed to be closing me in, preventing me from doing anything except shake with fear. These attacks were the worst I'd had since 1976. And they weren't the worst that I would face.

•

Two weeks before Christmas 1992 I was asked to play an acoustic set at the Universal Ampitheatre in LA for KROQ radio station's Acoustic Xmas. Marco flew over and rehearsed with me for a couple of days before, and we played on the second night, a Sunday. I was nervous at first, but the reception from the audience was great, and I soon relaxed and enjoyed the performance immensely. As the Los Angeles Times reported, 'Making his first concert appearance for nearly five years, the

English singer-turned-actor seemed genuinely overwhelmed by the wild response of young fans who had sat patiently through the three preceding acts on the bill.' It was a good review and, combined with the performance, filled me with optimism for the new year and new album.

That Christmas was one that I wouldn't forget. On the invitation of Cheri, who was a good friend of his daughter, I found myself spending Christmas Day at Jack Nicholson's house. He was dressed immaculately in a green shirt and tie and dark trousers. The picture of a perfect host, he leaned across a small coffee table in his immense living room, in front of the Picasso hanging over his fireplace (I'd passed a Jean Dufy in the hallway), arched those eyebrows, shook my hand, and said, 'Hi, Adam, I'm Jack.' I smiled and felt better than I had since walking on set at Universal for the first time. I passed much of the day in awe of this great actor whom I'd seen in *A Few Good Men* only a couple of weeks earlier. Of course I couldn't help but gush about how great I thought he was in it. He took all the praise graciously. Jack was a great host, attentive and always flashing *that* smile. Knowing that my old friend Dave Whiteing had dressed Jack for a couple of movies, I mentioned him, and we shared a few notes. The day ended with Jack asking me to bring Dave over next time he was in town. I never did, unfortunately.

In January 1993 I had a first date with a young actress who had joined my acting class with Harry Mastrogeorge. I had been almost mesmerised by her from the moment she had walked in. At first I had been a little disappointed to find that she was the girlfriend of the actor James Wood, but was encouraged when I heard a few weeks later that they had split up. Her name was Heather Graham, and she was about to change my life in many ways. With her pure blue eyes and soft, gentle smile, Heather seemed like an angel to me. She moved with a natural grace and seemed to be without a care in the world. She was beautiful, but unaffected by the effect she had on men, which I loved.

There was nothing precious about her, as there was about so many LA starlets.

We spent our first date at the Tam O'Shanter restaurant, chatting and getting on well before returning to her apartment and spending all night listening to a classical music station and talking. For the next three weeks we met for lunches, walks and dinner, always having fun and apparently liking each other. Yet I dared not make a move on her because it somehow didn't seem right – we were 'pals', it seemed. All the while I kept writing in my diary that she was almost too beautiful. Finally, she made the first move and I was gone.

On 25 January I wrote in my diary, 'A wave of joy comes over me in the shape of Heather.' I felt pure joy whenever we were together and spent most of my time thinking about her when we were apart. By the beginning of February I was sure that this was serious stuff. It didn't create the usual raging fear in my guts, accompanied by the desire to run a two-minute mile in the other direction, like other relationships had when they got 'serious'. That Heather felt the same kept me as happy as I had been for a very long time.

While we were getting to know each other, I was also planning a tour of America, playing small clubs with a band that included Marco, Bruce Witkin, Dave Barbarossa, Boz and Dave Ruffey. But while excited at the idea of playing music live again, I was also feeling that I didn't want to be away from Heather for too long. There was also the fact that I was personally paying for the tour, because there was no record company (yet) to underwrite it. Still, I felt that it was an important step forward for me to get my musical career back on track. I was also determined that this time the tour would be fun, and without having to worry about how any record release was doing, I didn't have any extra pressure on me.

After only eight days' rehearsal with the band we opened in Orange County, California, in late February. We played eight

shows back to back, including three sell-outs at the Henry Fonda
Theatre in LA, and then started a trek around America, beginning in Palm Springs. In mid-March we were snowed in, in
Atlanta, Georgia. My diary is full of my love for Heather – I was
using the word 'love' without fear. I was unafraid to admit that
I was head over heels about her, and it was getting better all the
time. I adored being with her. In her car the previous week,
when she had misheard what I'd said as 'I love you', I said I
did when asked if that was indeed what I'd said.

A week later, despite playing small clubs, some of which
didn't have dressing rooms, I was happy that as a band we were
performing well. We were a unit, together and having fun on
stage. The tour lasted five weeks, during which time I thought
constantly of Heather and wrote two or three letters a day to
her during the dull travelling bits.

When I returned to LA and Heather, I felt fit and strong
physically, and was determined to kick ass on the music front,
which meant getting the deal with EMI signed and sorted for
good. However, after four weeks in LA, during which time I
discovered that I could do nothing to hurry them along, I found
myself gardening a lot and becoming lethargic. Laziness was
always a sin to me. I hated it, not least because it usually
signalled a return of my depression.

•

In May I took Heather to London for a two-week visit. Amazingly
we spent every day together in my small Primrose Hill flat and I
loved every minute of it. I didn't feel trapped or crowded at all.
We visited my family (although not Les), friends and all my
favourite places – Chiswick House, Cookham and Greenwich
among them. The only business I managed to complete on the
trip was to agree with Clive Black, then head of EMI, that my
next album should be all new material (forget about *Persuasion*). And so I arranged to write new material with Marco and
work with a new drummer, John Reynolds (who was Sinead

O'Connor's husband and whom Marco had worked with previously). After Heather went back to LA, I spent three weeks working with them, and also squeezed in a trip to Seaford to spend some time with Jordan and her kittens, which always made me calm and happy.

During the times when I wasn't working on music in London, I began to feel tired, remote, and as if things were moving in slow motion. I put it down to missing Heather (I couldn't wait to return to LA and her arms). I was also experiencing a mounting, irrational fear in the mornings. I began to wake with fear knifing me in the guts, unable to get out of bed, where I lay stewing in my misery. All I could think about was getting away, running into the arms of Heather for love and comfort. So I did. On 23 June I flew to Montreal, where she was in the middle of making *Mrs Parker and the Vicious Circle*, directed by Alan Rudolph. In order to be there, I had blown out a part in a movie that was to be shot at the same time in LA, which naturally annoyed my agent, Ellen Drantch, but I genuinely felt that being with Heather was the right thing to do at that time. And for the first few days it was. I arrived as she had two days off from filming, and so we made love and laughed and spent every minute together. However, a couple of long days after that, during which she worked and I had nothing to do but think about my problems, I wasn't feeling as happy to be there. I felt like a spare part in her life, which worried me. But Heather was the subject of and the reason for all of the songs that I'd written with Marco and Boz in the previous three weeks, the escape from all my business and work problems. I had never felt this way about anyone before. I was determined to stay on set with her for as long as I could, which turned out to be five days.

I then decided to fly back to London to finish the songs and settle the EMI deal. Back in Primrose Hill, though, jet lag hit and I found myself unable to get out of bed through sheer bloody fear for the next couple of days. After a huge effort, I finally pushed myself into work, but then was too afraid to go to bed at night, simply because of the fear I knew I'd feel when I woke up the next day.

During my time in London I would force myself to get out of bed as soon as I awoke – usually at six-thirty – and then get on with doing things, anything. Until the things to do ran out, that is. With EMI bosses on holiday and no more songs coming together, I planned to be back in LA when Heather got there. Of course, I was putting her in the way of my fear and loathing, using her as a shield against my illness. She didn't know it, and I wouldn't admit it, but that was what I was doing. I even began to write in my diary that I could get engaged to Heather, that we could live together, get married. She was twenty-four years old and just starting to make a career for herself. I was thirty-eight and trying to restart mine, but that didn't mean I wasn't willing and wanting to give her as much help and support as I could.

Yet back in LA, after a few short days I was lying awake in my bed, alone, at six-thirty a.m., with cold sweats and the shakes.

•

When I was with Heather I felt happy and contented. When I was working, making music, I was happy. For the rest of the time between August and December 1993 I suffered terrible bouts of depression and fear. The reasons for the fear changed at different times. I was scared of losing all my money and that I didn't have the ability to make any more. I was scared of losing Heather to a leading man in one of the many movies that she was being offered. I was scared of not being able to write songs any more. Of course my fears were irrational, but I couldn't make that judgement. No one had ever told me that I was truly ill, that I couldn't help how I felt.

A stark entry in my diary for Friday, 13 August 1993, reads:

So sick of pissing about. Got to get the problem met + do something about myself. WHAT THE FUCK IS WRONG WITH ME? Shit scared of blowing my fucking brains out!

In an attempt to keep myself occupied, I hopped from LA to London several times in those three months, reworking songs with Marco and Boz when Heather was away filming. I even went on photo shoots with Heather in LA just to be doing something. She and I spent Thanksgiving that year at her aunt and uncle's farm in Arizona. Both of them are deaf, and I felt humbled by their amazing ability to communicate and get obvious joy from their life together. We had a fantastic time there, riding (I only had one small accident when a horse ran away with me) and breathing good, clean air, and I managed to sleep well and wake without the fear. But it couldn't last.

Not long after returning from Arizona, Heather and I went to Yoghurt Palace in LA, where a seemingly innocuous meeting almost floored me. Out front stood a young, mentally ill homeless guy with blond, dirty curls. He said 'Hi, Adam,' when I gave him two bucks on the way out. He looked almost embarrassed as he ate the free frozen yoghurt given him by one of the waiters (to get him to move on, I guess). He then asked God to bless me. I was shaken by his helplessness and hopelessness and was close to tears. Heather asked how someone could get so low like that, and I thought, 'I know how,' but said nothing. Back at her place that night, we talked about the homeless guy, about my fears and about our feelings for each other. Without really thinking about it, I suggested that we move in together. Not into her place and certainly not into my house in Meadow Valley, but somewhere new and fresh where we could start a life together from scratch. It would mean finding a new home for Elvis and Alfie, preferably a family with kids and a huge garden to run around in. That would be better for them than my constant running between my and Heather's places feeding them, not spending enough time with them.

Heather happily said yes to the proposal, and we agreed to think it over and make plans when I got back from my next trip to London.

A few days later, in London without Heather, on 6 December,

I finally signed a deal with EMI and arranged to release my next album in the spring of 1994, with a single ('Wonderful') released ahead of that. While it was good news, the fact that I had to hang around in London to record 'Wonderful' at Abbey Road Studios up until Christmas was not so welcome. In the end the sessions never happened because the producer, Dave Tickle, couldn't make it. So I flew back to LA for Christmas and to prepare for a one-off live show at the LA Forum as special guest on a Duran Duran date.

For three weeks over Christmas 1993 Heather and I enjoyed a blissful time, walking through the LA surf as if we were in a soppy, cliché-ridden movie. The bliss was briefly interrupted by the live show when the band and I found ourselves as the opening act (ahead of the Village People) on the bill, despite being promised a forty-five-minute spot before the headline act appeared. Our presence at the show had helped the show to sell out (it was struggling before the announcement that we'd play) as we filled the empty seats with a few thousand fans. So it was disappointing, to say the least, to be told that we had only twenty-five minutes on stage and a perfunctory sound check before that. Still, we played a storming set and raged off to collect our $20,000 fee. I had also booked us to appear at the Coachhouse in LA, where we played two sets in one night a couple of days after the Forum show and really enjoyed ourselves.

At the beginning of January 1994 I flew back to London to go into the Abbey Road studios to record my next album.

•

Abbey Road's Studio 2 was where the Beatles made so many of their greatest recordings, and it was still pretty much as they'd used it back in the 1960s. We played the songs 'live' while producer Dave Tickle rolled the tape. Tickle proved to be a calm and thorough producer throughout the recording, putting every-one at ease and coaxing the best out of us all. At various times both Michael Cox and Miles Copeland came into the studio and seemed happy with the progress we made that month.

The only slight hiccup we suffered during the recording came when Miles informed me that Clive Black, who had signed us to EMI, was leaving to join Warner Brothers. Wary of the same thing happening as had at MCA, I demanded a meeting with the new boss, a Frenchman named Jean François. Happily he said that he very much wanted to release the album and that, as a good pal of Clive Black, he had heard from him how great it was sounding.

When I had time off from recording I wrote long letters to Heather or talked with her for hours on the telephone. During one conversation she said that she really wanted us to live together and I eagerly agreed. Within days I had asked my great friend, Dangerous Jane, who now lived in Toronto, to find a new home for Elvis and Alfie. I had first met her at Camden's Music Machine nightclub in 1978, and had named her Dangerous because she had a gangster for a boyfriend at the time, so just talking to her was considered a danger to a man's health. I also talked via telephone with a couple of estate agents in LA about putting Meadow Valley on the market.

At the end of January my nan suffered an attack of angina and was hospitalised. I went down to Cookham to see her, full of worry, only to find her sitting up in bed happily joking about the food and looking more carefree than she had in years. We talked for an hour or so, and after agreeing that Les was apparently on the mend (i.e. not drinking too much) but still wasn't to be trusted, she asked if there was a chance that I would marry Heather. Without thinking about it, I said, 'Yes.' And meant it, for the first time in my life.

As February arrived, Nan seemed to be on the mend and left hospital to stay with my aunt and uncle in Cookham. Meanwhile, recording was beginning to slow down and I had more time off from the studio, which wasn't a good thing. So I flew to

Heather, and for four days we hardly left her apartment. After that I returned to my Meadow Valley house and prepared it for sale. I had rough mixes flown out to LA and took time at a studio to work on them, in between fixing the house and trying not to stay in bed for too long in the mornings, avoiding the fear. I managed it for a month.

But then I felt myself slowing down, sleeping for too long, feeling afraid of the telephone, not wanting to see anyone except Heather, not wanting to talk to anyone. I had begun to practise Transcendental Meditation – the first session had been a present from Heather – but somehow it didn't work for me. I couldn't empty my mind for long enough.

And this time there was plenty for me to do. I had been offered a part in a movie with Martin Kemp and Grace Jones that was well paid and worth doing, despite the script being decidedly B-movie (originally titled *Sailor's Tattoo*, it would be released as *Cyber Bandits* in 1995). Faxes from the UK about the album piled up on my creaking fax machine, all unanswered. I spent a few hours in the studio remastering old Adam and the Ants material, switching it from quarter-inch tape to DAT, but apart from that I spent as much time as I could with the love of my life. We spent days looking at houses to share, and eventually found one in Nichols Canyon that we agreed to rent. Then, on 21 March 1994, my beloved nan, the girl named Bill, died peacefully in her sleep at her Cookham home. Apparently she curled up on the sofa and simply went to sleep, for ever. I was devastated.

I helped to arrange Nan's funeral over the telephone as best I could, but couldn't bring myself to return to England for the service, which took place just three days after she passed away. I called Les and consoled him but he didn't seem to be as distressed about it as I was.

The day after the funeral, Dangerous Jane called from Toronto to let me know that she'd found a perfect family who would take Elvis and Alfie. And so, on the first weekend in April

1994, I put my dogs on a plane to Canada. Another part of my life was gone as I prepared for what I hoped would be a grand new life with Heather.

On 8 April we picked up the keys to our new house and drove over to see it, together. The night before, Kurt Cobain had killed himself. I wrote in my diary:

> The singer from Nirvana blew his brains out last night, leaving a note. Boy, did he have some courage.

It took another two weeks before I'd moved all of my stuff into our home. During that time I plotted the running sequence for the new album, which was temporarily titled *Slapdash Eden*, and finished doing up Meadow Valley in order to sell it. By the end of April Heather and I had unpacked all of the boxes and were settling in. At the beginning of May I started filming *Sailor's Tattoo* (or *Cyber Bandits*) in downtown LA. The location meant that I could be home every night or day off. Things were great and I didn't once feel cramped, suffocated or angry at living with someone else.

I enjoyed working with Martin Kemp on the film (we played two sailor pals), and, I reasoned, at least it was a movie. There hadn't been a lot of them to my name recently. The shoot lasted for three weeks, during which time we had a few scenes together. Martin was very focused and set on getting everything right. He seemed determined to become a working actor, which I admired. After the film wrapped I found myself with nothing to do. Despite my body feeling heavy and my movements slow, I decided that I had to go to London to get the album finished, the artwork created and ready for printing, to do anything to avoid having to do nothing. I phoned and booked a flight for the next day, 1 June.

I missed the flight. I awoke full of fear and feeling too slow and dull to summon the energy to get myself to the airport. The night after that, though, I stayed up all night working. I had more ideas for songs and scripts that night than I had had in six months. I started making lists of notes at half past midnight, and the ideas wouldn't leave me alone, so I went to the study in our house and jotted them down. It was like being hit by lightning, with ideas racing across the page as if from nowhere. I created visuals for the album cover, wrote four letters, two of them for Heather. I telephoned Marco, Boz and EMI, and then the sun came up and I was still roaring along. It was a rare, truly manic episode, and it lasted long enough to take Heather and me to London on a whim two days later. Once back in Primrose Hill, though, the lack of sleep hit me and I collapsed, sleeping for over twenty-four hours while Heather sat around, confused about what was going on with me. I awoke full of fear, shaking and shivering and asking Heather just to hold me. She was terrified, of course, and forced me to see a doctor after a couple of days with no change. We went to a Harley Street clinic where a doctor talked to me for a while, then gave me a prescription for some pills and a bill for £100, but no diagnosis. For the next two weeks I hardly spoke to Heather, just sat and cried, whimpering in my bed as she tried to feed me the pills. Marco, Michael Cox and other friends came round and were obviously shocked at my state, yet I couldn't and didn't care. Slowly I climbed out of the stupor and began to talk, to eat and make love with Heather. By the time she left for LA on 18 June I was back to a semblance of normality. It didn't last long, though, and soon enough I started to slip back into dark depression. 'The days are long, endless + surreal,' I wrote in my diary on 24 June, adding that 'nothing really matters to me. Haven't truly laughed since I don't know when.' The Harley Street doctor, disappointed with my progress, prescribed me some medication and asked me, looking me square in the eye, if I wouldn't prefer to be in hospital. I said no.

Somehow during this time I met with Anton Corbijn, the photographer, and arranged to shoot the *Wonderful* album cover in Regent's Park the next weekend. I made the shoot, and if you look closely at the images on the cover (which I toyed with calling *Bad All Over* as well as *Slapdash Eden*) you will see the public face of my illness.

With the photo shoot over and burning with a need to see Heather, I got a flight to LA. Once there, I collapsed again and lay in bed unable to speak. Heather had no idea what was wrong, and took to sleeping downstairs just so that she could get some sleep. I couldn't tell her, but all I wanted was for her to hold me.

After a few days of my helpless behaviour, unable to get me by telephone, Michael Cox came to the house and, seeing the condition I was in, decided that I really should go to Cedar's-Sinai hospital. He helped me to dress, which wasn't easy because I didn't want to go with him – I was torn between wanting the fear to end and being too scared to go into a hospital in case they never let me out. It took him over an hour to get me into his car. When we arrived at the hospital it took almost five more hours for him to talk me out of the car and up to the front desk for admission. Eventually I went. The amount of time it had taken for me to get inside meant the press had cottoned on that I was there, and as I entered the lift to be taken to the seventh floor, someone took a photo of me looking as terrible as I felt. The next day, as I lay in a hospital bed, the British tabloids ran a story about my collapse, which was how my mum and Tony got to hear that I was unwell.

I stayed in the psychiatric ward of Cedar's-Sinai for two weeks, and Heather came to see me every day and sat at my bedside until I told her to go, that she should get on with her life. I lay there, barely conscious most of the time, feeling scared, filthy and tired, and unable to speak. I was diagnosed as being 'bipolar' (at the time it was still called manic depression) and treated for it with medication, and by the middle of July I was well enough to be returned to London, where I was taken directly to the Charter Nightingale Hospital, a private place in Lisson Grove. Marco, my mum and other close friends visited me regularly and helped me to regain myself during this hellish time.

For the first time since 1977, my diaries are blank for that period, except for one entry. A spidery, heavy black-ink scrawl sits in the middle of the page, and written around it are four words: 'Fucking hell time buddy!' I was incapable of recording anything about what had happened to me. It was the darkest time of my life since waking up in Friern Barnett hospital that day in 1976. And it wasn't to be the last.

•

My diary entries begin again on Saturday, 20 August 1994. I'm back at home in Primrose Hill, taking the pills prescribed, but still unsteady. In a shaky, uncertain hand I've written:

> Scratching by the day
> By the day
> Fear please please
> PLEASE go away

Later that same day I began to analyse what had gone wrong. I came to the same conclusion that I had in 1976 – that love was killing me and that, while it was not Heather's fault, we should not have lived together.

Heather called me regularly from LA during the first few weeks of my recovery. We'd talk awkwardly, and I could never bring myself to tell her that I didn't want to go back to LA, that I was too scared to go back. I couldn't tell her that I privately referred to the house we had shared as Amityville, and couldn't separate it from my trip to hell. She sounded on the telephone as if everything was normal and happy in her life, which relieved me. After a couple of weeks, she then began to try to make plans for us to meet, possibly in New York, in September. I stalled, trying to think of a reason not to go. It almost freaked me out to realise that we had to go our separate ways, but I knew we did.

I had to occupy my time and my mind, so I went back to working on the release of the new album and planning a tour to promote it. Marco and I attempted to write new songs, and things began to get back to a kind of normality.

I was being kept stable by taking medication, which I was prescribed by my private doctor. She also gave me acupuncture and homeopathic powders to back up the medication. In September I began psychiatric therapy twice a week with a female therapist whom I liked enormously. She told me to think of what I had been through, not as a breakdown, but as a breakthrough, which I was very happy to do. She also told me that I had spent too much of my life looking after other people and not enough time looking after myself, which I now had to do. I agreed with her at the time, but I didn't do enough of the looking after myself. For a while, though, I felt stronger and was able to get on with my work, the music.

Calls still came regularly from Heather through the autumn of 1994, and she was now saying that I seemed to be stronger and well when I wasn't with her, and ill when I was, which I knew was true although I said nothing. I missed her like hell, and missed sex, too.

Getting myself back into shape, I made my usual lists of things to do, but added a list of things not to do as well. One thing on the list of 'No More's was 'listening to any more film offers'. I also decided to drop out of Harry's acting classes (which I had to pay for, even if I didn't show up), despite loving them. (Many of his directions and maxims have come to me at different times in different situations throughout my life – I will always be grateful to him for teaching me so much, and not just about acting.) I was determined to cancel my life in Los Angeles. It scared me to think about going back there.

As things progressed in London, I found my life becoming more interesting and strange. After meeting Carole Caplin for lunch in mid-September, I found myself at the 'clinic' of a friend of hers named Jack Temple. He looked like a classic nutty professor, and waved a small bottle of fluid on a chain over everything. He said I had vodka poisoning in my legs and that my brain was working at one per cent of its capacity. He made me sit in a field in a circle of stones on a chair, as he 'aimed' a force stone at me. Ten minutes later I went back in to his 'clinic' and discovered that I had twenty per cent of my brain working.

In my vulnerable state I was ready to believe in anything that might help me. I made several visits to Jack over the next few weeks, at times sitting in the pouring rain while he pointed his stone at me and 'restored' my brain capacity for me. I wanted to believe him, and the fact that I hadn't touched vodka since 1978 didn't enter my thoughts when he mentioned the 'poisoning' in my legs. Each visit cost me money, of course, but I considered it as well spent as the fees for my private doctor.

At the end of September I asked the doctor to help reduce my medication, and she lowered my dosage and upped the homeopathic powders until I gradually weaned myself off the pharmaceuticals. I managed to perform three songs at the EMI sales conference in Brighton that month without any extra stress, and met a new woman while there named Amy. We met at the restaurant she ran in Brighton and hit it off immediately. Sessions with my analyst were also helping me a lot, and as October began, I felt as if I was almost back to normal.

I was sleeping better and not waking up with the fear, and had started going out to clubs again (such as Soho House and the Groucho – private members' clubs rather than nightclubs). Heather and I still talked on the telephone, but neither of us was willing or able to end the affair, and we both kept on pretending that I was going to go back to her in LA at some point.

I listened to remixes of the 'Wonderful' single, looked over possible video directors' show reels to find someone to direct the promo for it, and even began working on new songs with Marco. I got Nan's house in Cookham sold, and agreed to make a film in New York at the end of October because the producers really wanted me.

When I made a two-day trip alone to Paris to be at the Vivienne Westwood couture show during Paris Fashion Week, I felt strong and almost happy. The only slight worry I had was wondering how my exorcism would turn out.

•

Being in contact with Carole Caplin again meant that I was in touch with her mother, Sylvia. I'd had a couple of chats with Sylvia before going to Paris and had told her about my hospital-isation. She had suggested that I have a session with a colleague of hers who performed exorcisms on people and removed bad spirits from them. Sylvia, who described herself as a Spiritualist, worked with a lot of people in that area and had introduced her daughter into the whole Spiritual world. Willing to try anything to ensure that I never again suffered the same horrible experi-ence, I agreed. Which is how I found myself going straight from Heathrow and the plane from Paris to meet Sylvia and the exorcist.

Sylvia met me as I sat by the Thames with my suitcase at my feet, feeling pretty tired but happy. We crossed a small bridge to a delightful house. A large, bulky man in a white shirt and dark slacks led us into the very homey, working-class interior. Pretty soon afterwards the 'exorcist' came in. She was plump with lovely eyes, a straight fringe and black hair.

''Ello, love, I'll just go get ready,' she said, and left.

'Er, hello . . .' I watched her go.

The big man then explained the routine. She'd come back in and sit down. When she put her hands forward I was to stand up and put mine in hers.

The exorcist came back in after a few minutes and sat in a corner, while a very serious Sylvia sat close by. 'This isn't going to be throwing up green bile or my twisting me neck around,' she joked.

Then it was down to business. She sat back and closed her eyes in deep concentration. After two minutes she extended her hands and I stood up to put mine between them. The moment I touched her she shouted and fell back in her chair. She held her head in her hands and her voice changed, getting lower. 'It's in my head. It's in my head. The pain,' she cried.

I was calm, but also excited. The big man said to her, 'We're your friends, here to help you. Listen to what we say.'

'No!' the voice shouted back petulantly. 'I'm staying here.'

This continued for a while, with the woman's face contorting, tears falling, the 'entity' refusing to go. The big man told it not to be silly and to behave. Then there was silence.

She finally breathed very heavily and waved her hands around the front of her head, neck and chin. The big man told me to shut my eyes and relax, which I did.

'I'm glad you got rid of him. He was a bad 'un,' the woman said to me. Then we had tea and she gave me instructions.

After a few questions about someone in my family who had been a 'bad 'un' – I mentioned Nan's evil husband, Tom – she told me that it was him who had got into my head. He'd been with me for a long time, maybe thirty years or more, she said. He entered when I took something or was knocked out (I didn't remember it happening, but it could have done). My neck or spine was damaged at birth, she told me (it wasn't). She also told me that I was looking for the wrong girl all the time, trying to find the love I felt I deserved but never got from my parents.

The rest of the things she said to me were in the same vague vein, all designed to make me feel that she understood me and could see into my head and soul. Until writing this I had forgotten entirely about this episode, and rereading it in my diary now makes me think I blanked it out because it was so dumb. I was in a very vulnerable state of mind at the time. I made several paid visits to her over the next six months and even introduced new clients to her (for which, she grandly told me, I had earned points in the Spiritual world. She earned straight pounds in the bank, of course). So much of what she told me was so general that it could have applied to anyone. At the time, though, she told me what I wanted to hear.

Immediately after the 'exorcism' I went through a manic phase that I interpreted as being the result of having Granddad Tom Goddard removed from my head. I agreed to travel to Brighton with a BBC film crew to get a tattoo done a couple of days later for the local London news programme which was broadcast the next night. After a couple of days' shopping and eating out in London, I packed my bags and flew to New York to film *Drop Dead Rock*, with Debbie Harry, among others. Although I was only booked for five days of actual filming, I felt so speedy that I stayed on at the Paramount Hotel and spent my time shopping, visiting clubs and enjoying encounters with various women I met. I also saw *Tommy* the musical on Broadway because the producers had approached me to play Uncle Ernie, but I decided that the show was not for me.

While at the Paramount I called Heather and told her that it was over between us and that I wouldn't be returning to Los Angeles. She was very polite and businesslike about it and had obviously been expecting the call. She agreed to stay in the house until the lease ran out and to help me get my stuff out and into storage, sold or shipped back to London. We both knew that it was the right thing to do, and I'm sure she felt as relieved to have ended the affair as I was.

I spent my fortieth birthday at the Paramount, where a small party was hosted for me by Downtown Julie Brown. I felt strong and happy. For the next three weeks I helped to arrange a US tour (for after the UK leg) for 1995 to promote *Wonderful*, and in the process agreed to play an acoustic show in San Francisco, with Marco, in November. That went well and we flew back to London, where I introduced Marco to the exorcist woman. She told us that we had been brothers in eighteenth-century France and that, like David Bowie and Bryan Ferry, I was a lizard. 'It's in the eyes,' she explained.

I eventually fell out with her after she became angry at me when I suffered a relapse in my mental health. She told me in strong language to stop being so stupid, that there was nothing really wrong with me because she'd exorcised the problem away.

I spent all of December in London, where we filmed a video for 'Wonderful' with me truly crying my eyes out as the camera turned. I was thinking of all of the sad times in my life, from my childhood to that day, and the tears fell easily. I also finished preparing for the single release of 'Wonderful' in late January, and agreed to play two songs with Nine Inch Nails at the Nassau Coliseum in New York on 6 January. They had recorded their version of my song 'Physical' a couple of years earlier, and their lead singer Trent Reznor had often spoken of how much he'd been influenced by my stuff. We were happy to say yes.

So 1995 kicked off with Marco and me enjoying the applause from more than 20,000 people as we played 'Physical' and 'Beat My Guest' with Trent Reznor and his Nine Inch Nails. God, it felt good to be playing live again, and I began to look forward to the tour that I'd be doing later that year.

Back in England two days later, though, things began to unravel. At a meeting to discuss promotion of the album, Miles Copeland told me in no uncertain terms that 'this album is your last chance' and that I had to do things his way. I was stunned, and reacted angrily. We agreed to part company.

Then I went on a five-day radio tour of Britain, being interviewed at stations up and down the country. Meanwhile Marco and our new intended manager, Grant Black (brother of Clive, and one half of Blackball Management with Kevin Ball), sent an official cancellation of contract for the UK and Europe to Miles.

January was spent promoting 'Wonderful'. On its release at the end of the month it entered the chart at number 32, which was slightly disappointing, but at least I was back in the charts.

Marco and I rehearsed with the band for the tour that would begin in late March, and by early February I was feeling tired and scared of breaking down, mostly because I feared that EMI would pull the album release if I was unable to promote it. I had stopped taking my medication altogether and was relying on the homeopathic powders from my doctor and twice-weekly therapy sessions to keep me healthy.

At the end of February I flew to New York to begin a promotional tour, because Capitol (who were EMI in the USA, and who had agreed to release the album when I refused to go with IRS) had become excited by the prospects of both the single and the album. Marco was unable to accompany me because he was rehearsing the band in London, so I used a fantastic pick-up guitarist named Michael Ward to play a number of acoustic shows at radio stations and record stores across the States from New York to Washington and San Francisco. There were fifteen in all (including the very hot *Howard Stern Show*) during a hectic nine-day period.

Back in London in mid-March I felt exhausted, but four days later the UK tour began in Stoke. My knee was swollen and I felt as if I could have slept for days. A week later, the London show ended the tour, and not a day too soon for my liking. It attracted a lot of attention and I had more requests for free tickets than I'd had in years. Two tickets went to Justine Frischmann and her boyfriend Damon Albarn, who at the time were considered the King and Queen of Britpop, a ridiculous, music press-created 'movement' that included their bands (Elastica and Blur, respectively) along with a couple of others, most notably Oasis and Supergrass. I had met Justine a couple of times over the past three months, and she was a fan, having grown up listening to my records. We had become pals, and nothing more, yet her boyfriend was certain that we had enjoyed more than a platonic affair. Unusually for me, we hadn't as much as kissed. After the London gig party, Damon acted like he thought a pop star should, while Justine was natural and fun. I thought there seemed to be a bit of pressure between them.

There was a lot more pressure on me, though. At a gig in Dublin, before London, I had wrenched my knee ligaments, and I now had to fit in a quick operation to fix the problem. I was feeling knackered but not sleeping too well. And then, on the morning of 28 March, I woke up at my Primrose Hill flat with Amy, the girl from Brighton whom I'd been seeing a lot of since Christmas. I was shaking again, and she held me tight in the way I had so wanted Heather to eight months earlier. When the fear didn't fade after three days, I took a limo to Seaford to stay at Jordan's house. For three days I drank tea, downed homeopathic powders and managed to get myself into a fit state to fly to America and begin the US tour. I even began to take my medication again, but just a low dosage.

For the first three weeks of the American tour I felt well enough to perform, and that was it. After a show I'd be so tired at first that all I could do was shower on the bus and then fall asleep. By the last week of April, however, I couldn't even manage the shower and change of clothes. Instead I'd collapse on my bunk and sleep in my stage clothes.

In May, I lay on my bunk during a twenty-hour drive to Florida hoping that we'd never arrive so that I wouldn't have to get up. In New Orleans I had chest pains and Marco had me rushed to hospital, where they put a tube down my throat and ran some tests, all of which were negative. Then Marco began to feel as lethargic and ill as I did.

Finally, after five weeks of a tour that became increasingly poor, with me barely able to sing, let alone perform, we hit New York and both Marco and I had a series of tests run at a hospital. We were both diagnosed with glandular fever and quarantined for two weeks. We finally got back to London in mid-June.

Throughout the summer of 1995 I suffered bouts of fear and loathing, and was often helped and comforted by Amy, who only left me alone when I told her that it was OK to. Unsure about the prescriptions that my doctor had been giving me, I asked my therapist for advice on finding another doctor. In July she arranged for me to see a psychiatrist at the Chelsea and Westminster Hospital. He proved to be a great help, but was unable to do anything for me until we were certain that the glandular fever had left my system. The symptoms of GF and depression are so similar that I spent many days asking myself whether it had gone and I was suffering depression, or the other way round.

There were still external pressures on me during that summer. Because we had had to cancel some of the American tour, my new management team, who were dealing with the insurers and promoters' claims against us, were in constant contact with me.

I decided in July that the cause of my breakdown on the US tour had been my going cold turkey after stopping my medication, and so I began taking it again, on prescription from my doctor. I had begun to suffer early-morning anxiety attacks and was unable to get to sleep at night, but by regulating different medications I was able to stabilise my sleeping routine. However, in September, in an attempt to lessen its bad side effects, I began taking it only every other day.

By October I had found a level of stability in my health, and although fear of the early morning creeps haunted me, I hadn't suffered any terrible attacks since August. Yet when Ellen Drantch, my film agent in LA, called to tell me that I was being offered a very well-paid role in a movie that began filming at the end of that month, I was reluctant to say yes. I didn't say no, though, until I saw my private doctor and asked her for an official note that stated I was unfit for work – it was my first sick note! I wanted a genuine reason to turn the film down, and didn't want Ellen to have to keep saying no on my behalf for no good reason. When I visited the doc, she happily gave me the note and then announced that she was giving up work for a year to go travelling. She looked me straight in the eye and asked, without a trace of irony, 'Do you think I'm nuts?'

I said no, and she gave me the details of a new (female) doctor in Cadogan Place, whom I went to see a few days later. She was very efficient and immediately sent me for tests to see if the glandular fever bug had gone (it had), and began to give me good advice on monitoring my medication. Despite the sick note, the film's producers said that they were willing to move the production date back in order that I could do it. At first it went back to the end of November, but eventually I wouldn't begin work on *Face Down* (with the great Joe Mantegna in the lead role) until April 1996.

Meanwhile, *Wonderful* the album had reached number 24 in the UK album charts in April 1995, and that was good enough for EMI to decide that my contract would be kept. Once more Clive Black was back in charge, having left Warner's. At a meeting with him and his brother, our manager, Clive said that he thought that Marco and I should record a version of Marc Bolan's 'Dandy In The Underworld'. I didn't think that was a great idea, but said nothing except 'OK'. Throughout November and December my new doctor oversaw the reduction of my medication dosage, with the happy results that my life returned to something approaching normal and I slept well again. I attended the Aberystwyth Film Festival where *Drop Dead Rock* made its UK premier, and I had two relaxed question-and-answer sessions with the audience. A couple of weeks later Marco, John Reynolds and I recorded 'Dandy In The Underworld', although it seemed to be a waste of time to me. Which is what it proved to be. Clive Black hated the recording. 'Where's the melody gone?' he asked his brother. (It has since been released as an extra track on the *Adam Ant Redux* CD, part of the *Adam Ant Remastered Collection* box set of 2005.)

As 1995 came to an end, I felt stronger and more optimistic

about the future than I had for a while. Marco and I parted
company with Blackball Management and set about getting the
tangled business deals of the past two years sorted out. Then
we hired James Wiley, a respected music business manager, to
look after our affairs.

I spent a relaxed and lovely Christmas with Jordan, her
kittens and her sister Sally in Seaford, before returning to Primrose Hill for the end of the year.

•

In January, having decided that I had to leave Primrose Hill and
all the terrible memories that my flat held, I took a walk around
Spitalfields in East London and looked at a Georgian house that
was for sale. The area, I discovered, was a treasure trove of old
houses and interesting people. The white-haired old lady who
opened her door and showed me round was sprightly and
clearly interested in art. On the second floor she introduced me
to her 'partner', a woman of about the same age who walked
with a stick. They were moving because of the difficulty she had
with stairs. It was a shame, they both said, because they loved
their 'roof terrace'. It was reached by a ladder up to their
butterfly roof, and gave a glorious view of the surrounding area.
'You used to be able to see St Paul's,' the first lady said, pointing
in the direction of Christopher Wren's masterpiece, 'until they
built the new Exchange.' I gazed around for a while up there,
imagining old London as it had once been – you could still see it
vaguely in the surrounding streets.

Walking back to Spitalfields market I spotted Gilbert (one
half of the artist partnership Gilbert and George) saying a polite
thank you to the postman as he handed over some letters. In
the market I found great young clothes designers and jewellers
and a thriving local community that I felt would suit me more
than Primrose Hill now seemed to. In the twenty years that I'd
lived there, the Hill had changed to become a kind of New

Hampstead. Where once there had been colourful characters there were now yuppie bankers and film and TV celebrities. The shops had changed with it and the place no longer felt like a village – more of a catwalk at times. I called the estate agent from my mobile phone and made an offer on the Spitalfields house. I would move in, I told myself, and find a wife and mother for the child I felt that I so desperately wanted. I was forty-one and getting broody.

And then there was Amy. She had now moved to London from Hove, and had a job as the manager of a West End restaurant. Amy had held my hand and my head, comforting me through my last bout of depression, and she'd done all of that even though her job made her as tired as I often felt.

I flew to Toronto to make *Face Down* in April. After an enjoyable shoot that took me into May, I returned to London and went straight into rehearsals for my part as Caulfield in Joe Orton's *Funeral Games*, which opened at the Drill Hall at the end of the month. Although originally an hour-long television play, Phil Willmott, the director of this version, had rewritten it as a two-hour musical, introducing a number of songs for each of the main characters. I got to sing the 1961 Neil Sedaka hit 'Calendar Girl', for instance, while my co-stars Bette Bourne (one of the best theatrical drag queens in the business) sang 'Walking After Midnight', the old Patsy Cline hit, and Sylvester McCoy, the old Doctor Who, sang Dietrich's 'Falling In Love Again'. The female lead was Aimi MacDonald, the delightful comedy actress whom I'd enjoyed watching on Marty Feldman's *At Last the 1948 Show* in the late 1960s. As a cast we had fun with the script, but the production was very difficult. The music proved particularly problematic and was hard to record and play back, and we missed lots of cues in rehearsal that were not cleared up until well into the run (despite Marco helping out with it, for which he was never properly thanked), by which time the press had passed their judgement, of course, and it wasn't good.

My busy work schedule in the first half of 1996 had meant

that I couldn't make the move to Spitalfields. I could never get the Primrose Hill flat sorted enough to put it on the market, and although my offer had been accepted, the Georgian house that I dreamed about moving into was bought by somebody else. The physically tiring rehearsals for *Funeral Games*, coming on top of the Canadian film and the work that I'd been doing on remastering my old albums for a proposed boxed-set release, had me slipping back into bad sleeping habits as summer arrived. By the time the reviews for *Funeral Games* appeared, I was sleeping for only a few hours each night. I asked myself why I was appearing in the play at all, and could only come up with two answers: insecurity and loneliness.

The reviews were depressing for everyone and had a disastrous effect on me. Throughout the summer I felt myself slipping back into disturbed sleep patterns and at times was unable to speak. Amy would visit me and look after me, but all I really wanted to do was sit in the flat with the blinds down, listening to the radio and seeing no one.

Then, in late October, I suffered my first truly bad episode of hypomania and couldn't sleep at all. Despite taking the medication I couldn't think straight and was terrified that I'd be arrested, that I'd go broke and that I'd lose everything. After four days without sleep, at dinner with my mum in her flat I collapsed completely. I raved at her and Tony between bouts of crying. She called Sylvi, who came immediately and found me lying on my old bed, making little sense. I reasoned at the time that I'd broken down because Amy had left me. Tired and unable to cope with my illness any longer she had returned to her parents' home in Hove and said that she needed space from me. I didn't blame her. Eventually, I turned on Sylvi and in a fit of mania said some terrible things to her, driving her away from me, for which I am truly sorry.

After that night at my mum's I asked Marco if I could stay with him. I couldn't go back to my flat. He said yes and I spent a week with him, slowly stabilising myself. After a visit to my psychiatrist and therapist, and with a new prescription, I felt well enough to return home. Amy came back to London and we resumed our relationship, as fractured as it was, enough for me to spend Christmas that year with her family. Unfortunately the calm wasn't to last long. Just after Christmas, feeling that my life was as bad as it had ever been and that I had nothing to live for, after three days of deep depression I crushed thirty paracetamol in my coffee grinder, mixed it with orange juice and attempted to drink the horrible white foaming brew. Within seconds I was throwing up in my toilet and crying my eyes out.

Amy, who was staying with me that night, was woken by the noise and came into the bathroom to see me on my knees by the bowl. She cleaned me up and put me back to bed. She had no idea what I'd tried to do until I told her days later.

That turned out to be one of the last nights that we spent together. She was working extremely hard, trying to carve out a career for herself, and (when I was capable of it) I didn't think that it was fair that she had to deal with my depressions and manic phases as well. It became too hard for us to maintain a relationship when we were both too tired most of the time to even speak to each other, and we drifted apart for a while before both admitting that, this time, it really was over. Before the New Year was very old, Amy and I were no longer lovers.

By the end of January 1997 my new medication had stabilised me to the degree that I felt better than I had for six months. I felt stronger and could make decisions about things. I had completed a publishing rights deal with MCA instead of EMI, and it had paid me a decent advance against future royalties. Although I wanted to make music and write new songs, I knew that I shouldn't ever tour as extensively and for as long as I had in the past. I was determined that I would not to be rushed back to work, and equally determined to eat as healthily as possible and get physically fit.

Then, in March, I got news that my father had died. One of his neighbours called me to let me know that he'd been found dead in his bed. The coroner later told me that he'd suffered a heart attack, which had killed him instantly. I felt relieved that he hadn't suffered and that he was finally at peace, but of course I was saddened by his passing. He was my father, and despite all the bad stuff, I had loved him. I set about arranging the funeral because there was no one else to do it.

It didn't take long before the terrible loneliness and sadness that Les must have suffered in his final days began to haunt me, even before I found myself standing over his cremated remains. I had to get busy, I thought, had to do something. In an attempt to get away from London, my flat and all of its awful memories I accepted an invitation from Vivienne Westwood to attend her show at Paris fashion week. It was to prove one of the most fateful trips I ever made. In the crush at the door to get into the show, with overzealous bouncers denying anyone access, I was about to give up and go for a walk when Lorraine Gibson, one of Vivienne's PR girls who I'd met in London at Westwood's shop, grabbed my arm and pulled me into the hall.

She smiled at me as I took in her long, long legs and beautiful 1940s-style glamour-girl outfit. That night we walked through the wet streets of Paris to the Eiffel Tower and talked and talked. I slept on the couch in her hotel room that night and awoke determined to see more of her when we got back to London.

After we got back from Paris, Lorraine and I spent every day together. In an attempt to escape my recent past, I asked Lorraine to come with me to America, telling her that I had to go so that I could keep my Green Card intact. She agreed, and we flew to America intending to visit Las Vegas after going to Elvis's home, Graceland, in Memphis and then on to LA. Instead, once we got to Atlanta, rather than catching a connection to Memphis, we got off the plane and hired a car. We drove south until hitting Dayton, Tennessee, where I fell in love with a house perched on top of a mountain that had a 'For Sale' sign out front. It was a timber, A-framed house with two bedrooms and a bathroom upstairs and an open-plan living area and kitchen on the ground. Out back there was an enormous porch with views far out over the Tennessee valley and a big garage in the yard. I loved it at first sight.

After a few weeks in a motel in Dayton, which was a small town with a main street that had a church on pretty much every corner, but only one general store and a big white town hall, I bought the house. A few days later, desperate to start a family, I asked Lorraine to marry me and I guess she wanted it as much as I did, because she said yes. I wanted to celebrate life some-how, and wanted to believe that this time marriage would be different, that I wouldn't go into a spiral of depression.

We were married in the Dayton court house a couple of weeks later. I didn't know it at the time, but that court house was famous. In 1925 it had been the setting for what was known as the Scopes Monkey Trial, in which a local teacher (John Scopes) was tried for illegally teaching Darwin's Theory of Evo-lution to school kids in Dayton. There was a play titled *Inherit the Wind* written about the trial that became a Broadway hit in 1955, and a very successful 1960 movie of the play starring Spencer Tracy. It seemed as if the town had barely got over the trial by the time we arrived. They still held regular main street parades on holidays, and everyone knew everyone else enough to say 'Hi' to when they passed one another.

I now think of this as my 'Hillbilly' period. We bought a dog, a Weimaraner puppy that we named Vivienne, and I set about making a home for us three. I bought a 1954 Dodge truck, a 1969 BMW motorbike and a 1952 Harley-Davidson motorbike and put them in the garage. I also bought various vintage guitars and planned to build a recording studio in the basement of the house. After a couple of months of marital bliss in the American South, Lorraine announced that she thought she was pregnant and I was overjoyed, especially when we found out that she was.

That joy didn't last, though, and by October we were back in Primrose Hill with me suffering terrible depressions, unable to speak or function. Lorraine handled my illness as well as I could have hoped during that time. However, it became increasingly difficult for her as her pregnancy continued.

Yet, as the baby's due date arrived, I managed to climb out of the depression, and when my daughter, Lily, was born in the spring of 1998, I was there to see her emerge and had the privilege of cutting the umbilical cord. I was also the first person to hold her, and it felt absolutely wonderful. As she looked into my eyes that first time, I felt that I had become a man at last. Lily became my reason to live and the one true love in my life.

For the first few months back at home in the summer of 1998 with my wife and child, I was happy and busy. I'd feed and change Lily, take her for walks and sit, just staring at her, as she slept. And then I began to feel the depression coming back and felt powerless to stop it. My relationship with Lorraine had become difficult most of the time, and things were getting on top of me.

The pressure of living in my small, one-bedroomed flat in Primrose Hill didn't help things for either of us. It was too claustrophobic. Lorraine made the decision to move out of our flat with Lily, and, naturally, I decided that I would support them financially, paying for their accommodation and living expenses – I would never have thought of doing otherwise. Of course I was distraught at losing them both, and of course with no one at the flat I soon slipped into a deeper depression. I had no alternative but to go into the Chelsea and Westminster hospital under the care of my psychiatrist.

For weeks I couldn't move – could barely think. Eventually I began to come round and could think only of seeing my daughter. Realising that I'd never get to see her regularly if I was in such a state, I knew that I had to get myself back into shape to be capable of looking after Lily on my own. I had to fight hard to get there, but I did.

For a while Lily's visits to my flat took place with her mother present, and then it became just me and my girl, and those were the happiest days of my life. When I was able to plan for her visits I'd buy paper, pens, glue and stuff that we could spend ages making into different things, from houses to spaceships and dinosaurs. We'd spend hours sticking, colouring and laughing at what we'd made. If only this could go on for ever, I'd tell myself, then everything would be OK. But not every day was like that. Not at all.

•

I spent much of the time between 1999 and 2001 suffering from terrible mood swings, shifting between hypomania and deep depression. When manic, I'd believe that I could conquer the world, that I could do anything. At those times I truly stretched the limits of my friendship with all and everyone that I knew well. I'd take off for anywhere, often not knowing where I was going, or why, and try to drag people along with me.

One time I found myself in a car bound for Scotland with three men and a woman I hardly knew. Apparently I was helping her to take herself and her things back home to Edinburgh from London. I had hired a car and asked one guy to drive, and two others had come along for the ride. At a service station somewhere on the M1 I spent over £200 on chocolate, CDs and God knows what else before becoming suddenly aware of where I was but not knowing why. I got scared and became abusive to them. The woman called the police after I refused to go any further. When two female police officers arrived to find me sitting on the kerb and this woman too 'scared' to get in the car, they simply asked me for an autograph and left, telling us all to stop being so silly. Somehow I persuaded the driver to go back to London that night, and ended up walking home from Highbury after demanding to be let out of the car in the early hours of the morning in my lovely London.

On another jaunt into London's West End late in 2000, I took two old friends on a three a.m. search for a pair of Chinese slippers. I told them that there was a place in Gerard Street where I could get them. We left the Groucho Club and walked toward Chinatown, not very far, which is probably why I didn't feel the cold for a while. I had taken off my shoes and socks and walked barefoot to Shaftesbury Avenue, where I then proceeded to play 'chicken' with the traffic, until one of my friends caught me and forced me into a cab home to Primrose Hill.

For long periods I ate only fattening, sweet things, often drinking countless buckets of sickly hot chocolate and cappuccino. I started to lose interest in my appearance, which was the most obvious outward sign of my illness. I had always cared deeply about how I looked and what I wore.

One evening I opened my door to come face to face with another stalker. A small, plain-looking, middle-aged woman, she rang my doorbell, and when I answered, just stood there, silently staring at me. That scared me a bit, but after a few similar appearances from her, I began to get truly freaked out and angry. I stopped answering the outer door to her, but on a couple of occasions she managed to get into the entrance hall of the house by ringing other doorbells. The first time it happened I opened the door and she tried to get into the flat, saying, 'I'm here, just as you asked.' She told me that the antenna I'd had planted in her head was working, that she could hear me talking to her, calling her to come and see me.

She also put notes through my letterbox saying that we were married, including wedding rings and photographs in the envelope. For months she made my life hell. A couple of times, Lily would have just dropped off to sleep for her afternoon nap when this deranged woman started ringing the doorbell and banging on the front door. After a few visits she had realised that there was a chance I'd have to open the door if she made enough noise, in order not to disturb Lily.

Eventually, after the stalker had tried to attack me and scratch my face, the police had to take action against her and she was arrested and placed in psychiatric care. Unfortunately she had caused enough disruption to my life to push me back under psychiatric care too. Not surprisingly, Lorraine found the stalker's actions terrifying and wanted me to move immediately, believing that Lily could be in danger.

It wasn't long after the arrest of the stalker that I experienced a prolonged period of hypomania followed by another acute depression. On my forty-seventh birthday I began to drink alcohol for the first time since 1978, when, at a birthday party in Soho, some 'friends' who didn't really know me gave me vodka laced with God knows what, and I swallowed it all. In my hypomanic state, alcohol had little effect on me, and as everyone else was downing drinks, so did I. After a while, even when calm, I began to drink bottled lager at home as well as when out.

In December 2001, I agreed to appear on a revue-type bill tour around the UK with a number of 1980s pop stars such as Belinda Carlisle (once of the Go-Go's) and half of Spandau Ballet. Because I'd never played the nostalgia game, the promoters thought that by making me the headline act they'd sell more tickets. They were probably right, but I clearly wasn't. I attended a press photocall to announce the Here And Now tour, and, while there, realised that this was not what I should be doing and almost told reporters as much. I was clearly not well, and had stopped taking my medication without telling my doctor. I was suffering from hypomania and ideas were bursting out of me as they had in the past.

In these years I managed at different times to frighten and upset good friends like Jordan, Dave Whiteing, Dave Gibb, Dave Pash and Marco. I'd insult them, swear at them, call them at all hours of the day and night and accuse them of all sorts of mad things. I scared my mum and upset Tony no end. I can never apologise enough to all of them for my behaviour.

Throughout this time Lorraine was pressing for a divorce settlement. I didn't tell anyone, of course, but I was stashing pills in a box in my bathroom and believed that I functioned better without them – the drowsiness and side effects they caused were, I thought, making my life a misery. I know now that it was stupid of me, and in January 2002, it led me to do the most stupid thing I've ever done.

12

RIDICULE IS NOTHING
TO BE SCARED OF

'THROW THE GUN OUT OF THE CAR.'

What? Where did all these police cars come from?

'Oi, driver, where are you going?'

The driver of the minicab jumps out of his seat in front of me and runs like a bat out of hell across the road.

There's a police patrol car parked diagonally across the road in front and two or three others behind and just to the right of me. There are policemen with bullet-proof vests on and black earpieces in, pointing their guns at the car I'm sitting in. The one closest to the minicab is shouting at me, 'Throw the gun out of the car and then get out of the car with your hands up.'

Fuck, they're talking to me.

'THROW THE GUN OUT OF THE CAR NOW!'

Shit, what gun? This one on the seat? 'All right, I'm throwing it out.'

'Now get out of the car with your hands up and kneel on the ground.'

Where am I, what's going on, why . . .

'GET OUT OF THE CAR NOW!'

'All right, all right, I'm getting out, don't shoot.'

'Put your hands on your head, together.'

I do it and immediately feel a size ten boot in my back and a pair of hands gripping my hands from behind. My face hits the wet tarmac of the Camden street and a knee thumps into the back of my neck. Another size ten boot kicks my legs apart and another knee lands in the small of my back.

Fuck. That hurts.

There's a lot of shouting and fast talking among the police, and a few nervous laughs as they stand around me, looking chuffed.

'All right, mate, we're picking you up now. Don't struggle.'

My arms are grabbed on both sides under the armpit and I'm wrenched to my feet. Two big cops half drag me to a patrol car and force me into the back seat. I have no idea why I'm here, how the gun got into that minicab.

And now I'm scared.

•

At around midday on 12 January 2002, in a fit of hypomania, I walked from Camden market to the Prince of Wales pub in Prince of Wales road. It's not very far and didn't take too long, certainly not long enough for my irrational anger to wear off.

I'd been to see a woman who ran a clothes stall in the market and whom I'd asked to make me a couple of things. I'd given her my telephone number so that she could call me. She'd told me that her husband had found the piece of paper with my name and number on and didn't like it and that he was going to 'fuck me up'. He had called my home about twenty times through the night, accusing me of having an affair with his wife; but far worse, he made threats towards Lily. I flipped and told him as calmly as I could to stop making that kind of threat, but he was having none of it. He made my blood boil.

The next day, I went looking for him in Camden market. Someone told me that he'd be in the Prince of Wales pub, so I walked there, dressed in a combat jacket, leather trousers and wearing a white cowboy hat. I was also wearing my blue-tinted glasses. As I walked into the bare, beer-stained pub, the handful of regulars sitting at the bar turned and looked at me. One of them laughed and another began to whistle the theme music from Sergio Leone's *The Good, the Bad and the Ugly*.

Already angry, this made me worse. I asked where the man I was looking for was and got a bunch of stupid answers. He wasn't there. And I had to leave because this wasn't a pub, it was a private members' club and I wasn't a member nor had I been invited in by a member. Royally fucked off, I left, shouting over my shoulder that I'd be back.

The rest of that day is lost to me. I have no idea where I went or what I did. Somehow I got hold of my father's World War II-era starting pistol and walked back to the pub. That part of Camden and Kentish Town is an odd area. At that time there were run-down, crack-filled council estates that sit behind streets of small, smart and expensive houses. On one side of the road leading up to the pub from Camden there is a big 1950s council estate and a pub, which had recently been torched by someone; opposite are a school for excluded kids and some heavily alarmed private houses built in the 1840s. There are also a building and plumbing supplies company not far off, and a bunch of cheap car repair shops. Somewhere on my walk to the Prince of Wales I picked up a car starter motor which had wires hanging out of one end.

When I got to the pub I took aim and threw the starter motor through the huge plate glass window of the pub. Some of the blokes I'd seen earlier came running out of the door into the street, shouting that they'd 'fucking murder' me.

I ran and they chased me. In an alleyway on the council estate nearby I found myself cornered by a bunch of them and so I pulled the 'gun' out of my jacket and pointed it at them. They stopped and ran back into the pub. I stood there shaking, in a kind of daze, wondering if they'd be back, still holding the gun. Had I not had the gun, I feel sure that they would all have attacked me.

I felt like I was in a film but had no script. After a while I wandered back into the road, still with gun in hand. Apparently a policeman spotted me and radioed for help from the armed response unit.

I didn't know that, of course, and went in search of a minicab with the intention off heading into Soho. A couple of roads up from the Prince of Wales, there's a minicab office that usually has a car waiting outside. It did. I got in and the car pulled away, but before we got 200 yards down the road we were surrounded by flashing lights and wailing sirens.

I was officially arrested, but at some point someone in the police station realised that I was ill and I was taken up the hill to the Royal Free Hospital, which houses one of the largest psychiatric outpatients departments in London. Once there I told them about my psychiatrist at the Chelsea and Westminster and calls were made. Within a few hours I was home in Primrose Hill, where there was a small welcoming committee of close friends waiting for me, plus my mum, close to tears and scared for me. They tried to tell me that I was ill and needed hospital attention. I wasn't ready to agree with them, though – I hated the idea of having to go back to hospital. They had arranged, they said, for me to go to the Chelsea and Westminster voluntarily until I got better. I wasn't having that and told them so, which was when they told me that if necessary they would have me 'sectioned'. In other words, with written permission from a relative or authority figure and two doctors, I could be forced into a psychiatric ward until fit to be released.

Feeling under threat, scared and not wanting to be imprisoned, which was my interpretation of a section order, I ran out of my flat and across to the canal path, and from there I went to Camden. God knows how long I was there, but I was picked up by the police again and taken directly to the Royal Free (missing out the police station this time). Once there, I was put into a secure ward (named Alice). I was furious and initially refused to take medication from the doctors and nurses. While my files were being transferred so that details of my medical history could be found, I managed to get to a pay phone in the ward, from where I called two of the country's biggest-selling tabloid newspapers. I ranted at them about being wrongfully arrested and imprisoned in what I called the Alice In Wonderland ward of the Royal Free. I kept repeating that I was innocent, that I'd been 'abducted' by the police, and that it was all a conspiracy against me. Of course none of it was true, but in my deranged state of mind I believed it.

The papers, naturally, had a field day with it all. Despite Marco telling the press that none of my accusations were true, the papers ran with their lurid headlines. By the time I had regained my sanity, I was mortified by what I'd done.

I was detained in the Alice ward for a couple of weeks and then moved to a private clinic for a further couple of weeks. Having agreed to keep taking my prescribed drugs, and still coming down from the heavy sedation that I'd been given during my hospitalisation, I initially set about carrying on with things where I'd left off when I got back to my Primrose Hill flat. I intended to rehearse for the Here and Now tour, but I soon realised that there was no way I could handle such a long live tour. In March my psychiatrist wrote a formal letter stating that I was in no fit state to take part. With his help I was beginning to realise what triggered off my fits of hypomania. Being tired and under stress, having to perform when I didn't want to and being away from home for long periods of time would all lead to a collapse.

The fit of hypomania that had led to my arrest had been triggered, as many of my fits were, by my not taking the prescribed medication. The first step on the road to my regaining any kind of control over my life had to begin with my taking it. The problem was that I still thought, at times, that I'd be able to manage things better without it. As the trial came closer I began to worry and fret over what might happen to me. This was serious, I knew, and it went straight to the heart of one of my greatest fears – being locked up.

•

My first visit to the Old Bailey was terrifying. It's a typical Victorian Hall of Justice with rococo painted ceilings and stern, dark wood panelling offset by marble. There are bars on the windows and bullet- and bomb-proof doors, and I was very aware that the hallways had reverberated with the footsteps of some of the country's most notorious criminals. I quaked as I sat in the court and looked at the judge and lawyers before me.

At the first hearing my lawyer attempted to have my various charges dismissed because of temporary insanity. I had been charged with some serious crimes – causing affray, using threatening behaviour, criminal damage, possession of a firearm and assault occasioning actual bodily harm. Being found guilty of any of them could have seen me imprisoned. During the course of the several hearings that I had to sit through over the space of several months, my psychiatrist testified to the court that I was suffering a period of hypomania and therefore unable to control my actions by reason of temporary insanity. He also told the court that public revelation of too many of the facts of the hearing could result in another hypomanic episode, depression and even attempted suicide. The court issued an order limiting the press coverage.

My case was adjourned until August 2002 for psychiatric reports. Unfortunately, the judge didn't agree with my lawyer's argument about temporary insanity, and when it finally came to it, after months of worrying, I pleaded guilty to affray, the other charges having been dropped. The Crown had reduced the charge to one not requiring a 'specific intent' so that it was easier for us to accept, and I was placed on probation for six months without having to sit through a trial in the dock.

In the period between hearings I took my medicine and, because of it, gained weight. As the final court appearance approached I knew that there would be photographers waiting for me to appear, and I worried increasingly as the date approached. With a few weeks to go I decided that I'd grow a beard like Ernest Hemingway or Jim Morrison had done, believing that no one would recognise me. Which is why, dressed in my most sensible clothes, wearing a flat cap and my Hemingway beard, I entered the Old Bailey through the front door. Of course I was recognised, and the subsequent headlines depressed me. Soon, though, the beard was gone and I worked on my weight.

During this terrible time I had been lucky enough to get to know better a designer I'd met a year or so before. Clare not only stood by me in some of my times of greatest need, but began to fight for me, and with me. As the newspapers and media heaped ridicule on me, Clare supported me and helped me to overcome it. I found myself falling in love with her. During lucid and 'up' times we had great fun together. During my fits of crippling depression she would help me as much as she could, and in manic phases she would try to keep me under control. The only trouble was, Clare lived in Oxford, ran her own design company and couldn't be with me at all times. Which is why I occasionally went out of control.

As time went on, I began to miss out my medication for days on end, once again going into the bathroom to 'get some water', but instead spitting the pills into a box that I kept in a cupboard for just that purpose. As a result, my behaviour became erratic again. I had not told Clare everything, and she had little real medical information about my condition at the beginning. As she learned how serious it was, she began to research as much as she could about bipolar illness on the internet. Eventually, by talking to my doctors and nurses and reading up about it, she came to know as much as anybody could who isn't medically trained. It would be a while before she knew enough to be able to advise me on my health, though.

I did many irrational things that summer, the most extreme

being in June, when I was alone at my flat suffering a hypomanic episode and I attempted to force my way into the flat of my downstairs neighbour by smashing in his patio door with a shovel. I had finally snapped after weeks of arguing with him. He naturally ran out the front of the building as I came in the back. It was so early in the morning that I'd woken him up and he was in his underwear as he ran down our road to the main street, where he stopped a passing police car. I followed him out of the front door but went in the opposite direction, to a café around the corner that I knew well. Once inside, I decided that I wanted to go to sleep and so, naturally, took off my trousers, half fell down the stairs into their basement, lay down and closed my eyes. A little while later the police found me curled up in a foetus-like ball on the concrete floor. They led me back upstairs and covered my Union Jack boxer shorts with a blanket before leading me out to the car while a small crowd watched. All I wanted to do was sleep.

Once again I was taken to Kentish Town police station and charged with affray and causing criminal damage. After a while I was taken to a psychiatric ward in what had been the hospital for tropical diseases in King's Cross. A dark and dour Victorian building, the strip lights never went out and the beds were steel and couldn't be moved. It was a truly terrifying place with its pale lime walls, battered furniture and broken TV. Just as in the Jack Nicholson film *One Flew Over the Cuckoo's Nest*, every day the patients had to queue up for pills to be handed out by the nurses in the day room.

I needed clothes for my stay in hospital, so Richard Cohen, my accountant and business manager, was called. It was a Saturday night and he lived a fair way away, but he got in his car, picked up a bag of clothes from my flat and came to see me, for which I'll always be grateful. Clare came to see me the next day, as soon as she heard where I was.

Thankfully my suspended sentence had expired by this time, or I would have been banged up in a prison psychiatric ward.

However, I would have to face the courts again. I spent a month in St Pancras, and, although released by them, wasn't completely well medicated, which led to another silly episode, when I recorded a new version of 'Stand and Deliver', using as the chorus the line 'Save the Gorilla' for the Dian Fossey gorilla fund. I wasn't exactly out of control, but it wasn't a rational thing to do, either. The fund had been based in Primrose Hill, just around the corner from my flat, for as long as I could remember, but I'd never been into their offices until one day when I suddenly felt the urge to help them. I did help them to raise over £100,000, but my last record company, EMI, prevented the single from being released and before I could do anything about that, I had been 'imprisoned' again.

In September 2003, at Highbury Corner Magistrates' Court, my lawyer entered a plea of 'not guilty' in my absence and the case was adjourned until psychiatric reports could be made. I was sectioned under the Mental Health Act 1983.

I spent six months in hospital, and underwent various tests and numerous drug regimes and different therapies. To begin with, all I could do was walk, eat, shit and breathe. I was so heavily sedated that I couldn't think coherently. At various times, so Clare told me, I was hallucinating and could 'see' birds flying. At others I'd 'see' my daughter Lily running across the room playing hide-and-seek under the table. Of course she was only there in my imagination.

The first three months was a difficult time as I lost interest in everything. The end of the section seemed like a lifetime away and I had no motivation for anything. I was at an all-time low, and if it hadn't been for Clare, who would visit me every day, I would have had nothing at all to keep me interested in living. It can't have been easy for her. I understood why she had to go back to Oxford for weekends, but I truly missed her when she did. Feeling drowsy and tired most of the time, I would long to fall asleep in the comfort of her arms.

Gradually, as time passed, my medication was modified and

I came out of the deepest part of the depression and more aware of my circumstances. I would spend the days resting and looking forward to Clare's visits; she helped prepare me for monthly ward round assessments which would consist of my psychiatrist and a few other doctors talking to me, assessing my condition, asking questions and discussing my treatment and progress. I underwent therapy, which basically involved the analysis of my thoughts, the balance of medication and the progress of my recovery. After a while I was allowed hours out of the hospital in the company of Clare. The time away from the hospital was good; it was difficult being there, especially when other patients kicked off about their issues. After spending the first few weeks alone in my small room, I gained a roommate, which was not an easy thing to accept at first. The rooms were never designed to hold more than one bed, being on an isolation ward, so when another was brought in there was barely room to walk between them. My roommate was a ballet dancer; at least that was what he told other patients. I don't think we ever spoke a sentence to each other while we were there.

Unfortunately there always seemed to be a shortage of beds for new patients at the hospital, especially around Christmas, when people seemed more likely to 'snap'. I was there over the holiday period of 2003 to 2004 and saw a lot of new patients come and go. Yet, whatever the situation, I have to say that the nurses did their best to calm things down and keep the place running as smoothly as could be expected. Their staffroom never had its door closed, they didn't wear white uniforms, and they listened to patients no matter how irrational or emotional they were being.

The highlight of an average day at the hospital proved to be the meals, although they weren't anything to really savour. The bland, tasteless food reminded me of school dinners, but there were days when we would be served custard or rice pudding – which must have been OK since they remain two of my favourite dishes.

After three months inside, the doctors allowed me one hour a day out of hospital under Clare's supervision. Eventually, as I progressed, I was allowed a whole day out. On those days we would go for walks, and I could feel the cool breeze and fresh air on my face, which was what I needed to wake me up. For the first time in a long while I could see everyday life passing by and hear the sounds of the streets. We went to a coffee shop and I remember distinctly the smell of my first cappuccino for three months – it tasted like a sweet memory. Of course, I often didn't want to go back to the hospital to be confined to my bed in a secure unit, but I knew I had to.

The days I got to spend out of the hospital helped me realise how fragile I still was – that I still had a long way to go. I would take each day at a time, I told myself constantly. Slowly I began to realise how much I wanted my life back – to be sitting in the comfort of my home and to be able to sleep in my own bed. My medication was monitored constantly over those first six months and bit by bit, as I began to feel better, it was duly adjusted. With Clare's patience and support I was eventually granted weekend visits home, where she would take good care of me and encourage me in my recovery, for my daughter Lily's sake as much as my own.

In February 2004 I was released. In June my case was heard again at Highbury Magistrates' Court. After representations from my lawyer, the Crown reduced the affray charge to one under Section 4 (1) of the Public Order Act 1986. I pleaded guilty to those charges and received a sentence of conditional discharge. That meant that the court would not punish me for the offence on condition that I stayed out of trouble for a specified period. If I committed – and was convicted of – a new offence during that period then the sentencing court would sentence me for both the new offence and the original one.

Thankfully I had been helped by Clare to keep to a strict medication regime, which, combined with exercise and healthy eating, has since helped me to grow stronger and more confi-

dent every day. With the unconditional love of Lily, Clare's love
and support and a few good friends by my side, I have been able
to look forward and find a clarity in dealing with the events that
have taken place in my life and understand how to manage my
condition. I am reclaiming my life from bipolar illness. I know
now what the warning signals are, and when I am in danger of
feeling depressed or manic I can, with help, manage to avoid
both states. I am in recovery.

•

Just as I finished writing this book, Clare asked me what the
difference was now, compared with all the other times in my
life when I've been in control and in love. 'What's to say that
you won't have another relapse?' she asked uncertainly. 'Is there
a happy ending to this? What's different?'

I thought for a minute and then realised that the difference
is her. For the first time in my life I am in a relationship with
someone where everything is equal. I don't feel that I have to
look after her, or hide anything from her – how could I? Clare
has seen me at the lowest I've ever been, yet she is still here,
by my side. And I truly do love her for that, as much as for
everything else. Ever since I had to go to the orphanage at the
age of seven, I have felt that I had to look out for those closest
to me as well as myself. Part of what drove me on to fame and
success was the urge, the need, to be able to look after my mum,
my family and my friends. I cannot imagine how anyone who
was in the state I was in in 2003 could ever get themselves back
together and become capable of living a 'normal' life unless they
had the kind of support and love that I have had from Clare.

I understand that it must have been scary for my friends
and family when I was suffering my worst phases of hypomania
and depression. Any kind of mental illness is scary for people
who do not suffer from it. It's impossible to reason with someone whose sense of reason is gone, and mine had definitely
gone at times. I sincerely hope that anyone who suffers from

bipolar illness (or any mental illness) has someone who can help them to overcome it and live with it. It makes a huge difference to the quality of life for the sufferer, and lessens the strain on them. If you'd like to help people living with mental illness, then please contact www.mind.org. They'll be happy to hear from you.

The writing of this book marks an end of one part of my life, and the beginning of another. I feel confident and happy that I can look to the future with some optimism. I have begun to feel like writing songs and making music again, and hope that in time there may be a new Adam Ant album out.

Thirty years after waking up in the emergency ward of a mental hospital as Adam Ant, it feels as if life is only really just beginning. This time, though, I've been awakened by a kiss and not a slap on the face. It's a kind of fairy-tale ending – I fully intend to live happily ever after.

Epilogue

IT WAS MY FIRST 'TOUR' for ten years and I was really nervous. I sat in the back of the car with Clare as we drove through the heavy London traffic, heading towards the huge Waterstone's on Piccadilly. The hardback edition of this book had just been published and this was my first signing. I kept thinking, what if no one turns up? All morning I'd had this picture in my head of me sitting in the shop with a big pile of books and no one to buy them. The closer we got, the more I worried. I hardly dared look as we inched towards the art deco building that houses the flagship store of Waterstone's.

And then I saw them – a queue of people snaking along the street and around the corner. Looking at the costumes some of them were wearing – guys in outfits similar to my 'Kings' gear, complete with white stripe across their faces – there was no doubt these were Adam Ant fans. For the first time that day, I felt myself smiling.

To be honest, I had no idea what to expect. Publishing a book isn't like releasing a single or an album; it takes so much longer to actually get it out there. I could have cut a single one week and had it in the shops a few weeks later back in the 80s. Even today, a newly recorded song can be on internet release within days of being finished. But books take longer. Much, much longer. Between my finishing the first draft and the publication date stretched almost six months during which I was supposed to do ... what? The manuscript would come back to me several times with different queries from the editor and often I'd remember other stuff that should go in and so made a few late amendments. But with most of the work done, for a short time I felt as if I was in a kind of limbo state, worrying about what people would think when it did come out, worrying if I'd remembered things correctly, if friends and family were going to like it or hate it. But it soon became clear that there were still so many things to do that within weeks of finishing the writing it almost felt as if I'd been caught up in a hurricane, though the feeling was increased no doubt by my last few years of inactivity.

The first thing on my post-writing agenda was the audio version of the book. So the book was cut down to a length that made it possible to fit onto a double CD, which had its own problems, or course. What would I leave out? The editor thought that my childhood memories should be edited down in order to keep most of the music years, while also keeping as much of the story as possible. It wasn't easy and we went to and fro on that one before coming to an agreement and booking a recording studio for me to read it through on mic. Yup, I had to go into a studio and record the thing myself, which made me a little nervous. On the first day, I found myself stumbling over words and phrases for a couple of hours, constantly stopping and starting again. But then I relaxed and it seemed to get easier. The producer was telling me that it sounded good and I had to trust her. I thought that it sounded a bit stilted, as if I was reading in a dull monotone, bereft of energy, but since I also felt a bit fuzzy from my medication, I knew that I had to take other people's word for how it was really going. Those three days in a small, smart and cool (it was boiling outside in the sun) studio in west London passed pretty quickly for me, though I can't speak for Clare who sat there every day listening to me. But I did it all. In some ways it had been harder than actually writing the book, and once I'd finished I felt not just relieved but a bit stronger.

That summer of 2006 felt like a slow reawakening for me. People started approaching me to do all sorts of things as soon as they knew about the book coming out in September. Would I

appear on television shows talking about this and that? Could
I present a section of an MTV celebration of the 1980s? Radio
stations in America were emailing to ask if I'd do interviews
down the line; magazines and newspapers were asking for
interviews. It was all flattering and reminded me of what was
about to come my way. I had to look forward to being interviewed by journalists for different newspapers, talking to DJs on
air and making a documentary for ITV – all stuff that I hadn't
done for years and I wasn't sure how I would cope.

The first press interview I had to do was with Jon Wilde for
Uncut magazine and while we talked we were being filmed for
the documentary. Jon managed to ignore the camera, which was
more than I could do for the first half an hour. Before agreeing
to any interview I had asked for the journalists to send me a list
of questions or general areas of discussion, and almost all of
the writers and DJs who I met with agreed to do that. I asked
not because I wanted to vet the questions (though I did ask for
some to be reworded or dropped), but simply because it would
allow me to focus and give as good an interview as possible. It
was difficult for me to form answers immediately when asked
questions out of the blue, and I knew that my hesitation in
responding could make people nervous, that they could think
that I didn't want to answer them, when in truth it was simply
that the answers took time to come to me. I wasn't trying to
avoid the question, it just took time. But armed with the questions beforehand, I could have the basis of what my answer
would be ready for them. I hope that the interviews I did to
promote *Stand & Deliver* read well.

With the documentary, I wasn't just talking about my past;
I got to literally revisit it. The producers took me to Luxe, the
house in Hertfordshire that I'd lived in back in the mid-1980s.
It had passed through a few hands since I sold it but each
owner had preserved everything pretty much as it was. The
people who live there now sweetly allowed me to trek through

the place with camera in tow. The 'AA' monogrammed carpets were still there, as was all my Egyptian-themed decoration, from the crystal pyramid outside the front door to the hieroglyphics on the walls at the foot of the staircase leading up to the only bedroom. The bedroom door opening mechanism – a small blue pyramid atop a column which, when pressed, released the 'hidden' entrance – still worked. And, inside the bedroom, the Bedouin tent effect was all as it had been when I'd had it painted. I remembered that it had taken two men over a year of living in the place to finish all that work and I'm so glad that their efforts have been preserved – they certainly deserved to be. There were some changes to the place of course, with a new house having been built in the garden (the new owners' parents lived there). My jukebox had also gone along with the gym equipment that had filled a small room which the new owners were about to turn into a nursery for their first child. Still, sitting on the imitation Napoleonic bed in the old place brought back so many memories of that particular time in my life and I really wish that I'd spent more time living in the house. Of course, I was so busy then that I couldn't settle in just one place. But if I could, that would have been it.

I also visited the storerooms at the Victoria & Albert museum with the camera crew and we went through all my old costumes. The 'Kings' hussar jacket and Prince Charming outfits, like all the other shirts and boots and jackets, are being kept in pristine condition by a wonderful team of people who love their job. And they're in great company among past artefacts of theatrical greatness. At one point Guy Baxter, the man in charge of the theatrical section, brought out the final manuscript of *School for Scandal* by Richard Brinsley Sheridan. It dated back to 1777 and it was amazing to see this historical document in fine handwriting (though not Sheridan's apparently) from the time that had so influenced my designs for 'Prince Charming' and 'Goody Two Shoes'.

For the camera I also ran through my original sketch books

from the early 1980s in which I'd laid out, scene by scene, frame by frame, storyboards for all of the videos that Mike Mansfield had directed so expertly for the camera. Mike and his producer Hillary were also interviewed for the documentary and I'm very grateful to them for agreeing to appear. Amazingly they said that no one had ever asked them to talk about our work before. They were a mine of great stories about our time spent filming together and I only wish that there had been time on the final cut to include more of them. They remembered things that I'd forgotten, such as Boy George turning up with Marilyn to be extras in the crowd on the set of 'Prince Charming', for instance. I don't remember that, but if Mike and Hillary said that they were there then they must have been. They're not in the final video though. I'm also very grateful to Mike Smith, the first A&R man to sign Adam and the Ants (to Decca) and his wife, the lovely Sally James (of *Tiswas* fame) for saying such nice things about me for the camera. It was kind of odd hearing the views of that time from other people. To me of course it was simply all part of my life then, and didn't seem at all unusual or extraordinary, but of course it was. Different perspectives throw up different memories.

And then, after a summer spent filming the documentary, it was finally September and time for publication. Coming back into the public eye after two years of living quietly was not easy, but in the end it wasn't as hard as I thought it would be. One of the first things I did was go on air with Steve Wright at Radio 2. He was extremely kind to me – as was David Jensen at Capital Gold and a whole load of local station DJs, and I thank them for that. They all played vintage Ants songs, most of which were included on a new greatest hits CD also titled *Stand & Deliver*.

The day after my autobiography was finally published, I had my first signing at Waterstone's Piccadilly. As I walked from the lift to the desk where I was to sit, the front of the queue started clapping; it gave me the most fantastic buzz and feeling of warmth. Unfortunately, because so many people had turned up (including two women who had flown over from America just for this), I could only sign the books and not write dedications, otherwise I and everyone else would have been there all day. As it was, over 400 people bought books and audio CDs that day. The shop ran out of stock and couldn't get any more so we had to limit people to buying just the one copy. There was a space directly in front of the desk which had been penned off using metal barriers and after having their book signed people were just standing there, staring at me or taking photos and digital film. Every half an hour the security people had to clear that area to allow others in.

It was fascinating to meet all these people. Some had been fans since the early days and came with their kids (some of whom claimed also to be fans of my music, which I guess must have been the result of their parents brainwashing them). Others were too young to have been there in the 80s but were big fans nonetheless. People showed me their tattoos, photos of themselves and family and brought gifts for me, including CDs, cards and even a tin of rice pudding because they knew it was my favourite. I got to meet many of the people who had been fans for a long time, and who have been busy keeping Adam Ant in the mind and on the screens of people around the world. They all made it to the first signing and it was good to have time to chat with them and tell them what a great job they've been doing. Some will be happy to hear that Sony had the great idea of compiling a box set of all my old singles, which should be out in time for the thirtieth anniversary celebrations of the first single release. Allan Ballard also came – the man who took all of those great photos of me in 1982. It was good to see him again and I thanked him for the photos in this book.

That first signing was a memorable day for me and I didn't think that it would be repeated. I was wrong. In Oxford, Birmingham, Manchester, Edinburgh, Glasgow and Milton Keynes the same thing happened. There were queues of people who waited hours to get a book signed and I am grateful to every one of them for doing so. In Milton Keynes I met up with Terry Lee Miall, my old drummer. He'd brought his family along and it was great to see him and them, looking good and healthy. We hugged, swapped numbers and wished each other well.

As much as I wanted to chat with people at the signings though, time was always short. The publishers kept getting me into their offices to sign more copies of the book because they'd been asked for them and someone worked out that I signed over 4,000 copies, which certainly built up my writing arm, I can tell you. If there are that many people who really wanted a signed copy of my book then I am a lucky man to have such dedicated fans.

If I seemed a bit ghost-like at the signings and in the documentary, that was because only slowly did I feel myself returning to a kind of normality. But I could sense that I was improving, day by day. While I was out doing signings and interviews, different ideas and positive thoughts came to me and I felt that I was becoming more lucid. And then the publicity was over and my life was back to its usual routine.

During the next few months I visited the gym and went on lovely long walks with Clare. We moved out of my flat in Primrose Hill to a completely new place, in a very different part of England, and we would walk for hours exploring the surrounding area. We visited family regularly, which I always look forward to, and everyone we met seemed to be very understanding and encouraging to me. Every little bit helps a great deal and it has all added to my positive frame of mind.

I've been asked before (and again, recently) if I'd like to appear on a 'greatest hits' live tour with a band, and while I agreed once to do it and couldn't physically make the dates, I have to say that I'm not tempted any more. When I play live music again it has to include new material. Music is a part of me as much now as it ever has been – I've never really stopped writing songs – and I want to share that new music with fans, along with some of the old stuff, of course. But I do not want to put on the old make-up and outfits and trawl the country pretending that it's 1982 again, because it's not and never can be. That was then and it was truly fantastic, but this is now and can be just as fantastic in a different way.

I'm hoping to get back into a recording studio soon with some new collaborators and lay down some new tracks. It's been a long time since I went into a recording studio with instruments and I miss it. It gives me such a natural high composing new songs and hearing them develop and grow in the studio. The desire to do it might ebb at times but it's always there deep within. I'm now at the stage where I need to let the songs flow again and there are melodies and lyrics beginning to surface from my mind.

Technology has moved on incredibly since I made *Wonderful* and I am trying to embrace and master all of that. Now I can work at home as well as in a studio. The internet means that I can begin to communicate with fans around the world from the comfort of my living room and playing live is no longer such an organizational nightmare. There's even been talk of my making 'narrowcast' performances. We'll see. The basics are all still there, you see. An acoustic guitar. A voice. And the song. The main thing is always the song.

And the muse.

Thanks, Clare.

Index